The Silver

Art and lettering by
Michael Walsh

1 "The Ticket" written by
Chip Zdarsky

2 "Girls of Summer" written by
Kelly Thompson

3 "Death Rattle" written by
Ed Brisson

4 "2467" written by
Jeff Lemire

5 "Covenant" written by
Michael Walsh

Colored by
Michael Walsh and
Toni Marie Griffin

Edited by
Chris Hampton

Additional linework by
Gavin Fullerton

The Silver Coin is created by
Michael Walsh, Ed Brisson, Jeff Lemire, Kelly Thompson, and Chip Zdarsky

IMAGE COMICS, INC. • Todd McFarlane: President • Jim Valentino: Vice President • Marc Silvestri: Chief Executive Officer • Erik Larsen: Chief Financial Officer • Robert Kirkman: Chief Operating Officer • Eric Stephenson: Publisher / Chief Creative Officer • Nicole Lapalme: Controller • Leanna Caunter: Accounting Analyst • Sue Korpela: Accounting & HR Manager • Marla Eizik: Talent Liaison • Dirk Wood: Director of International Sales & Licensing • Alex Cox: Director of Direct Market Sales • Chloe Ramos: Book Market & Library Sales Manager • Emilio Bautista: Digital Sales Coordinator • Jon Schlaffman: Specialty Sales Coordinator • Kat Salazar: Director of PR & Marketing • Drew Fitzgerald: Marketing Content Associate • Heather Doornink: Production Director • Drew Gill: Art Director • Hilary DiLoreto: Print Manager • Tricia Ramos: Traffic Manager • Melissa Gifford: Content Manager • Erika Schnatz: Senior Production Artist • Ryan Brewer: Production Artist • Deanna Phelps: Production Artist • IMAGECOMICS.COM

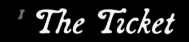

The Ticket

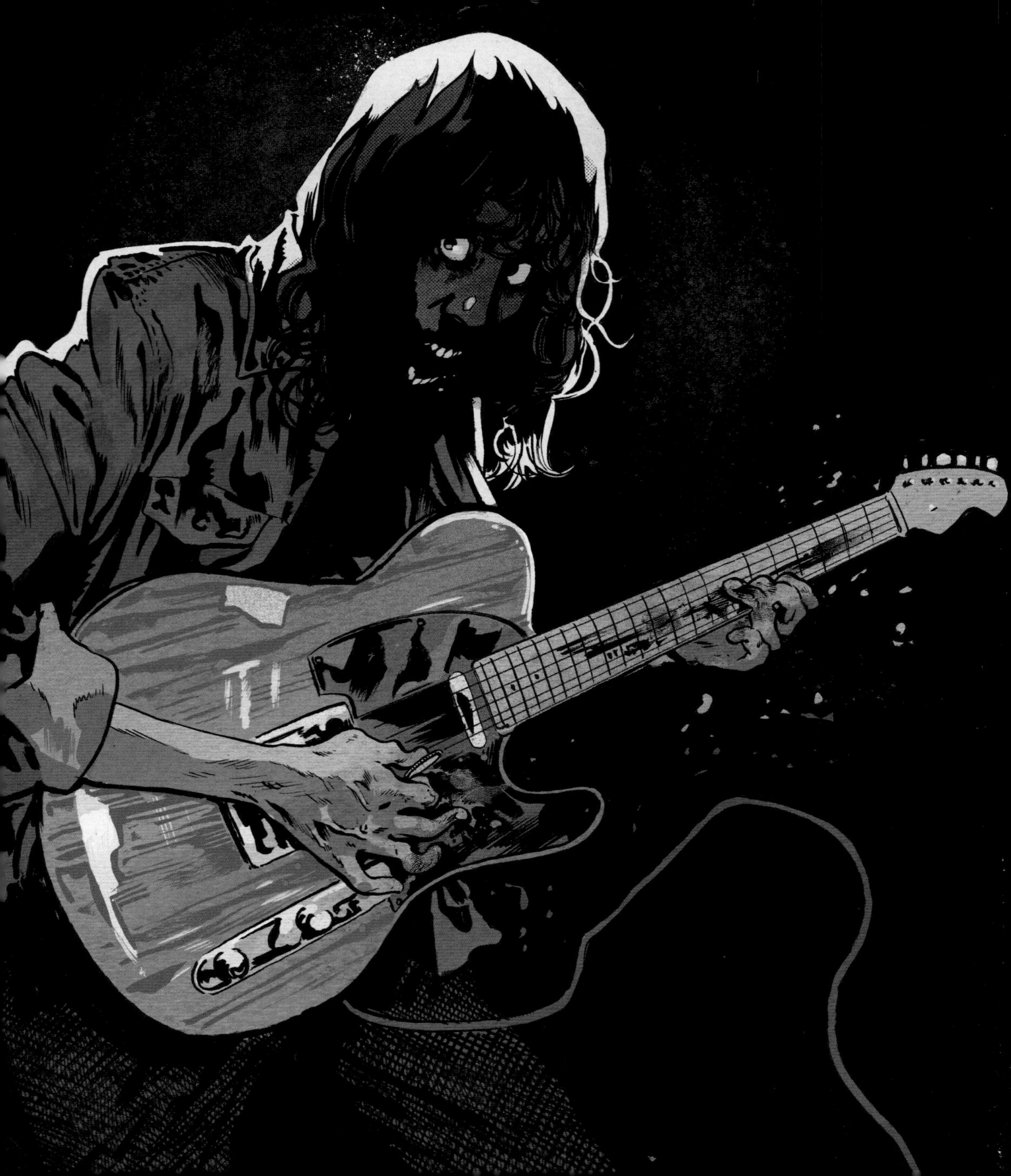

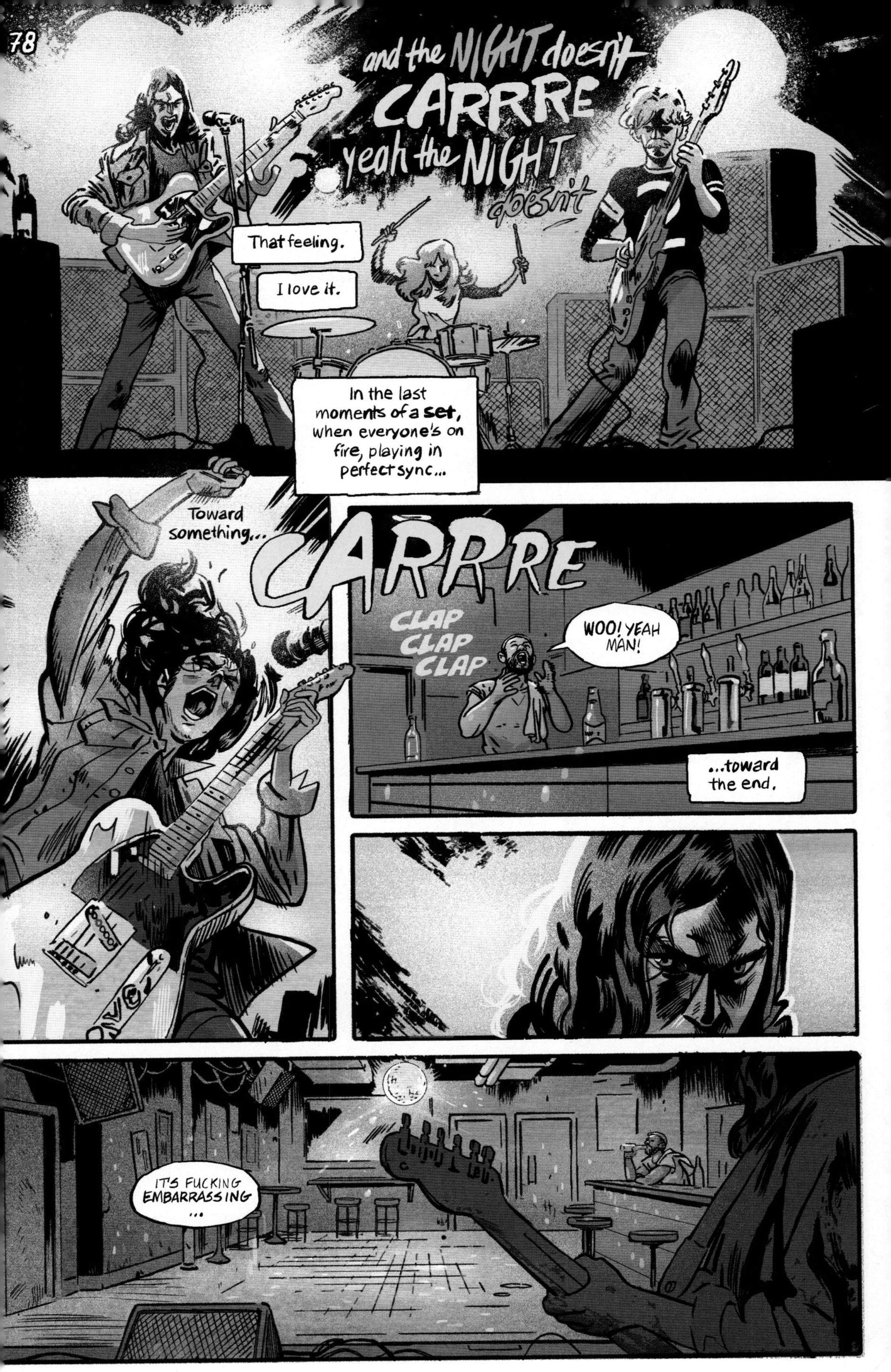
and the NIGHT doesn't
CARRRE
yeah the NIGHT
doesn't
That feeling.
I love it.
In the last moments of a **set**, when everyone's on fire, playing in perfect sync...
Toward something...
CARRRE
CLAP
CLAP
CLAP
WOO! YEAH MAN!
...toward the end.
IT'S FUCKING EMBARRASSING ...

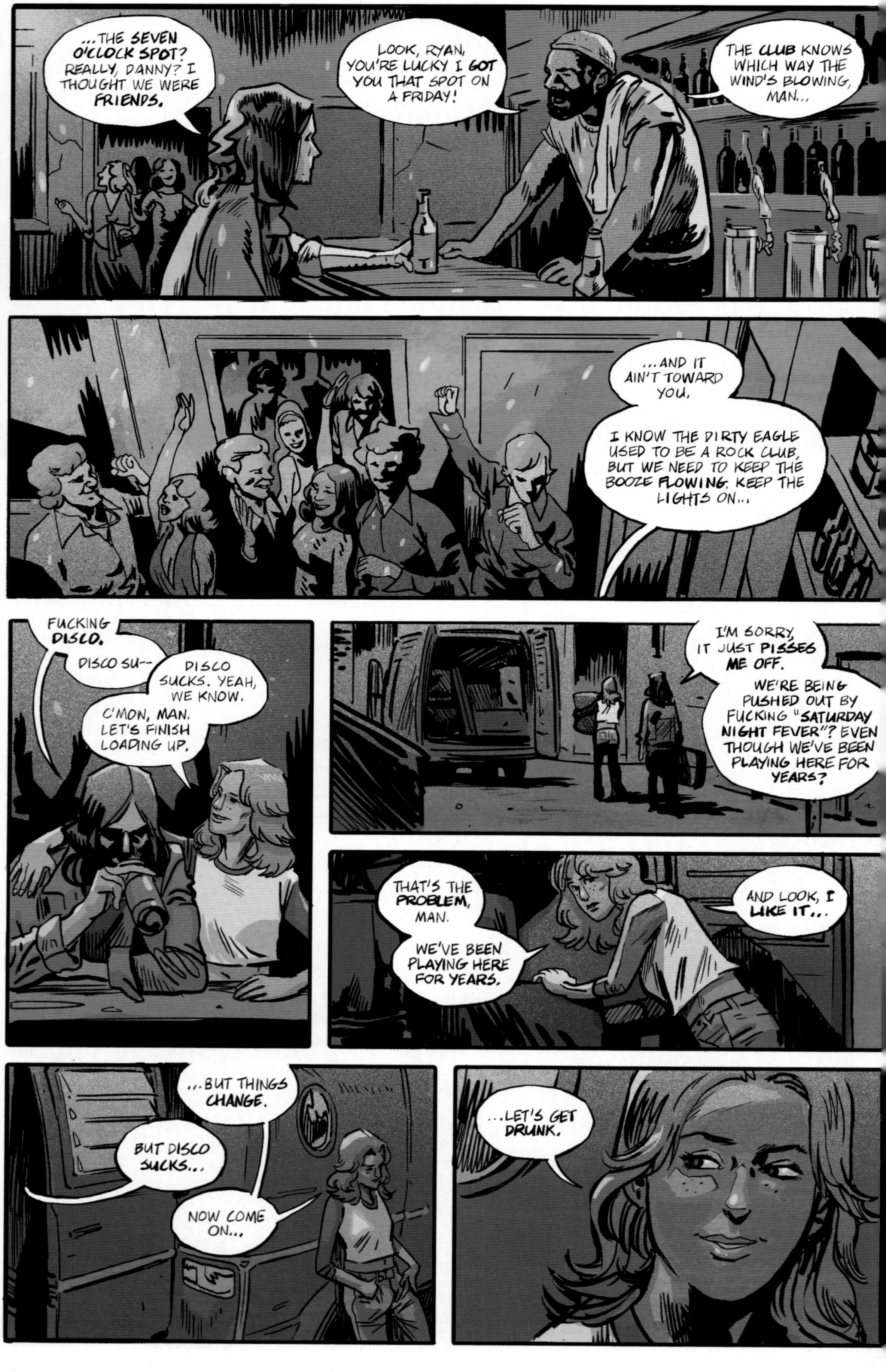
...THE SEVEN O'CLOCK SPOT? REALLY, DANNY? I THOUGHT WE WERE FRIENDS.
LOOK, RYAN, YOU'RE LUCKY I GOT YOU THAT SPOT ON A FRIDAY!
THE CLUB KNOWS WHICH WAY THE WIND'S BLOWING, MAN...
...AND IT AIN'T TOWARD YOU.
I KNOW THE DIRTY EAGLE USED TO BE A ROCK CLUB, BUT WE NEED TO KEEP THE BOOZE FLOWING. KEEP THE LIGHTS ON...
FUCKING DISCO.
DISCO SU--
DISCO SUCKS. YEAH, WE KNOW.
C'MON, MAN. LET'S FINISH LOADING UP.
I'M SORRY, IT JUST PISSES ME OFF.
WE'RE BEING PUSHED OUT BY FUCKING "SATURDAY NIGHT FEVER"? EVEN THOUGH WE'VE BEEN PLAYING HERE FOR YEARS?
THAT'S THE PROBLEM, MAN.
WE'VE BEEN PLAYING HERE FOR YEARS.
AND LOOK, I LIKE IT...
...BUT THINGS CHANGE.
BUT DISCO SUCKS...
NOW COME ON...
...LET'S GET DRUNK.

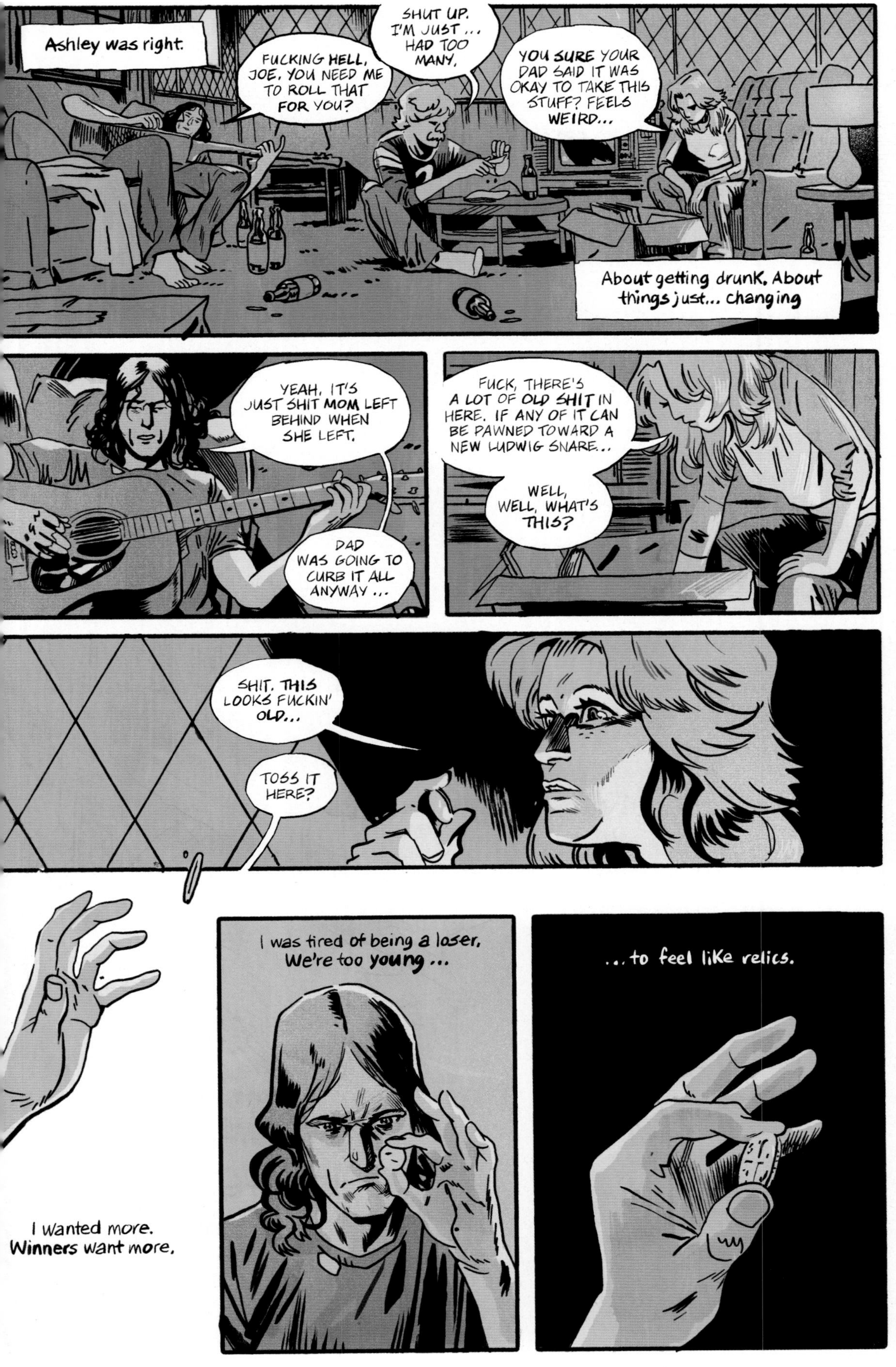

Ashley was right.
FUCKING HELL, JOE. YOU NEED ME TO ROLL THAT FOR YOU?
SHUT UP. I'M JUST... HAD TOO MANY.
YOU SURE YOUR DAD SAID IT WAS OKAY TO TAKE THIS STUFF? FEELS WEIRD...
About getting drunk. About things just... changing
YEAH, IT'S JUST SHIT MOM LEFT BEHIND WHEN SHE LEFT.
DAD WAS GOING TO CURB IT ALL ANYWAY...
FUCK, THERE'S A LOT OF OLD SHIT IN HERE. IF ANY OF IT CAN BE PAWNED TOWARD A NEW LUDWIG SNARE...
WELL, WELL, WHAT'S THIS?
SHIT. THIS LOOKS FUCKIN' OLD...
TOSS IT HERE?
I wanted more. Winners want more.
I was tired of being a loser. We're too young...
...to feel like relics.

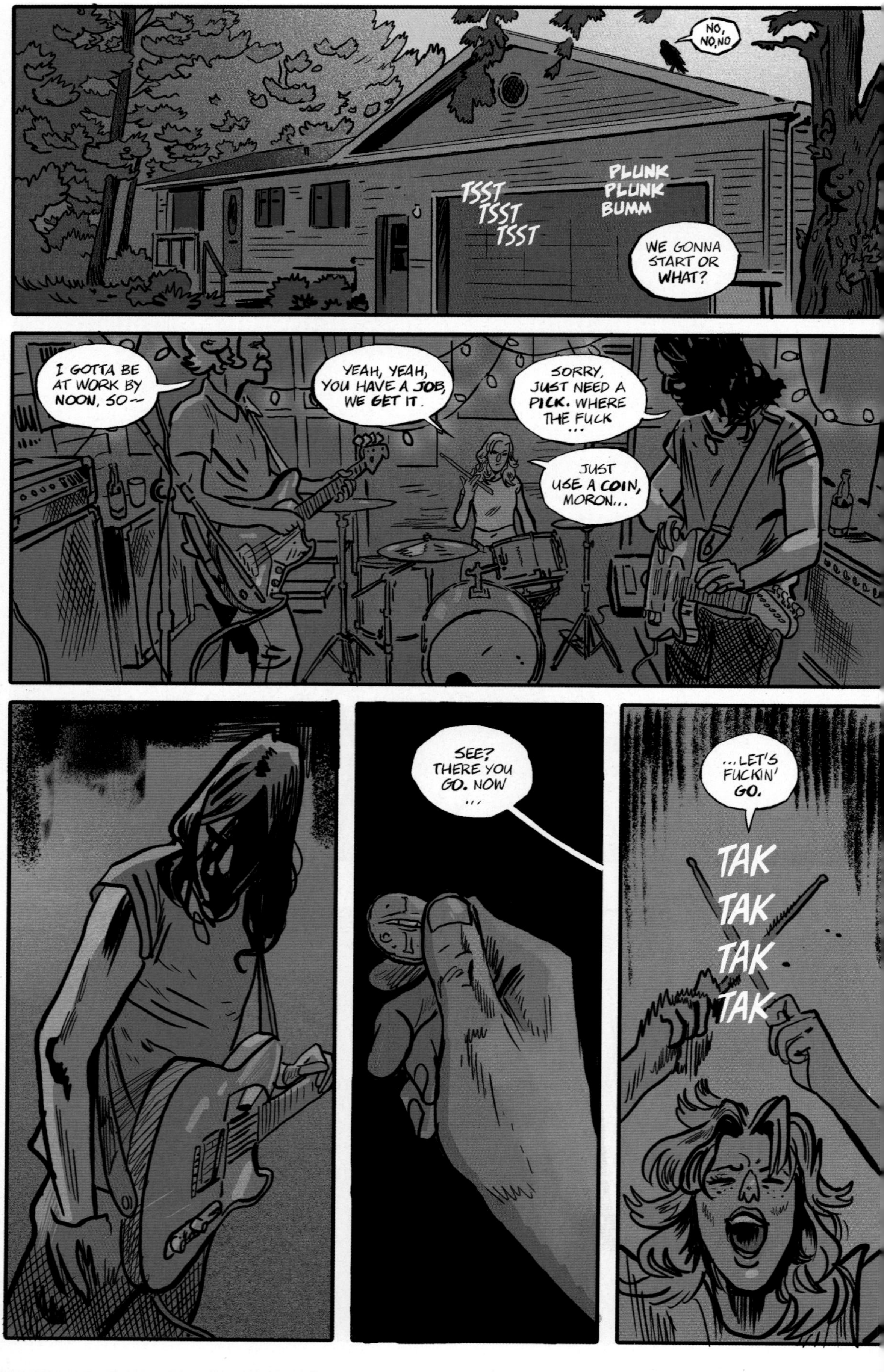
NO, NO, NO
TSST TSST TSST
PLUNK PLUNK BUMM
WE GONNA START OR WHAT?
I GOTTA BE AT WORK BY NOON, SO--
YEAH, YEAH, YOU HAVE A JOB, WE GET IT.
SORRY, JUST NEED A PICK. WHERE THE FUCK ...
JUST USE A COIN, MORON...
SEE? THERE YOU GO. NOW ...
...LET'S FUCKIN' GO.
TAK TAK TAK TAK

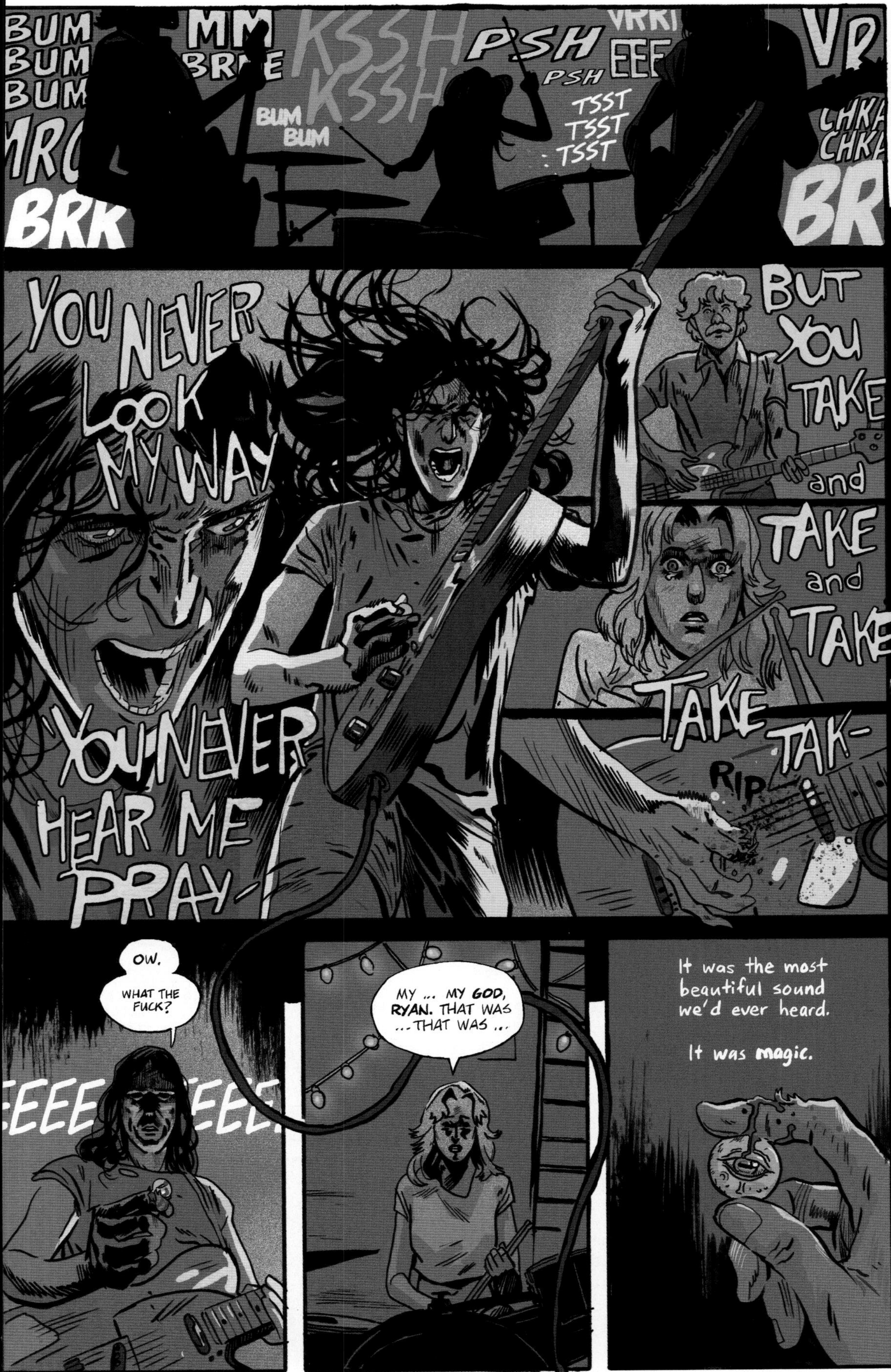
BUM BUM BUM
MRO
BRK
MM BREE
KSSH KSSH
BUM BUM
PSH
PSH
TSST TSST TSST
VRR EEE
VR
CHKA CHKA
BR
YOU NEVER LOOK MY WAY
YOU NEVER HEAR ME PRAY-
BUT YOU TAKE
and
TAKE
and
TAKE
TAKE TAK-
RIP
OW.
WHAT THE FUCK?
EEEE EEEE
MY ... MY GOD, RYAN. THAT WAS ... THAT WAS ...
It was the most beautiful sound we'd ever heard.
It was magic.

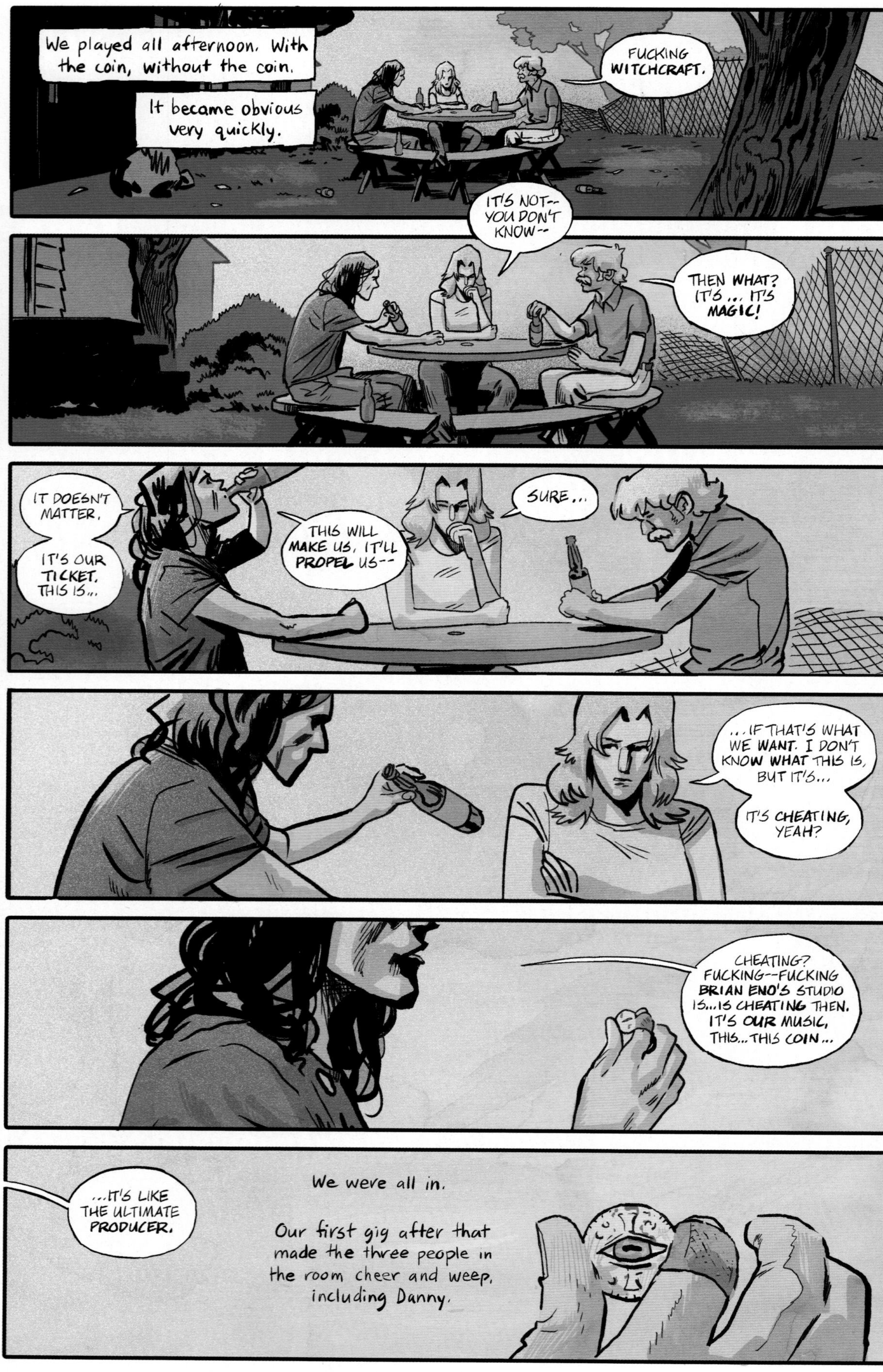

We played all afternoon. With the coin, without the coin.
It became obvious very quickly.
FUCKING WITCHCRAFT.
IT'S NOT-- YOU DON'T KNOW--
THEN WHAT? IT'S... IT'S MAGIC!
IT DOESN'T MATTER.
IT'S OUR TICKET. THIS IS...
THIS WILL MAKE US, IT'LL PROPEL US--
SURE...
...IF THAT'S WHAT WE WANT. I DON'T KNOW WHAT THIS IS, BUT IT'S...
IT'S CHEATING, YEAH?
CHEATING? FUCKING--FUCKING BRIAN ENO'S STUDIO IS...IS CHEATING THEN. IT'S OUR MUSIC, THIS...THIS COIN...
...IT'S LIKE THE ULTIMATE PRODUCER.
We were all in.
Our first gig after that made the three people in the room cheer and weep, including Danny.

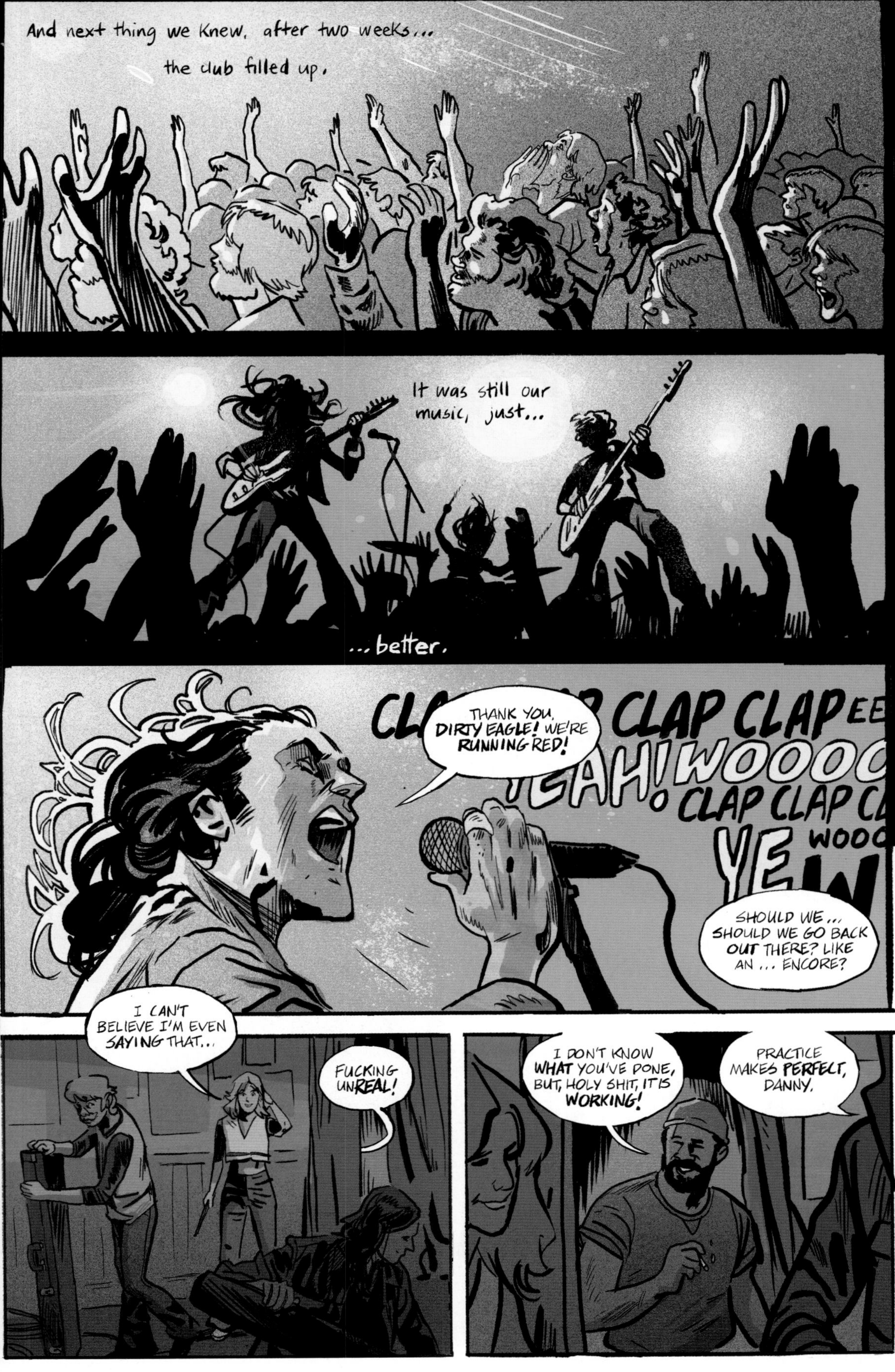

And next thing we knew, after two weeks...
the club filled up.
It was still our music, just...
...better.
CLAP CLAP CLAP CLAP
THANK YOU, DIRTY EAGLE! WE'RE RUNNING RED!
YEAH! WOOOO
CLAP CLAP CLAP
WOOO
SHOULD WE... SHOULD WE GO BACK OUT THERE? LIKE AN ... ENCORE?
I CAN'T BELIEVE I'M EVEN SAYING THAT...
FUCKING UNREAL!
I DON'T KNOW WHAT YOU'VE DONE, BUT, HOLY SHIT, IT IS WORKING!
PRACTICE MAKES PERFECT, DANNY.

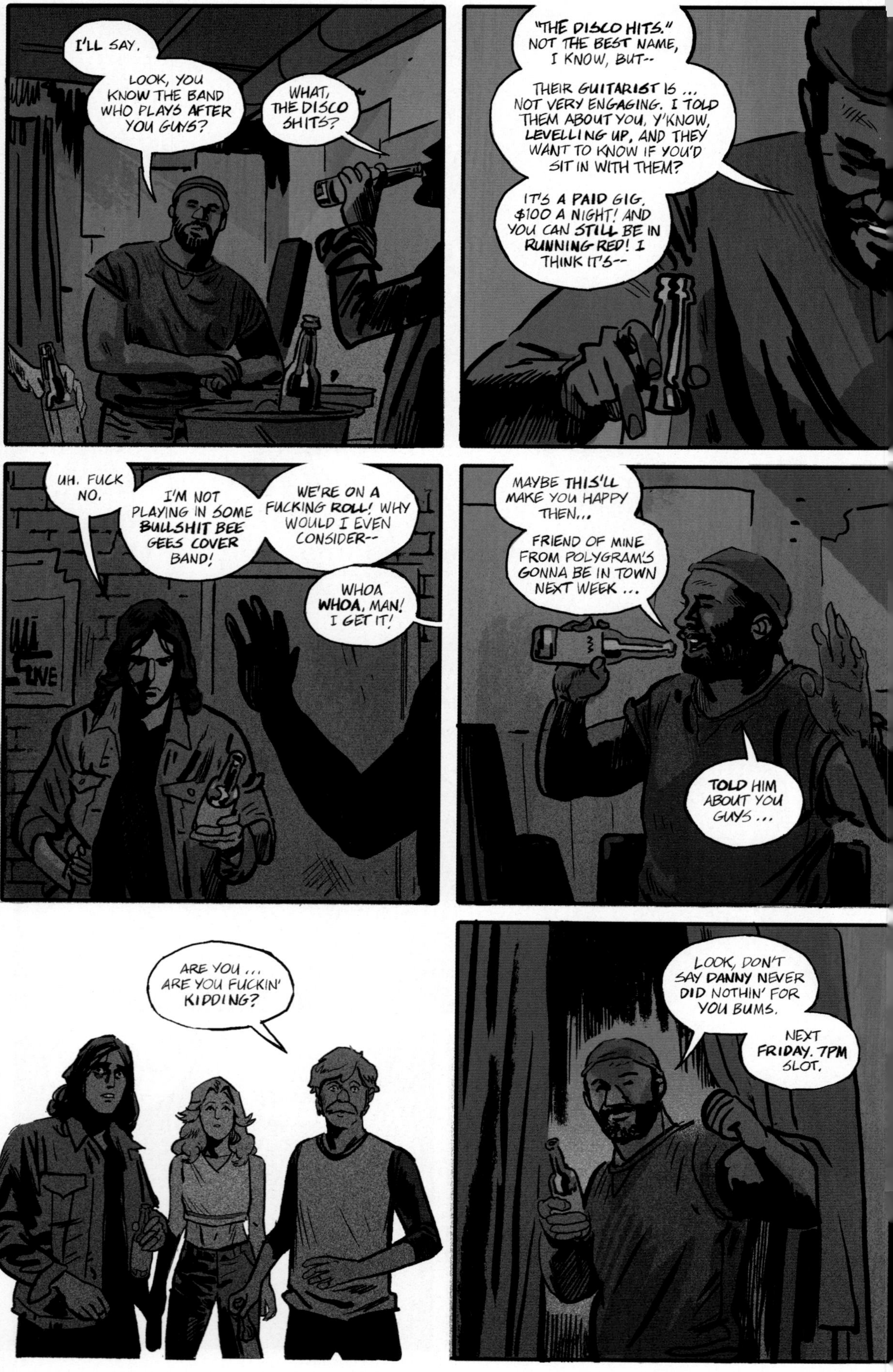

I'LL SAY.
LOOK, YOU KNOW THE BAND WHO PLAYS AFTER YOU GUYS?
WHAT, THE DISCO SHITS?
"THE DISCO HITS." NOT THE BEST NAME, I KNOW, BUT--
THEIR GUITARIST IS ... NOT VERY ENGAGING. I TOLD THEM ABOUT YOU, Y'KNOW, LEVELLING UP, AND THEY WANT TO KNOW IF YOU'D SIT IN WITH THEM?
IT'S A PAID GIG. $100 A NIGHT! AND YOU CAN STILL BE IN RUNNING RED! I THINK IT'S--
UH. FUCK NO.
I'M NOT PLAYING IN SOME BULLSHIT BEE GEES COVER BAND!
WE'RE ON A FUCKING ROLL! WHY WOULD I EVEN CONSIDER--
WHOA WHOA, MAN! I GET IT!
MAYBE THIS'LL MAKE YOU HAPPY THEN...
FRIEND OF MINE FROM POLYGRAM'S GONNA BE IN TOWN NEXT WEEK ...
TOLD HIM ABOUT YOU GUYS ...
ARE YOU ... ARE YOU FUCKIN' KIDDING?
LOOK, DON'T SAY DANNY NEVER DID NOTHIN' FOR YOU BUMS.
NEXT FRIDAY. 7PM SLOT.

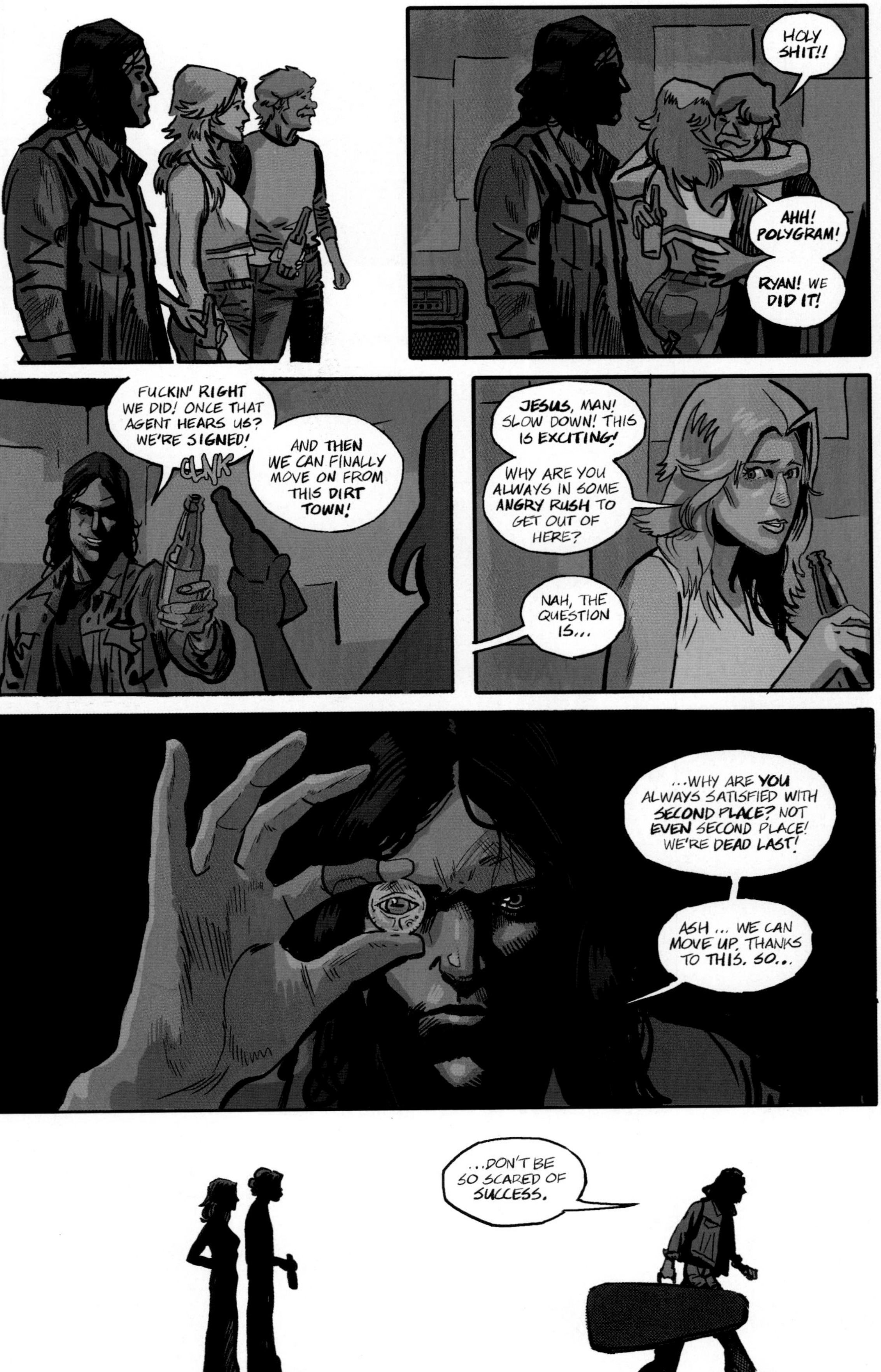
HOLY SHIT!!
AHH! POLYGRAM!
RYAN! WE DID IT!
FUCKIN' RIGHT WE DID! ONCE THAT AGENT HEARS US? WE'RE SIGNED!
CLNK
AND THEN WE CAN FINALLY MOVE ON FROM THIS DIRT TOWN!
JESUS, MAN! SLOW DOWN! THIS IS EXCITING!
WHY ARE YOU ALWAYS IN SOME ANGRY RUSH TO GET OUT OF HERE?
NAH, THE QUESTION IS...
...WHY ARE YOU ALWAYS SATISFIED WITH SECOND PLACE? NOT EVEN SECOND PLACE! WE'RE DEAD LAST!
ASH ... WE CAN MOVE UP, THANKS TO THIS. SO...
...DON'T BE SO SCARED OF SUCCESS.

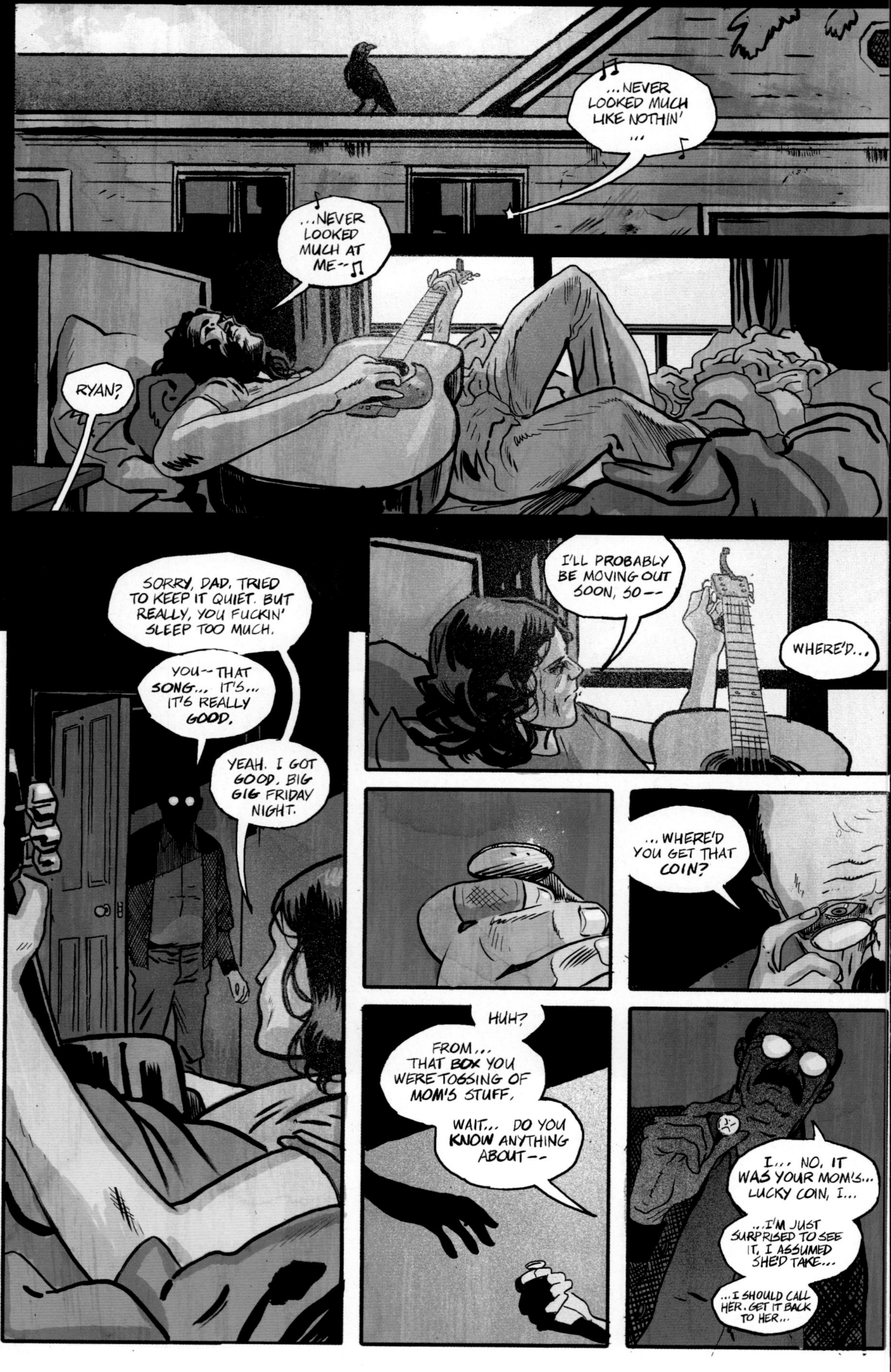
...NEVER LOOKED MUCH LIKE NOTHIN' ...
...NEVER LOOKED MUCH AT ME--
RYAN?
SORRY, DAD. TRIED TO KEEP IT QUIET. BUT REALLY, YOU FUCKIN' SLEEP TOO MUCH.
YOU--THAT SONG... IT'S... IT'S REALLY GOOD.
YEAH. I GOT GOOD. BIG GIG FRIDAY NIGHT.
I'LL PROBABLY BE MOVING OUT SOON, SO--
WHERE'D...
...WHERE'D YOU GET THAT COIN?
HUH?
FROM... THAT BOX YOU WERE TOSSING OF MOM'S STUFF.
WAIT... DO YOU KNOW ANYTHING ABOUT--
I... NO, IT WAS YOUR MOM'S... LUCKY COIN, I...
...I'M JUST SURPRISED TO SEE IT, I ASSUMED SHE'D TAKE...
...I SHOULD CALL HER. GET IT BACK TO HER...

APRIL 4 8PM AT THE COLISEUM
UH, NO.
FUCK NO.
GRAB
SHE LEFT YOU! SHE LEFT US!
SHE DOESN'T GET SHIT!
YOU WON'T UNDERSTAND, BUT THIS COIN? IT'S MY-- OUR TICKET.
I... I DO UNDERSTAND,
...I REALLY DO...
Mom leaving made Dad weak.
Did she leave the coin to help him or did the coin help her to leave and she just didn't need it anymore?
This is what was going through my mind, but the overriding thought was...

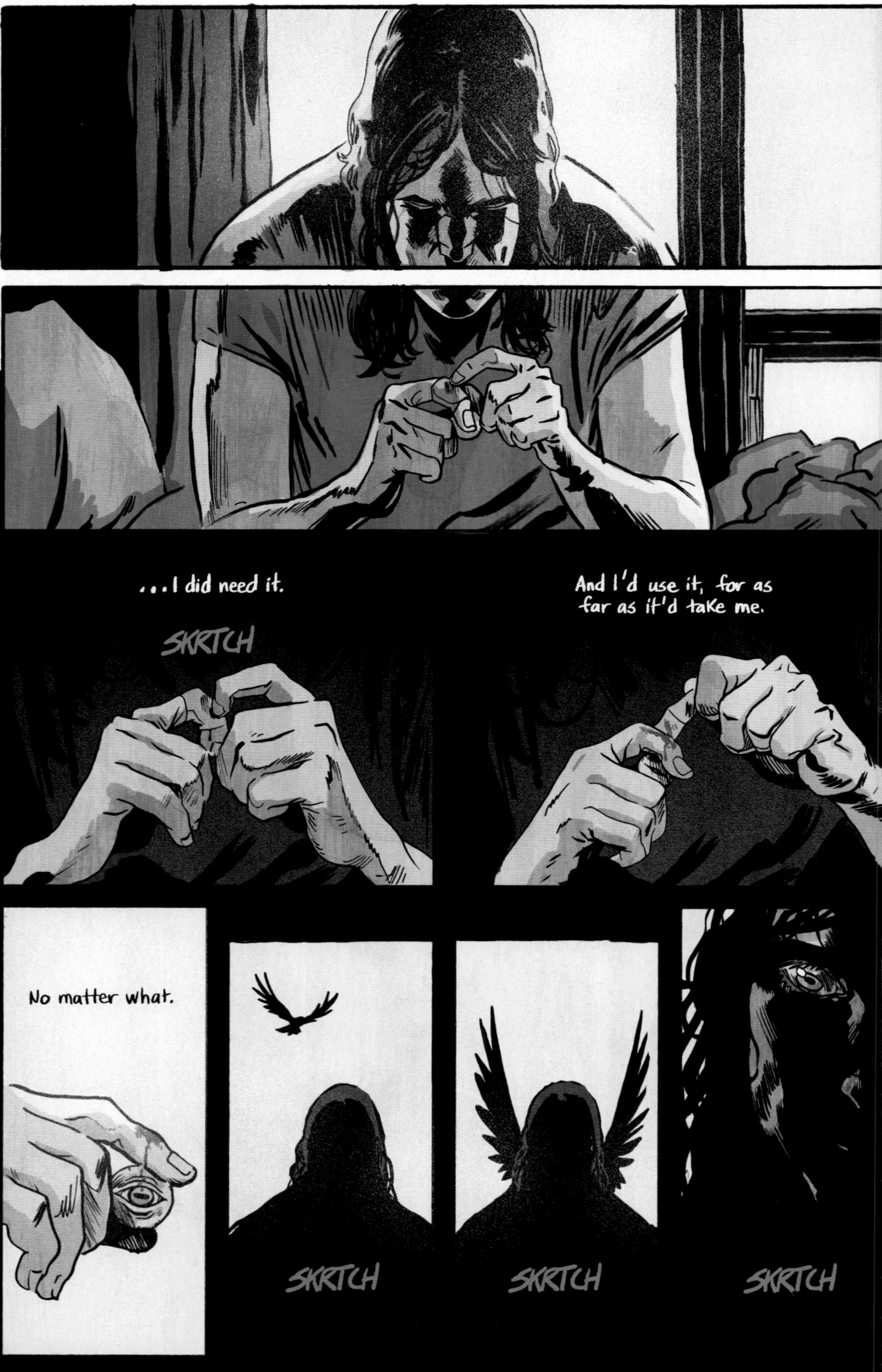
...I did need it.
SKRTCH
And I'd use it, for as far as it'd take me.
No matter what.
SKRTCH
SKRTCH
SKRTCH

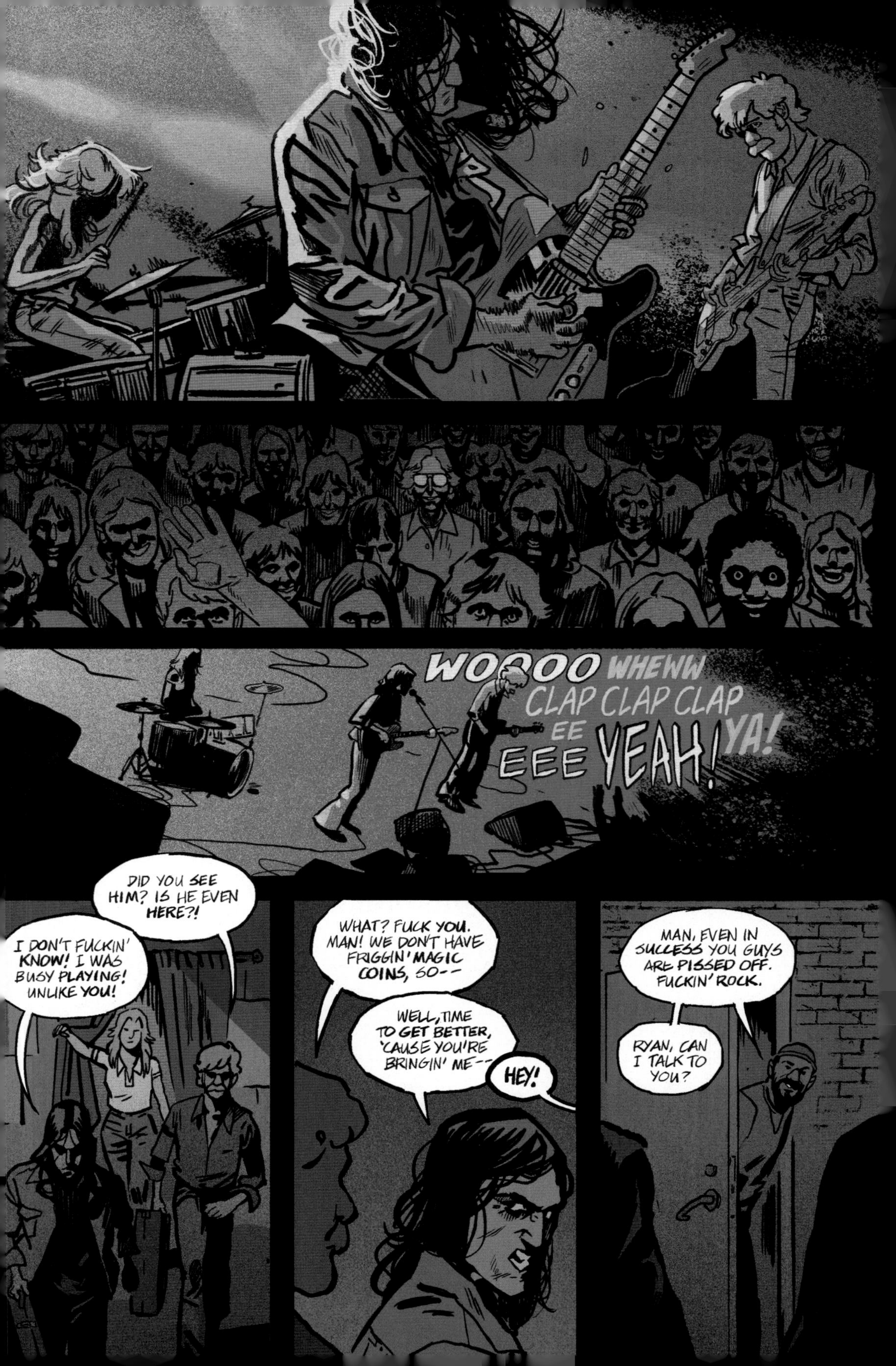
WOOOO WHEWW
CLAP CLAP CLAP
EE
EEE YEAH!
YA!
DID YOU SEE HIM? IS HE EVEN HERE?!
I DON'T FUCKIN' KNOW! I WAS BUSY PLAYING! UNLIKE YOU!
WHAT? FUCK YOU. MAN! WE DON'T HAVE FRIGGIN' MAGIC COINS, SO--
WELL, TIME TO GET BETTER, 'CAUSE YOU'RE BRINGIN' ME--
HEY!
MAN, EVEN IN SUCCESS YOU GUYS ARE PISSED OFF. FUCKIN' ROCK.
RYAN, CAN I TALK TO YOU?

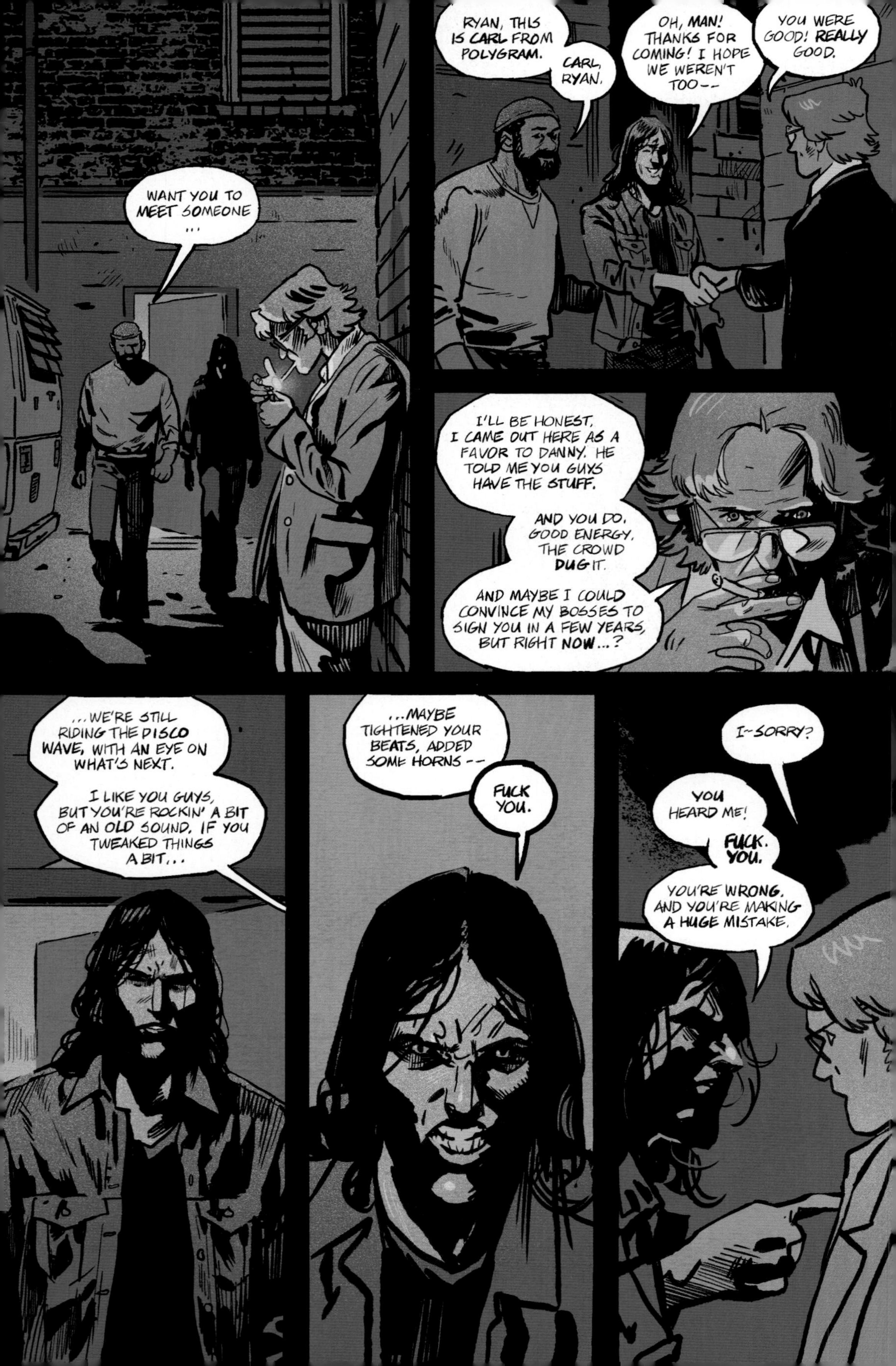
WANT YOU TO MEET SOMEONE ...
RYAN, THIS IS CARL FROM POLYGRAM.
CARL, RYAN.
OH, MAN! THANKS FOR COMING! I HOPE WE WEREN'T TOO--
YOU WERE GOOD! REALLY GOOD.
I'LL BE HONEST. I CAME OUT HERE AS A FAVOR TO DANNY. HE TOLD ME YOU GUYS HAVE THE STUFF.
AND YOU DO. GOOD ENERGY. THE CROWD DUG IT.
AND MAYBE I COULD CONVINCE MY BOSSES TO SIGN YOU IN A FEW YEARS, BUT RIGHT NOW...?
...WE'RE STILL RIDING THE DISCO WAVE, WITH AN EYE ON WHAT'S NEXT.
I LIKE YOU GUYS, BUT YOU'RE ROCKIN' A BIT OF AN OLD SOUND. IF YOU TWEAKED THINGS A BIT...
...MAYBE TIGHTENED YOUR BEATS, ADDED SOME HORNS --
FUCK YOU.
I-SORRY?
YOU HEARD ME!
FUCK. YOU.
YOU'RE WRONG. AND YOU'RE MAKING A HUGE MISTAKE.

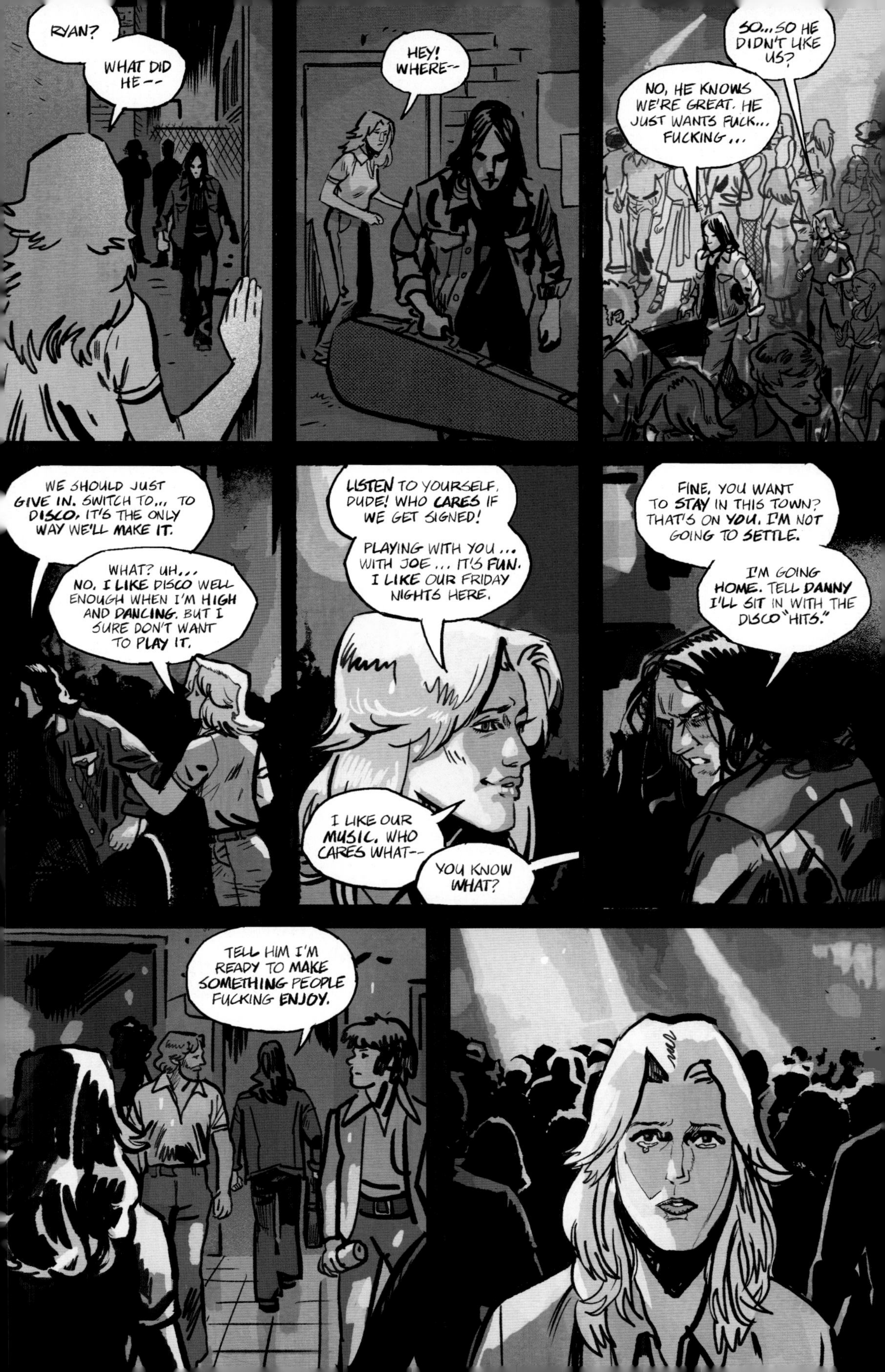
RYAN?
WHAT DID HE--
HEY! WHERE--
SO...SO HE DIDN'T LIKE US?
NO, HE KNOWS WE'RE GREAT. HE JUST WANTS FUCK... FUCKING...
WE SHOULD JUST GIVE IN. SWITCH TO... TO DISCO. IT'S THE ONLY WAY WE'LL MAKE IT.
WHAT? UH... NO. I LIKE DISCO WELL ENOUGH WHEN I'M HIGH AND DANCING. BUT I SURE DON'T WANT TO PLAY IT.
LISTEN TO YOURSELF, DUDE! WHO CARES IF WE GET SIGNED!
PLAYING WITH YOU... WITH JOE... IT'S FUN. I LIKE OUR FRIDAY NIGHTS HERE.
I LIKE OUR MUSIC. WHO CARES WHAT--
YOU KNOW WHAT?
FINE. YOU WANT TO STAY IN THIS TOWN? THAT'S ON YOU. I'M NOT GOING TO SETTLE.
I'M GOING HOME. TELL DANNY I'LL SIT IN WITH THE DISCO "HITS."
TELL HIM I'M READY TO MAKE SOMETHING PEOPLE FUCKING ENJOY.

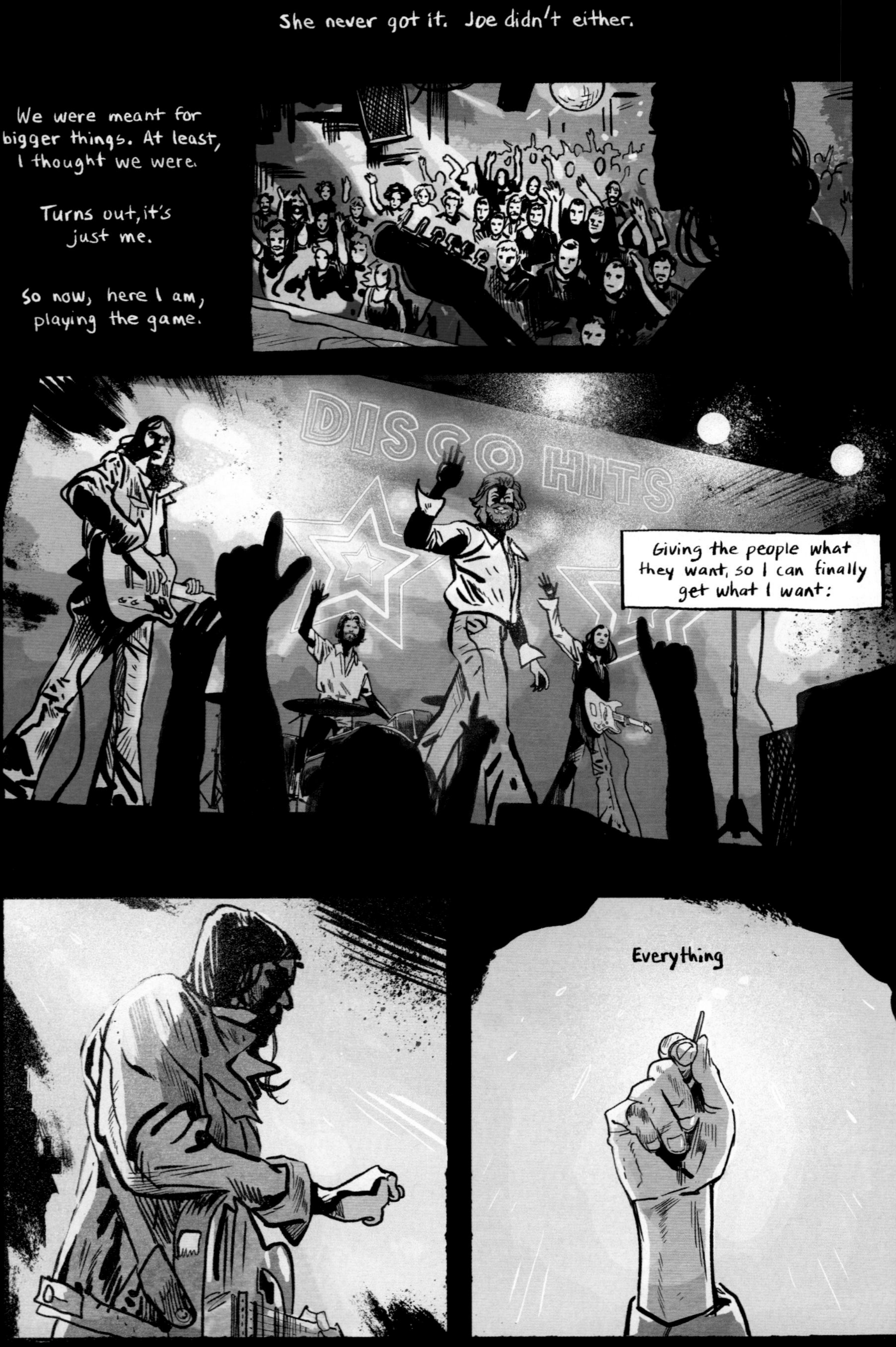
She never got it. Joe didn't either.
We were meant for bigger things. At least, I thought we were.
Turns out, it's just me.
So now, here I am, playing the game.
DISCO HITS
Giving the people what they want, so I can finally get what I want:
Everything

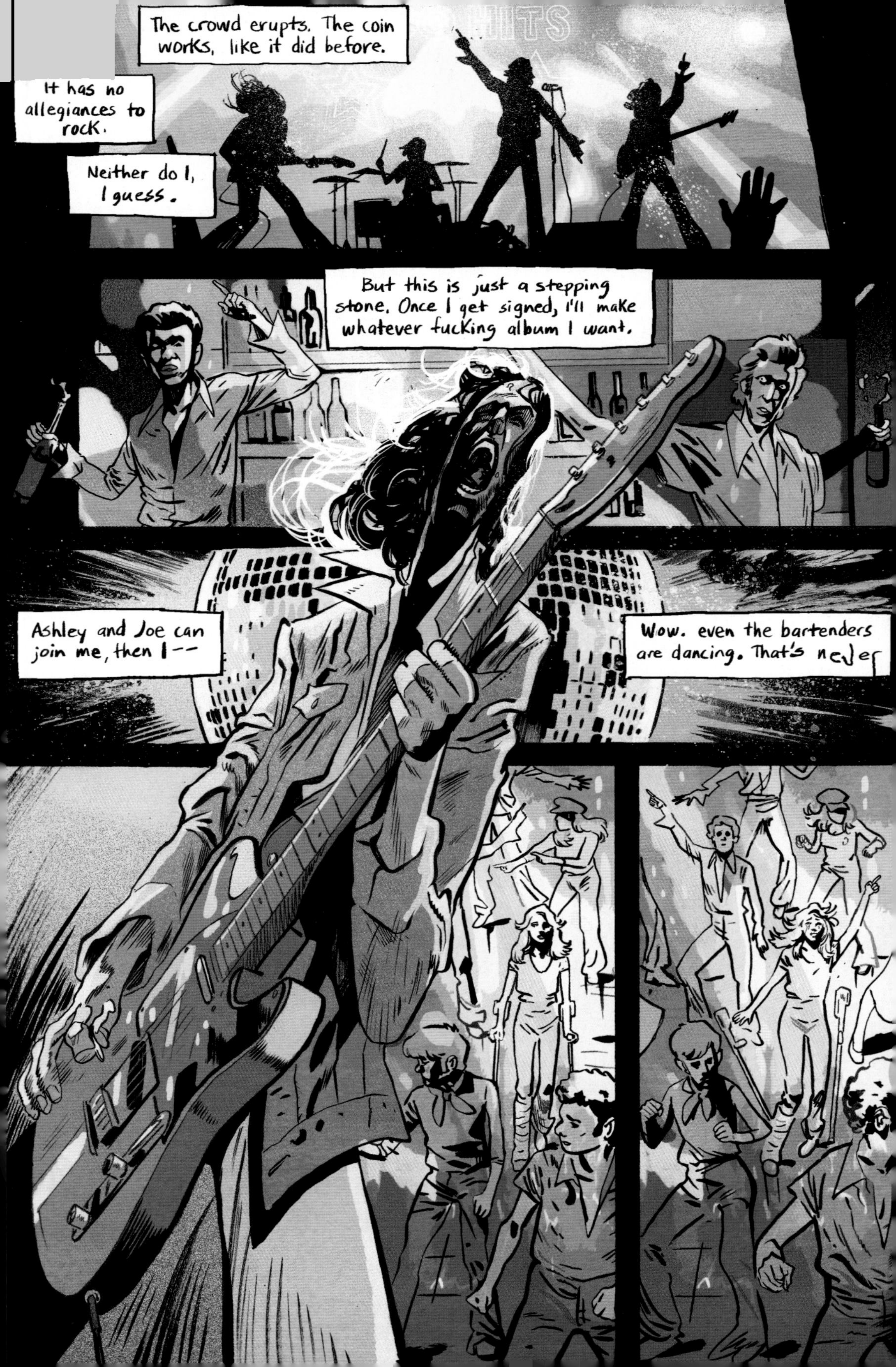

The crowd erupts. The coin works, like it did before.
It has no allegiances to rock.
Neither do I, I guess.
But this is just a stepping stone. Once I get signed, I'll make whatever fucking album I want.
Ashley and Joe can join me, then I --
Wow. even the bartenders are dancing. That's never

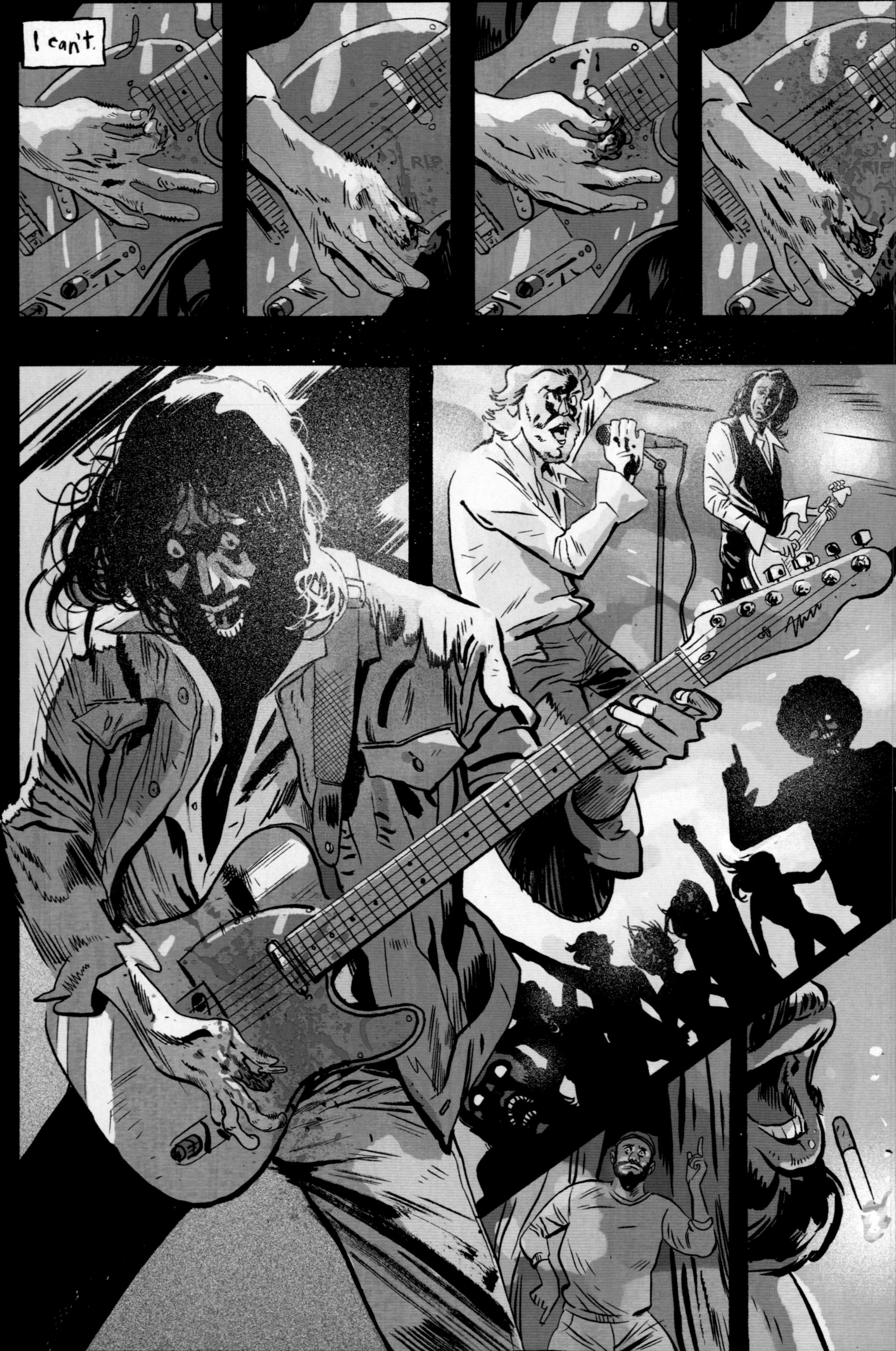
I can't.
RIP

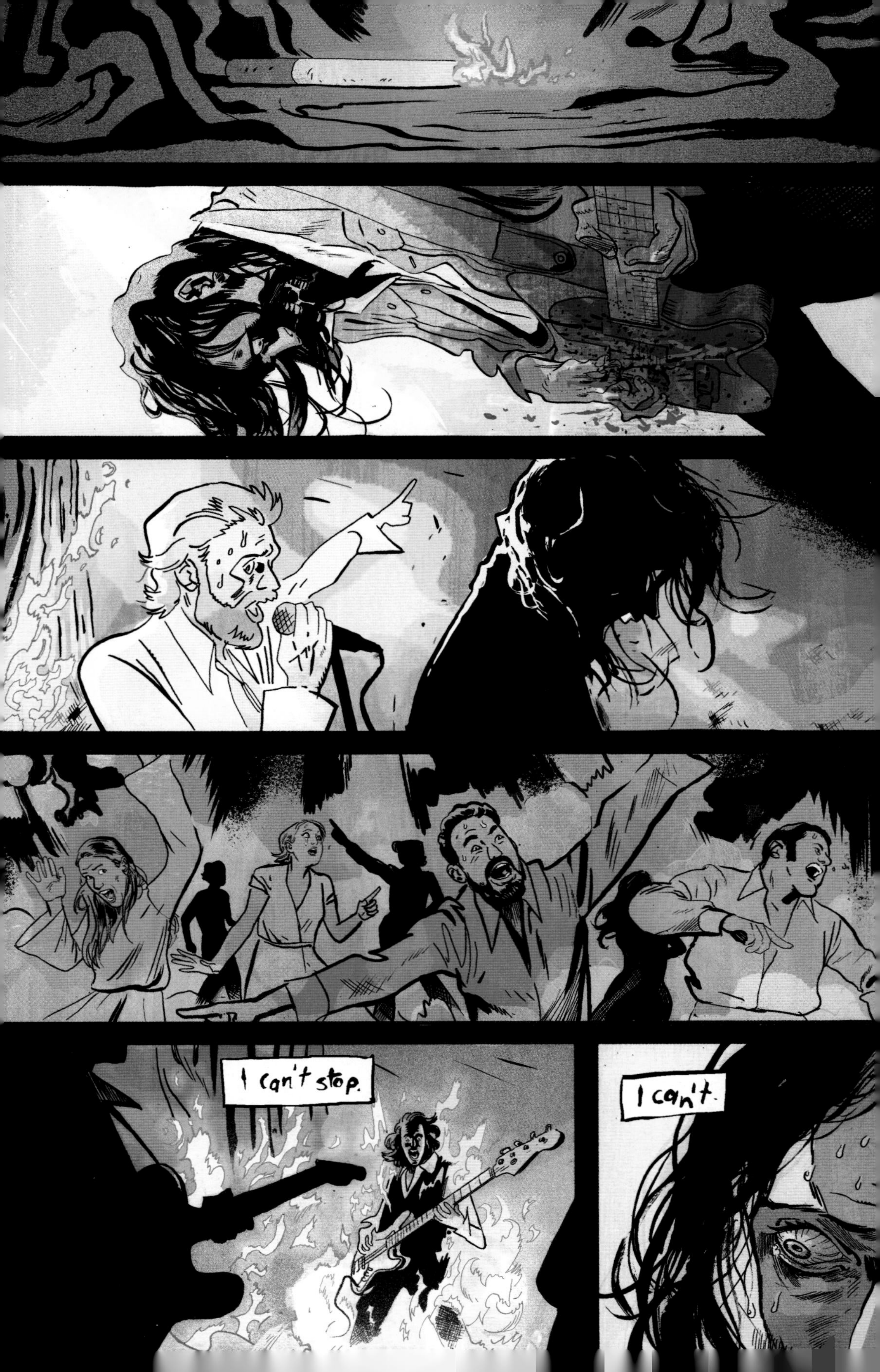
I can't stop.
I can't.

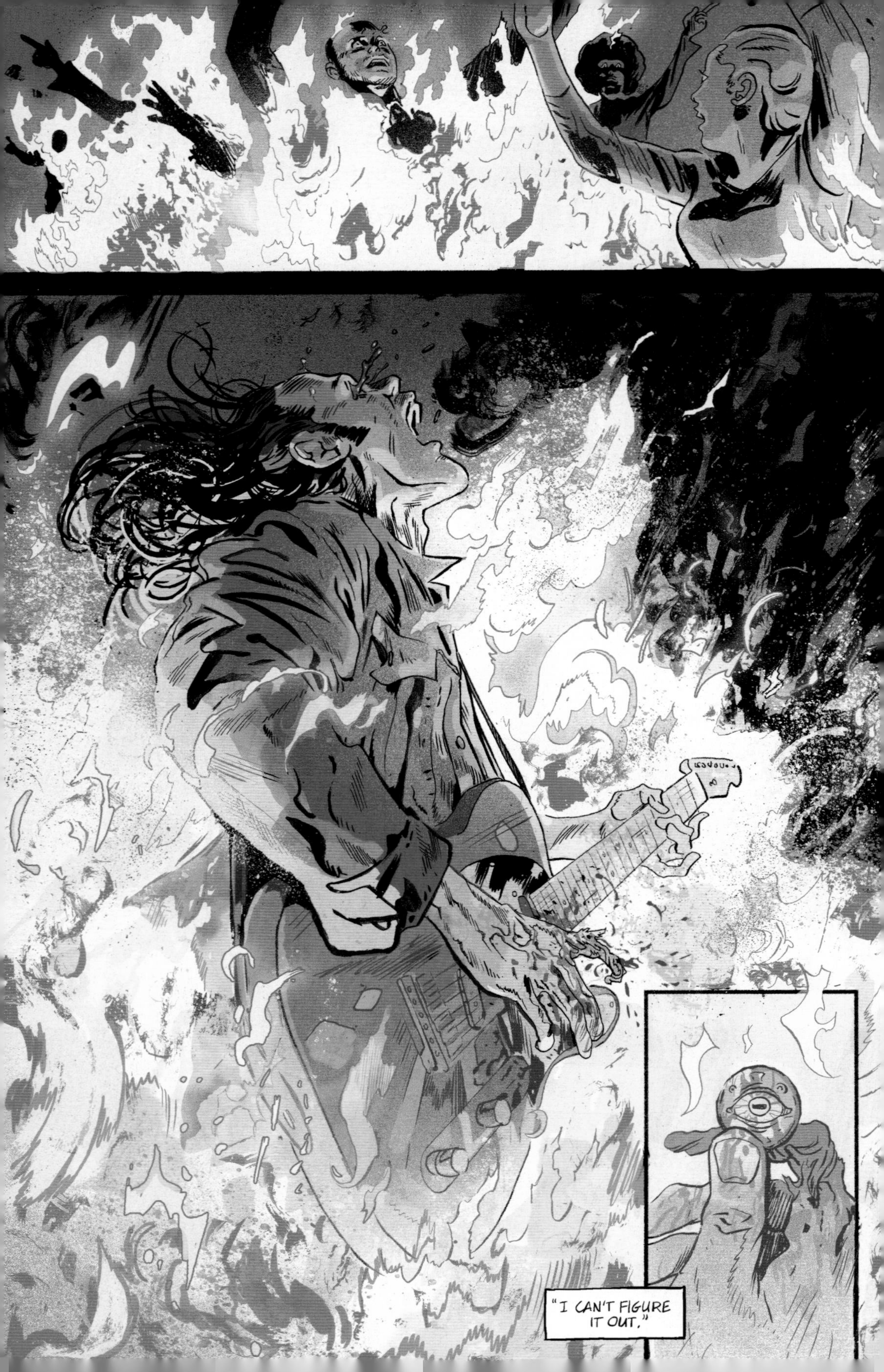
"I CAN'T FIGURE IT OUT."

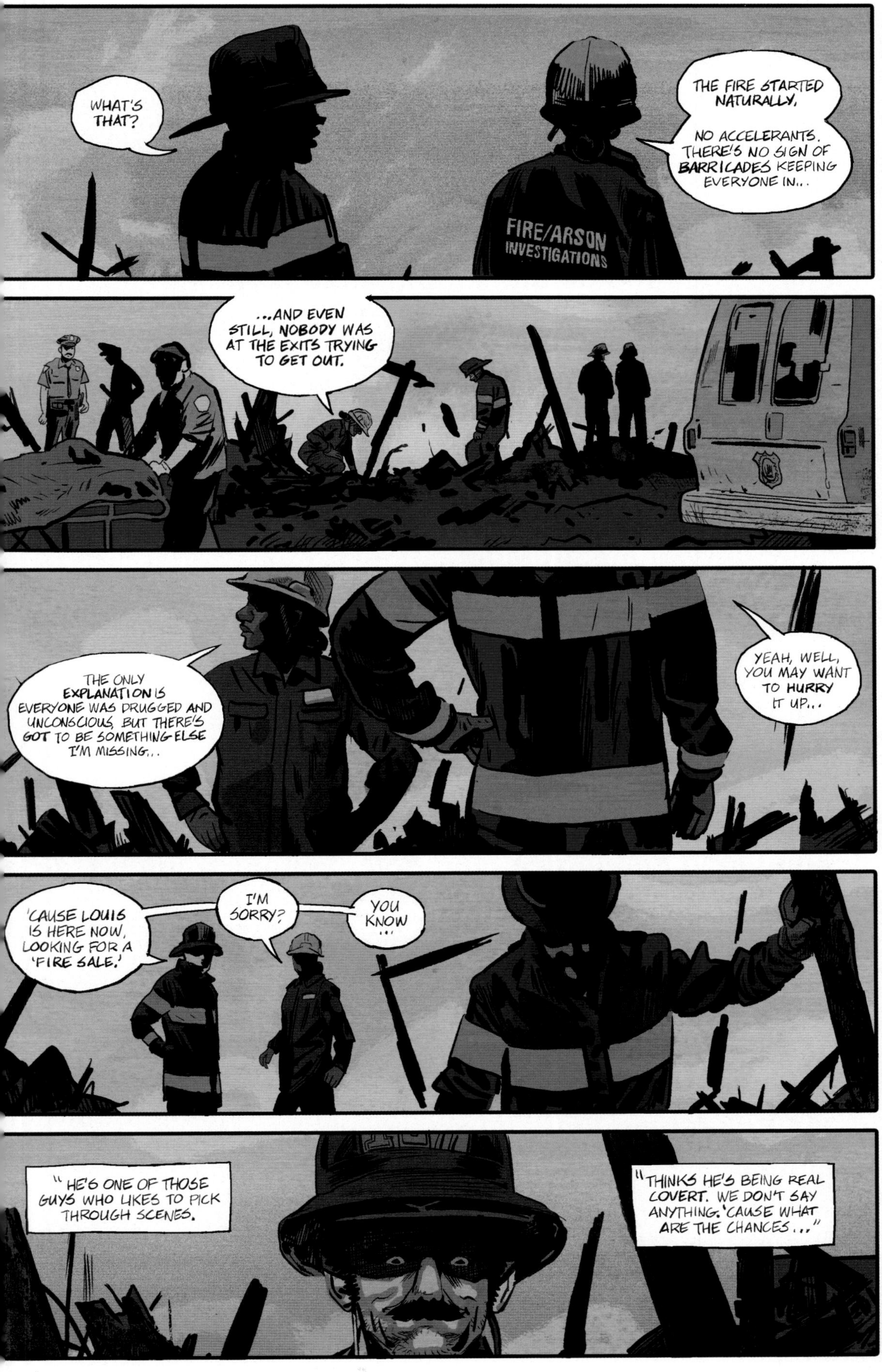
WHAT'S THAT?
THE FIRE STARTED NATURALLY,
NO ACCELERANTS. THERE'S NO SIGN OF BARRICADES KEEPING EVERYONE IN...
FIRE/ARSON INVESTIGATIONS
...AND EVEN STILL, NOBODY WAS AT THE EXITS TRYING TO GET OUT.
THE ONLY EXPLANATION IS EVERYONE WAS DRUGGED AND UNCONSCIOUS, BUT THERE'S GOT TO BE SOMETHING ELSE I'M MISSING...
YEAH, WELL, YOU MAY WANT TO HURRY IT UP...
'CAUSE LOUIS IS HERE NOW, LOOKING FOR A 'FIRE SALE.'
I'M SORRY?
YOU KNOW...
"HE'S ONE OF THOSE GUYS WHO LIKES TO PICK THROUGH SCENES.
"THINKS HE'S BEING REAL COVERT. WE DON'T SAY ANYTHING. 'CAUSE WHAT ARE THE CHANCES..."

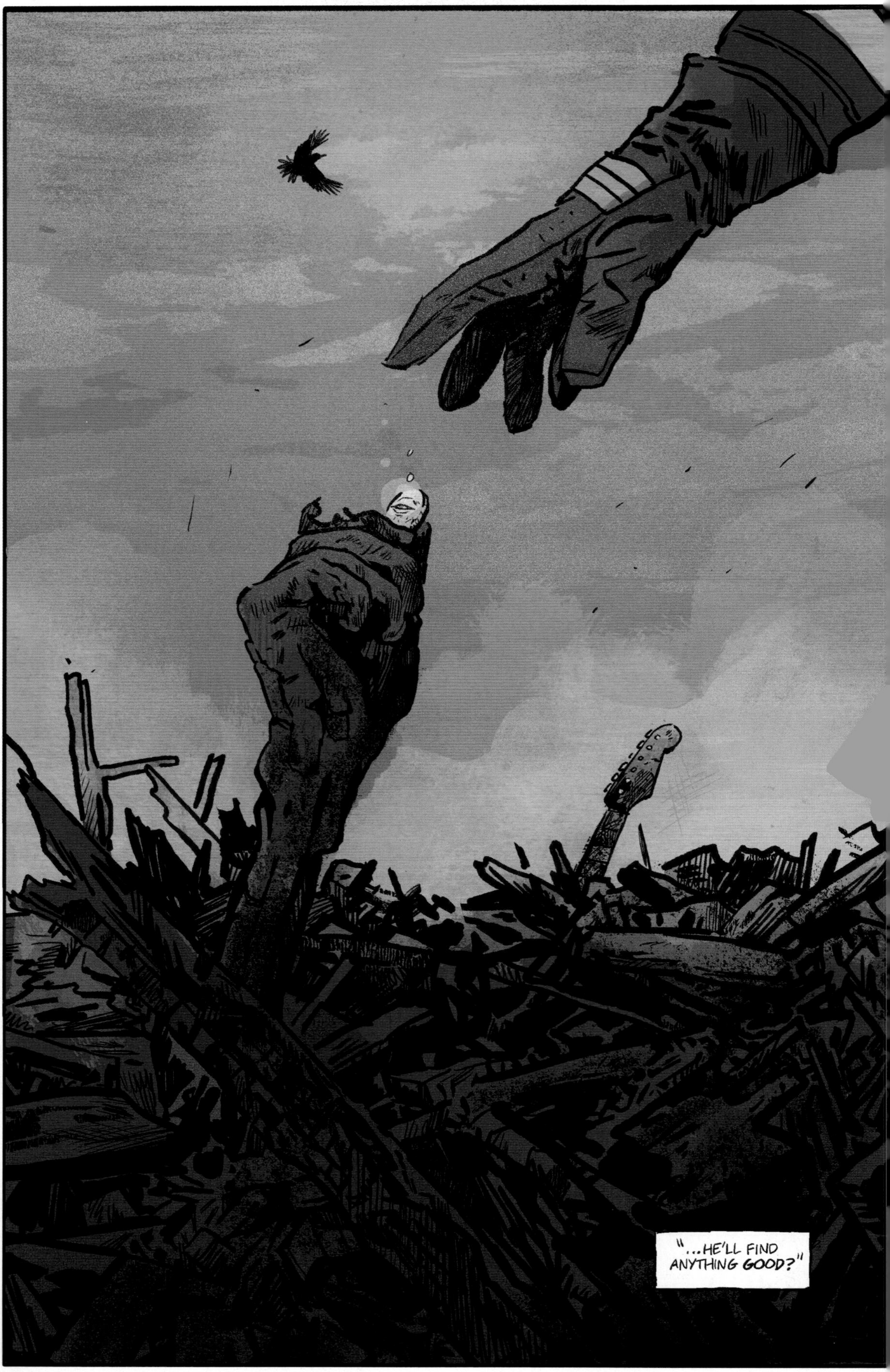
"...HE'LL FIND ANYTHING GOOD?"

"I'd use it, for as far as it'd take me."

² Girls of Summer

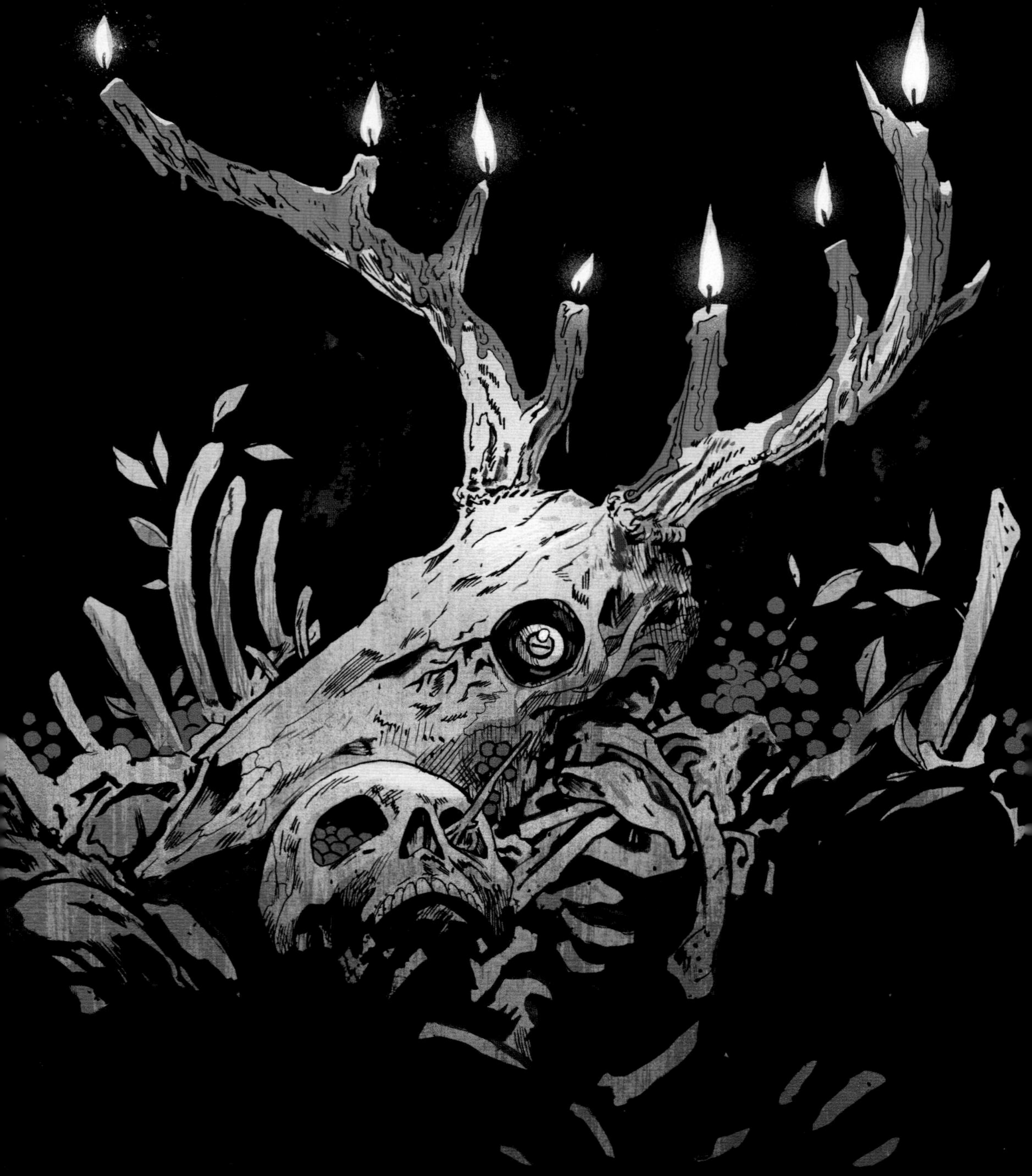

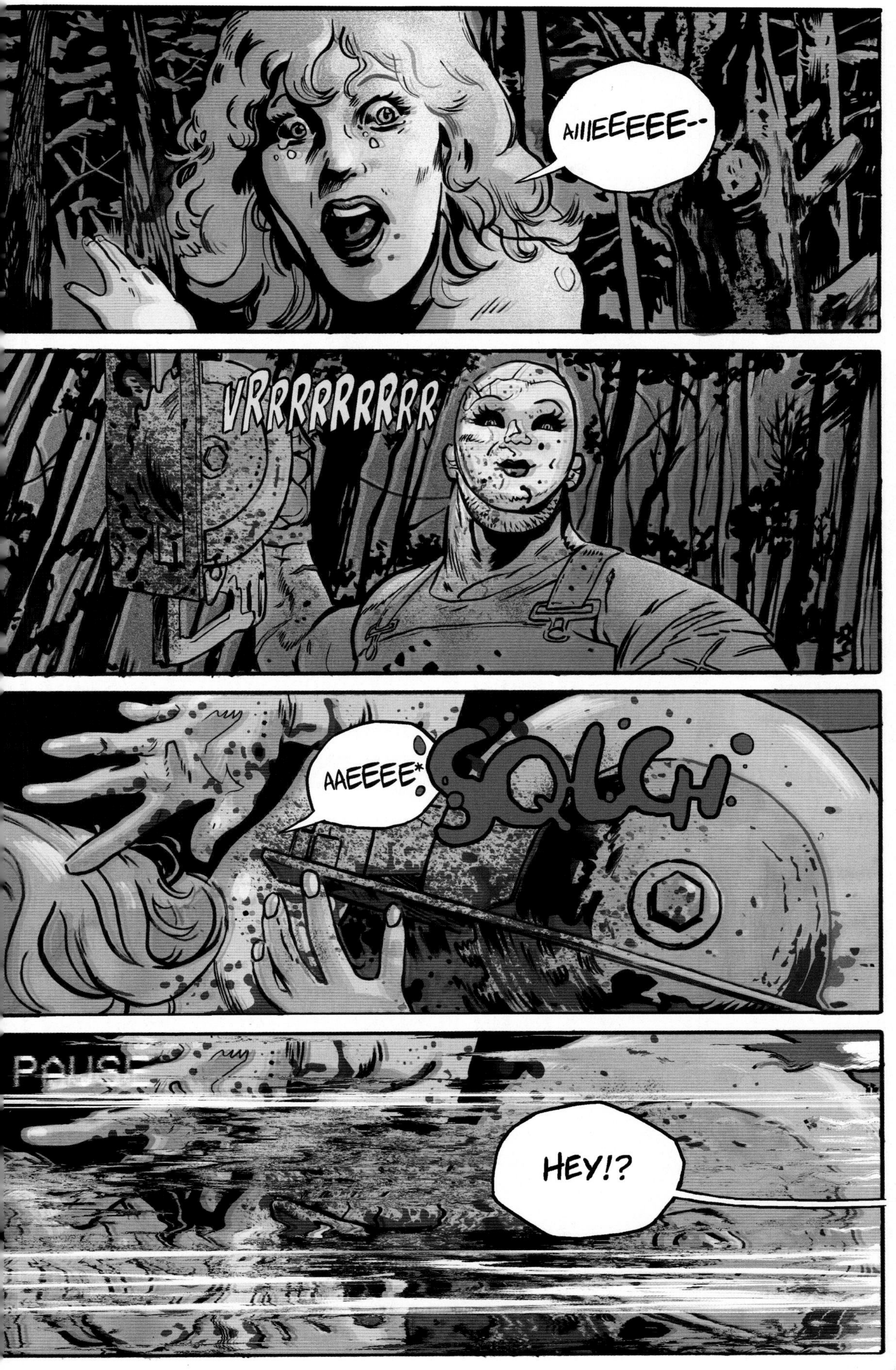
AIIIEEEEE--
VRRRRRRRRR
AAEEEE*
SQLCH
PAUSE
HEY!?

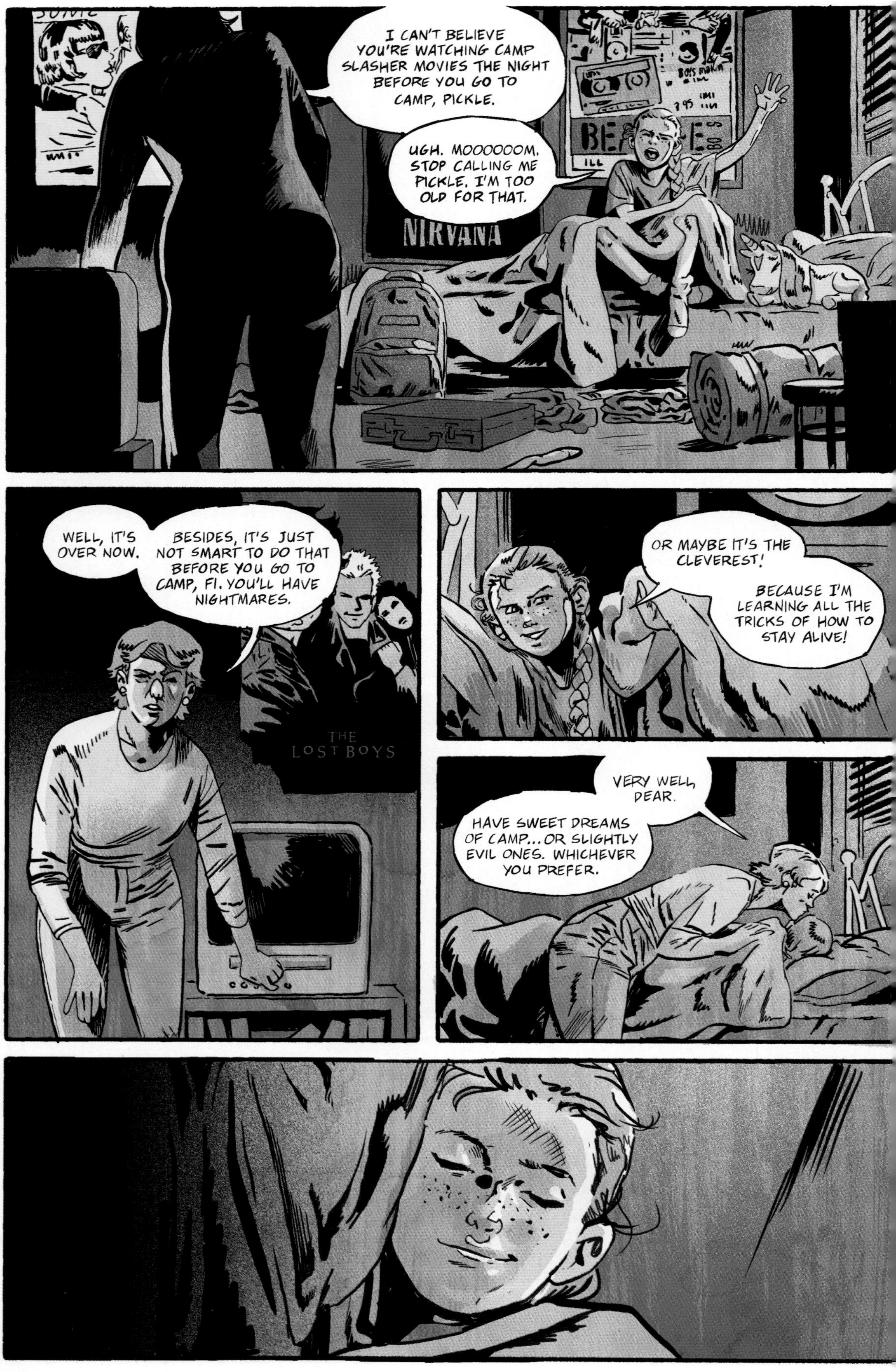
I CAN'T BELIEVE YOU'RE WATCHING CAMP SLASHER MOVIES THE NIGHT BEFORE YOU GO TO CAMP, PICKLE.
UGH. MOOOOOOM. STOP CALLING ME PICKLE. I'M TOO OLD FOR THAT.
NIRVANA
WELL, IT'S OVER NOW.
BESIDES, IT'S JUST NOT SMART TO DO THAT BEFORE YOU GO TO CAMP, FI. YOU'LL HAVE NIGHTMARES.
THE LOST BOYS
OR MAYBE IT'S THE CLEVEREST!
BECAUSE I'M LEARNING ALL THE TRICKS OF HOW TO STAY ALIVE!
VERY WELL, DEAR.
HAVE SWEET DREAMS OF CAMP... OR SLIGHTLY EVIL ONES. WHICHEVER YOU PREFER.

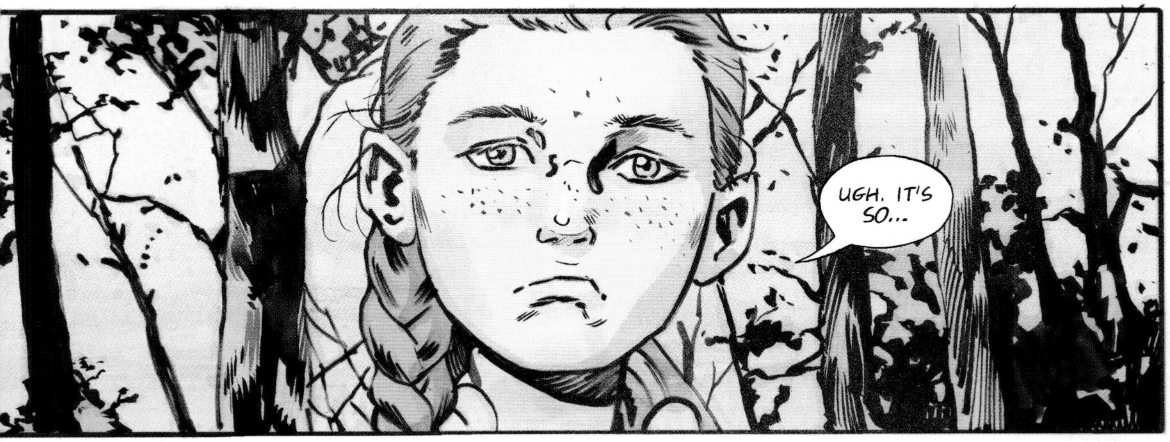
UGH. IT'S SO...

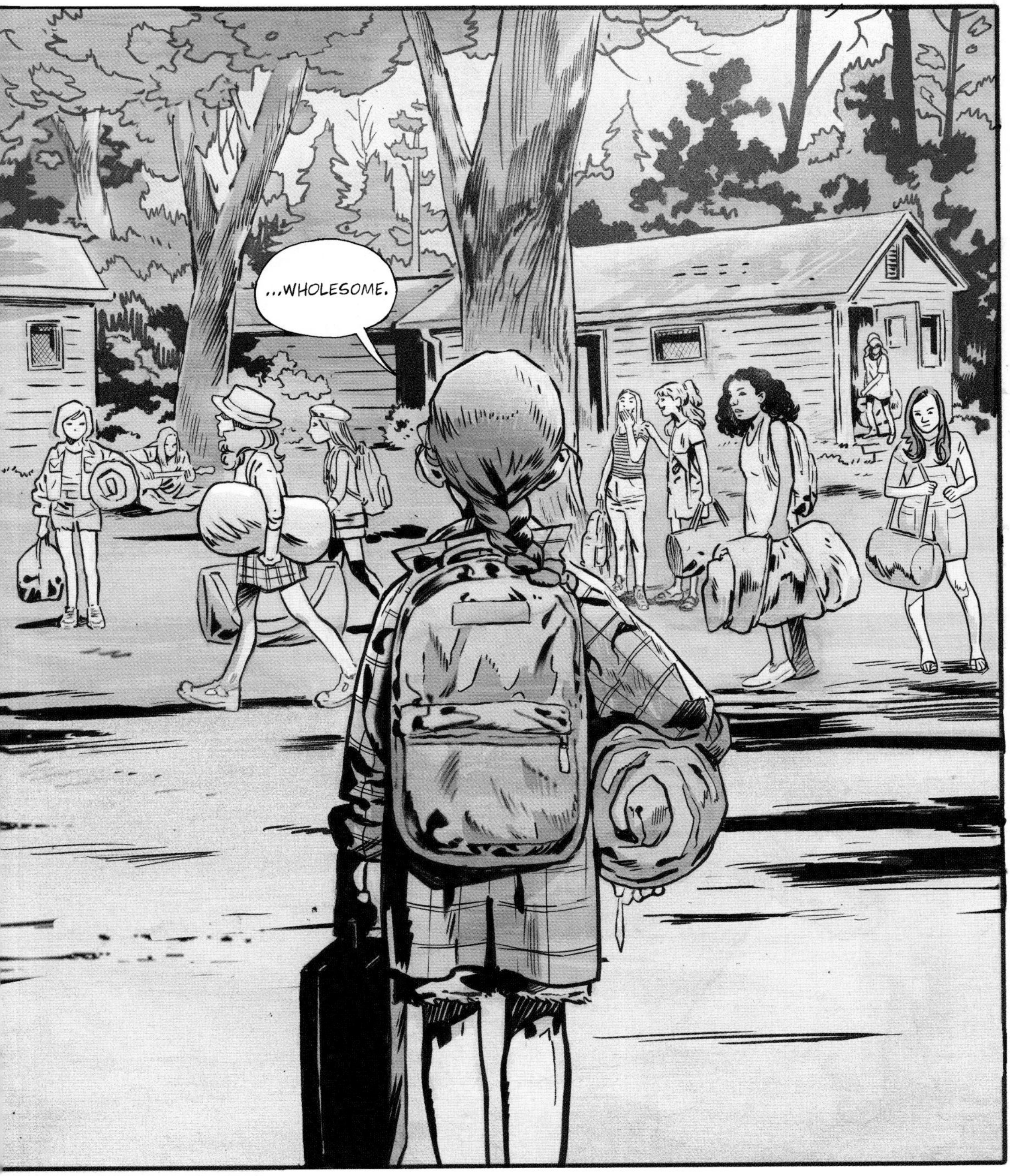
...WHOLESOME.

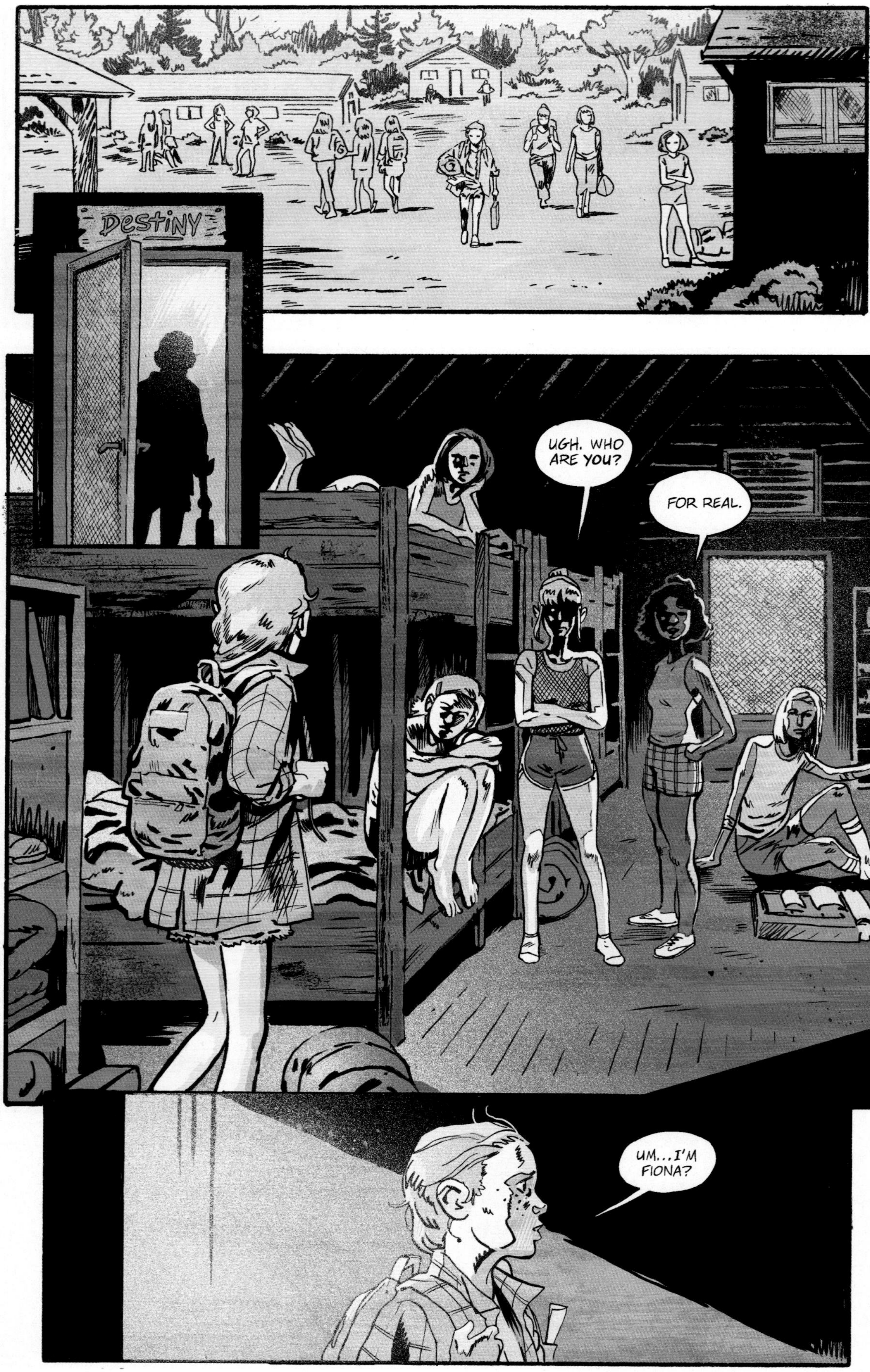
DESTINY
UGH. WHO ARE YOU?
FOR REAL.
UM...I'M FIONA?

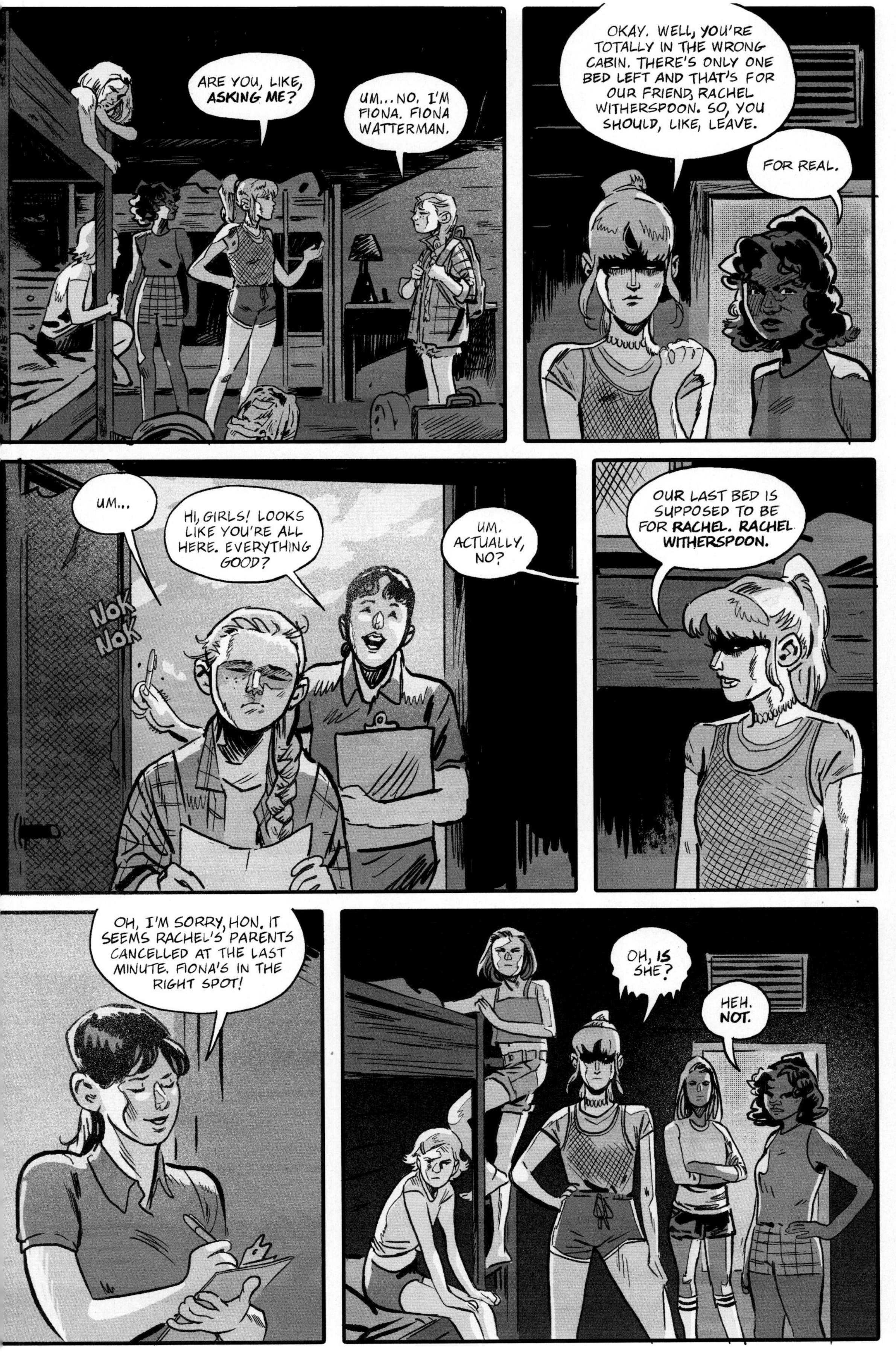
ARE YOU, LIKE, ASKING ME?
UM...NO, I'M FIONA. FIONA WATTERMAN.
OKAY. WELL, YOU'RE TOTALLY IN THE WRONG CABIN. THERE'S ONLY ONE BED LEFT AND THAT'S FOR OUR FRIEND, RACHEL WITHERSPOON. SO, YOU SHOULD, LIKE, LEAVE.
FOR REAL.
UM...
NOK NOK
HI, GIRLS! LOOKS LIKE YOU'RE ALL HERE. EVERYTHING GOOD?
UM. ACTUALLY, NO?
OUR LAST BED IS SUPPOSED TO BE FOR RACHEL. RACHEL WITHERSPOON.
OH, I'M SORRY, HON. IT SEEMS RACHEL'S PARENTS CANCELLED AT THE LAST MINUTE. FIONA'S IN THE RIGHT SPOT!
OH, IS SHE?
HEH. NOT.

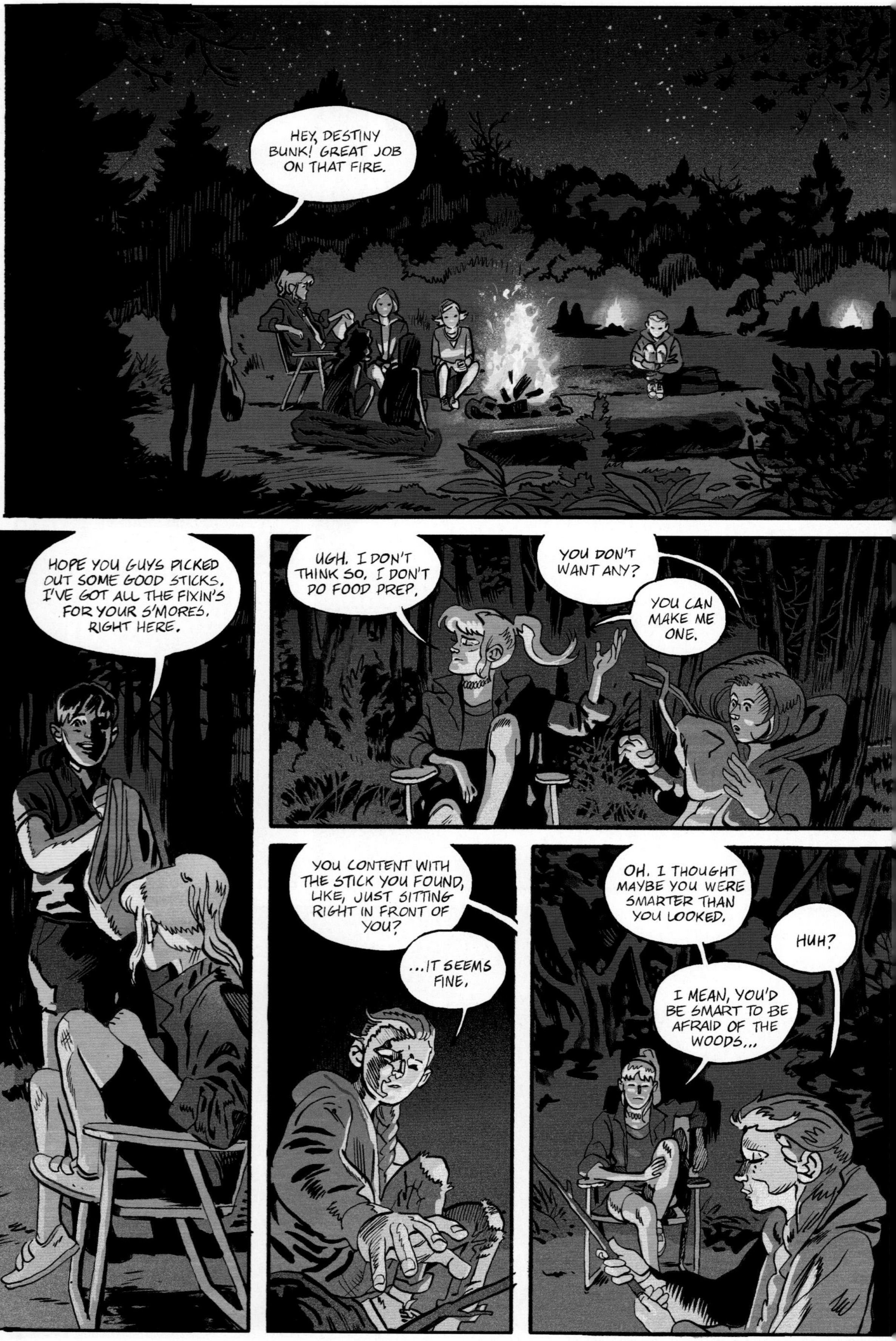
HEY, DESTINY BUNK! GREAT JOB ON THAT FIRE.
HOPE YOU GUYS PICKED OUT SOME GOOD STICKS. I'VE GOT ALL THE FIXIN'S FOR YOUR S'MORES, RIGHT HERE.
UGH. I DON'T THINK SO. I DON'T DO FOOD PREP.
YOU DON'T WANT ANY?
YOU CAN MAKE ME ONE.
YOU CONTENT WITH THE STICK YOU FOUND, LIKE, JUST SITTING RIGHT IN FRONT OF YOU?
...IT SEEMS FINE.
OH. I THOUGHT MAYBE YOU WERE SMARTER THAN YOU LOOKED.
HUH?
I MEAN, YOU'D BE SMART TO BE AFRAID OF THE WOODS...

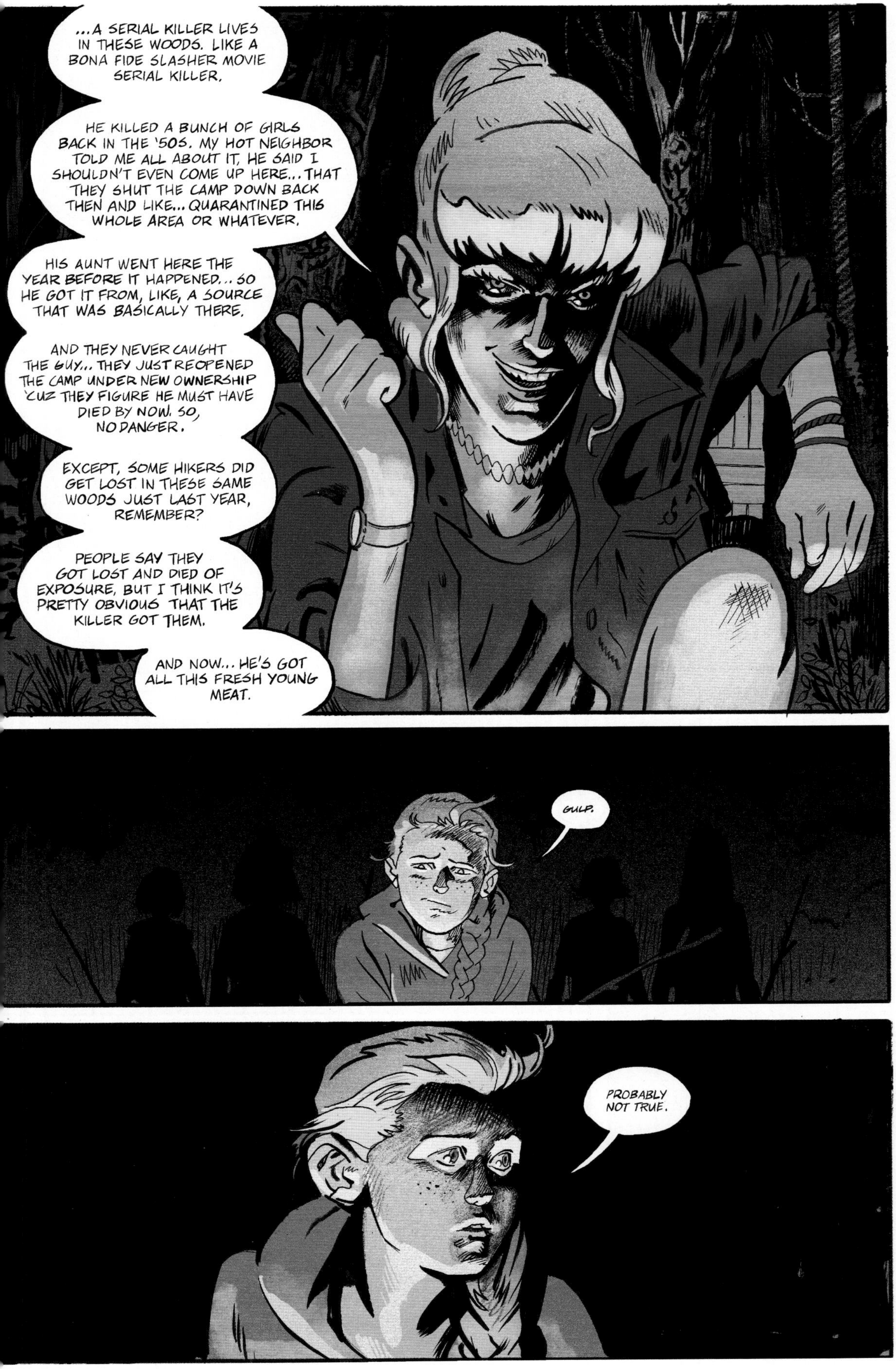
...A SERIAL KILLER LIVES IN THESE WOODS. LIKE A BONA FIDE SLASHER MOVIE SERIAL KILLER.
HE KILLED A BUNCH OF GIRLS BACK IN THE '50S. MY HOT NEIGHBOR TOLD ME ALL ABOUT IT, HE SAID I SHOULDN'T EVEN COME UP HERE... THAT THEY SHUT THE CAMP DOWN BACK THEN AND LIKE... QUARANTINED THIS WHOLE AREA OR WHATEVER.
HIS AUNT WENT HERE THE YEAR BEFORE IT HAPPENED... SO HE GOT IT FROM, LIKE, A SOURCE THAT WAS BASICALLY THERE.
AND THEY NEVER CAUGHT THE GUY... THEY JUST REOPENED THE CAMP UNDER NEW OWNERSHIP 'CUZ THEY FIGURE HE MUST HAVE DIED BY NOW. SO, NO DANGER.
EXCEPT, SOME HIKERS DID GET LOST IN THESE SAME WOODS JUST LAST YEAR, REMEMBER?
PEOPLE SAY THEY GOT LOST AND DIED OF EXPOSURE, BUT I THINK IT'S PRETTY OBVIOUS THAT THE KILLER GOT THEM.
AND NOW... HE'S GOT ALL THIS FRESH YOUNG MEAT.
GULP.
PROBABLY NOT TRUE.

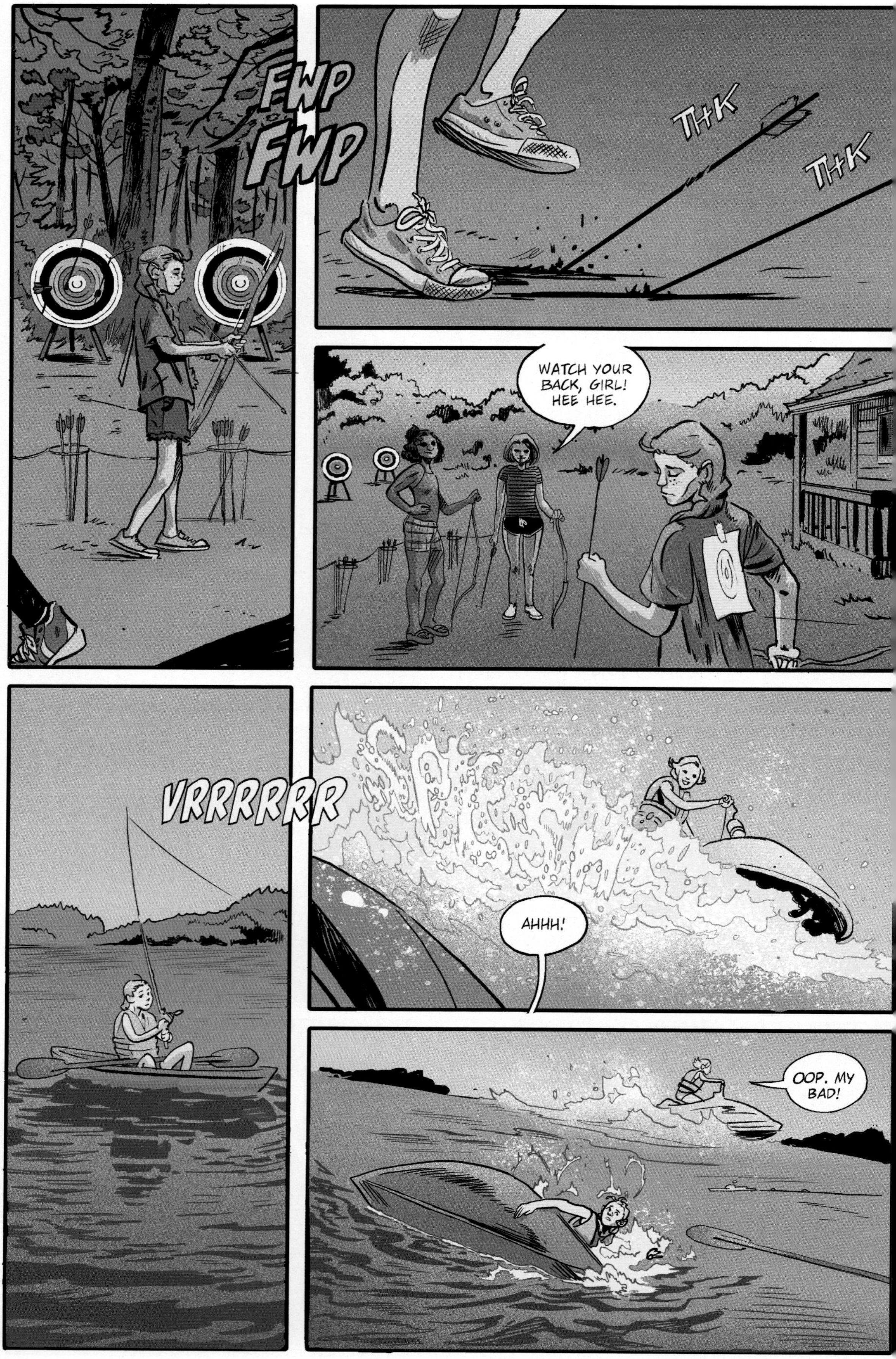
FWP
FWP
THK
THK
WATCH YOUR BACK, GIRL! HEE HEE.
VRRRRRRR
AHHH!
OOP. MY BAD!

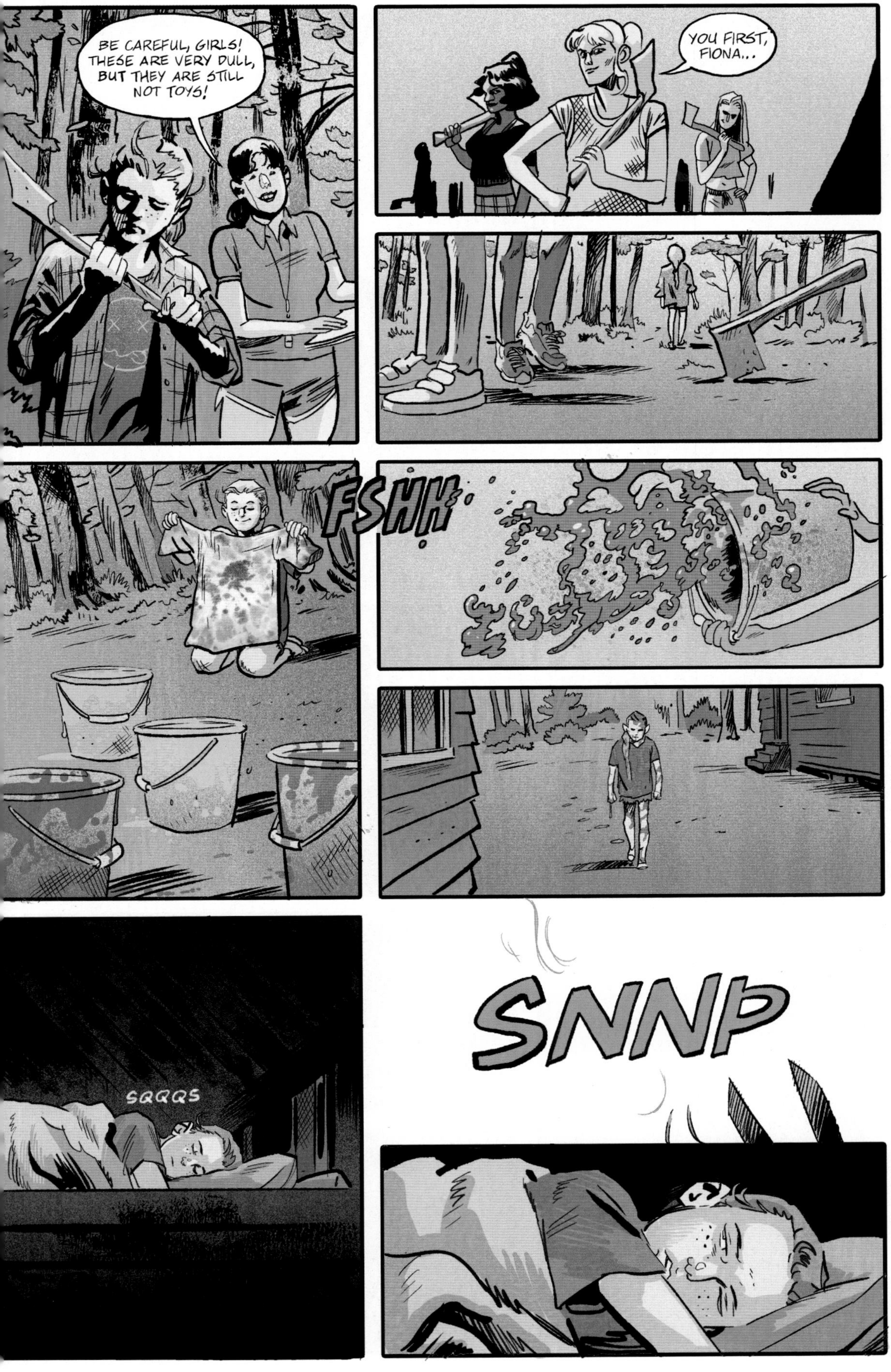
BE CAREFUL, GIRLS! THESE ARE VERY DULL, BUT THEY ARE STILL NOT TOYS!
YOU FIRST, FIONA...
FSHH
SQQQS
SNNP

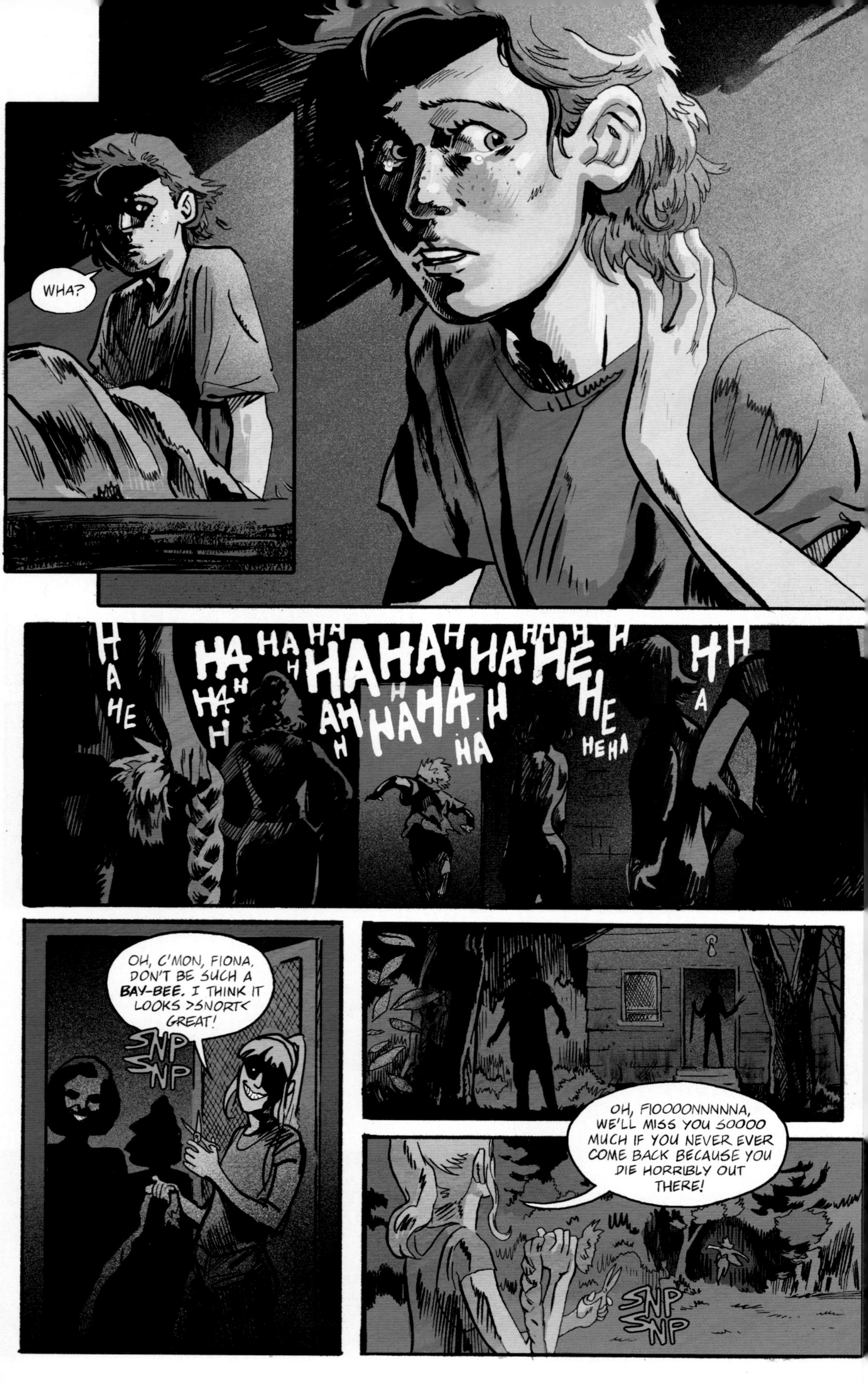
WHA?
HA HA HA HAHA HA HE HA HE HEHA
OH, C'MON, FIONA, DON'T BE SUCH A **BAY-BEE.** I THINK IT LOOKS >SNORT< GREAT!
SNP SNP
OH, FIOOOONNNNNA, WE'LL MISS YOU SOOOO MUCH IF YOU NEVER EVER COME BACK BECAUSE YOU DIE HORRIBLY OUT THERE!
SNP SNP

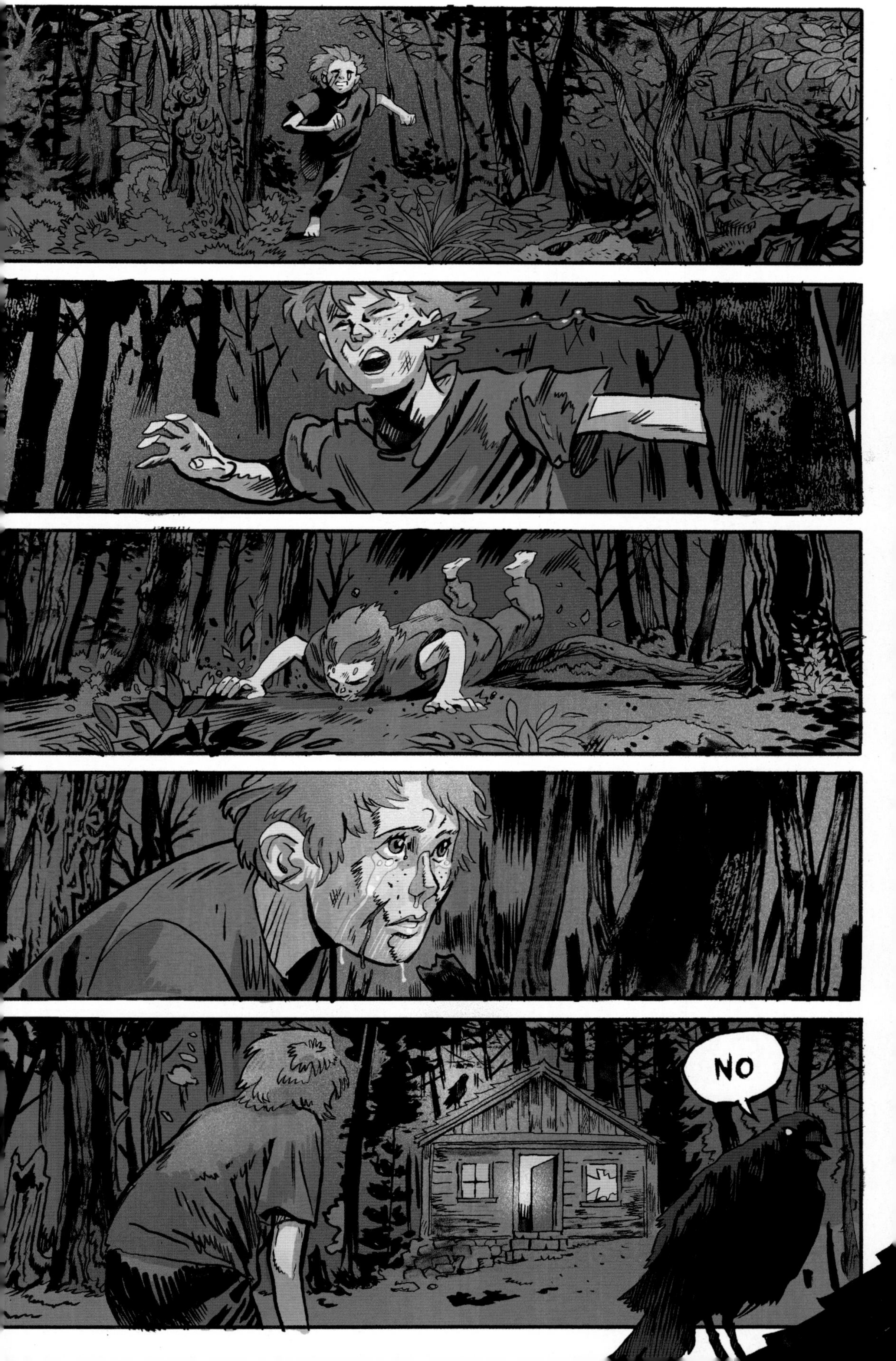
NO

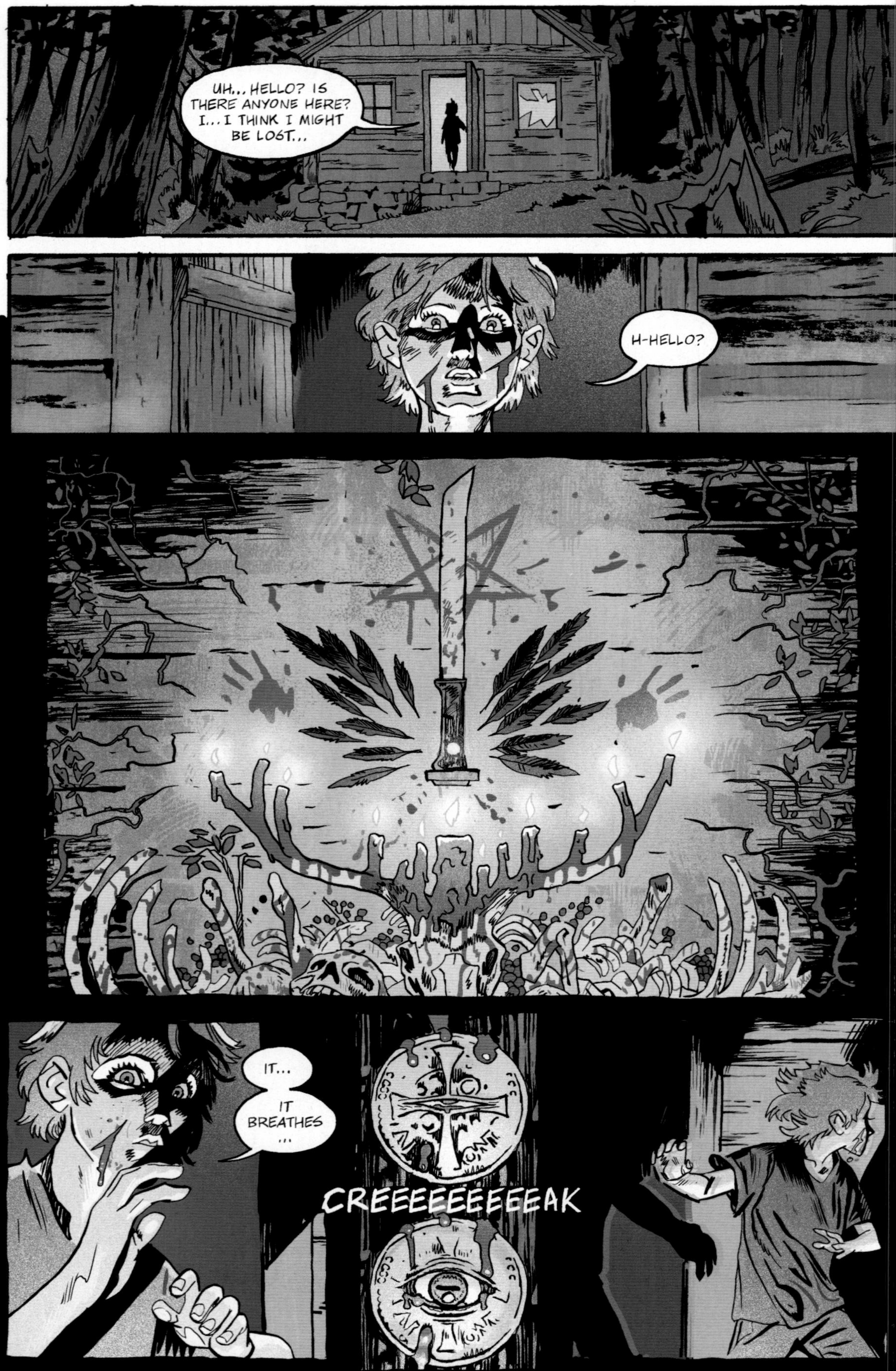
UH... HELLO? IS THERE ANYONE HERE? I... I THINK I MIGHT BE LOST...
H-HELLO?
IT...
IT BREATHES ...
CREEEEEEEEEEAK

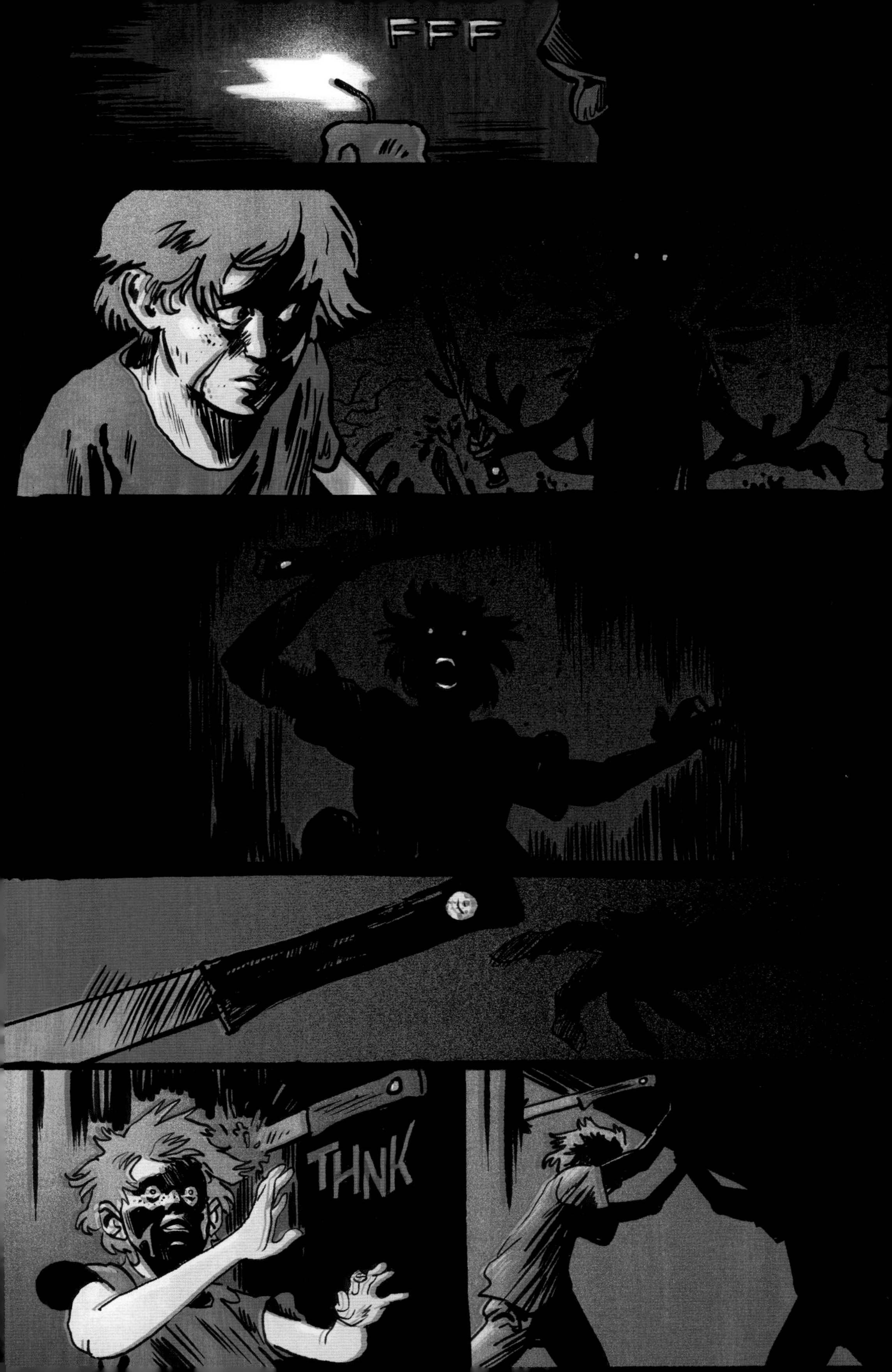
FFF
THNK

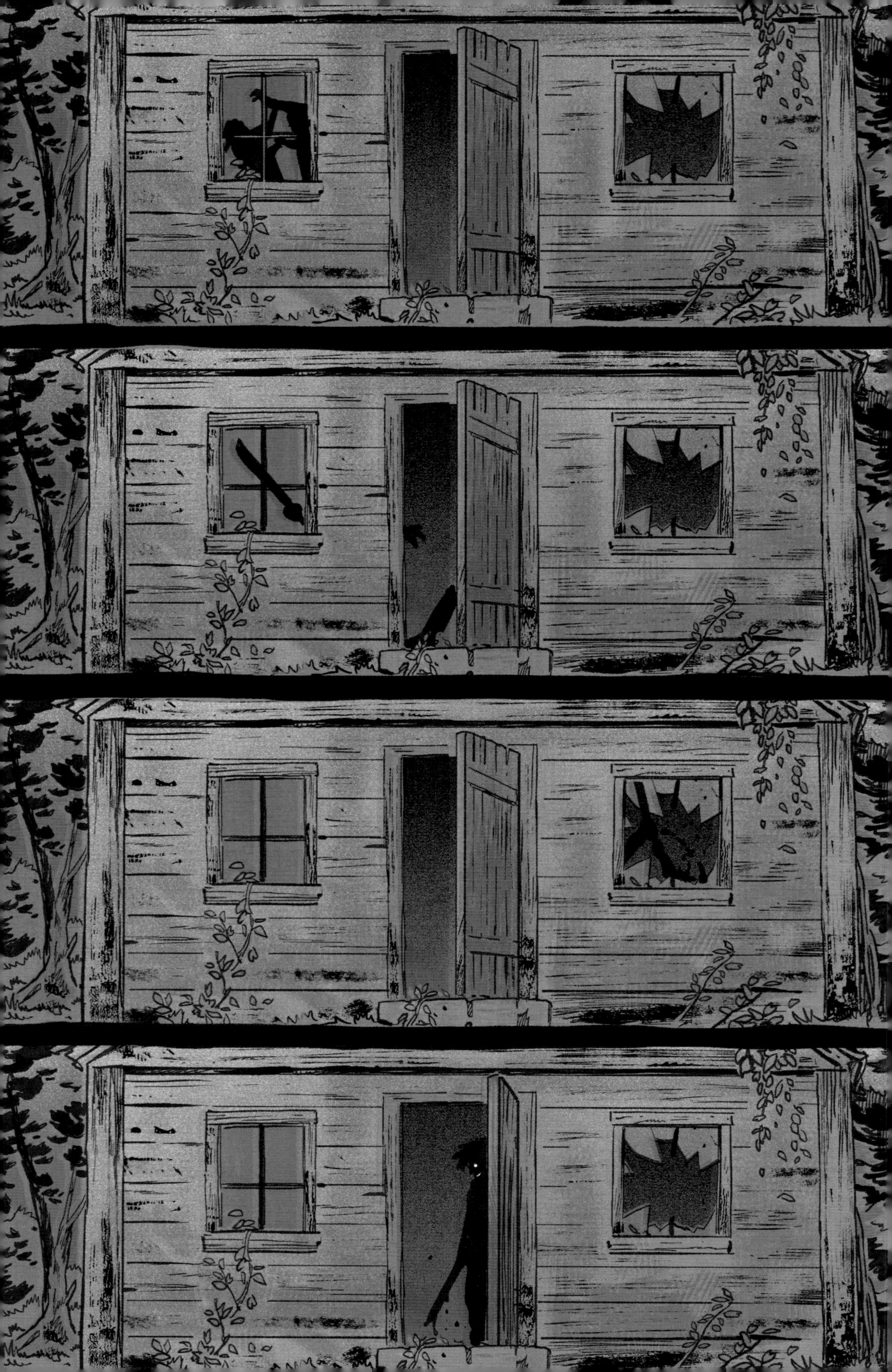

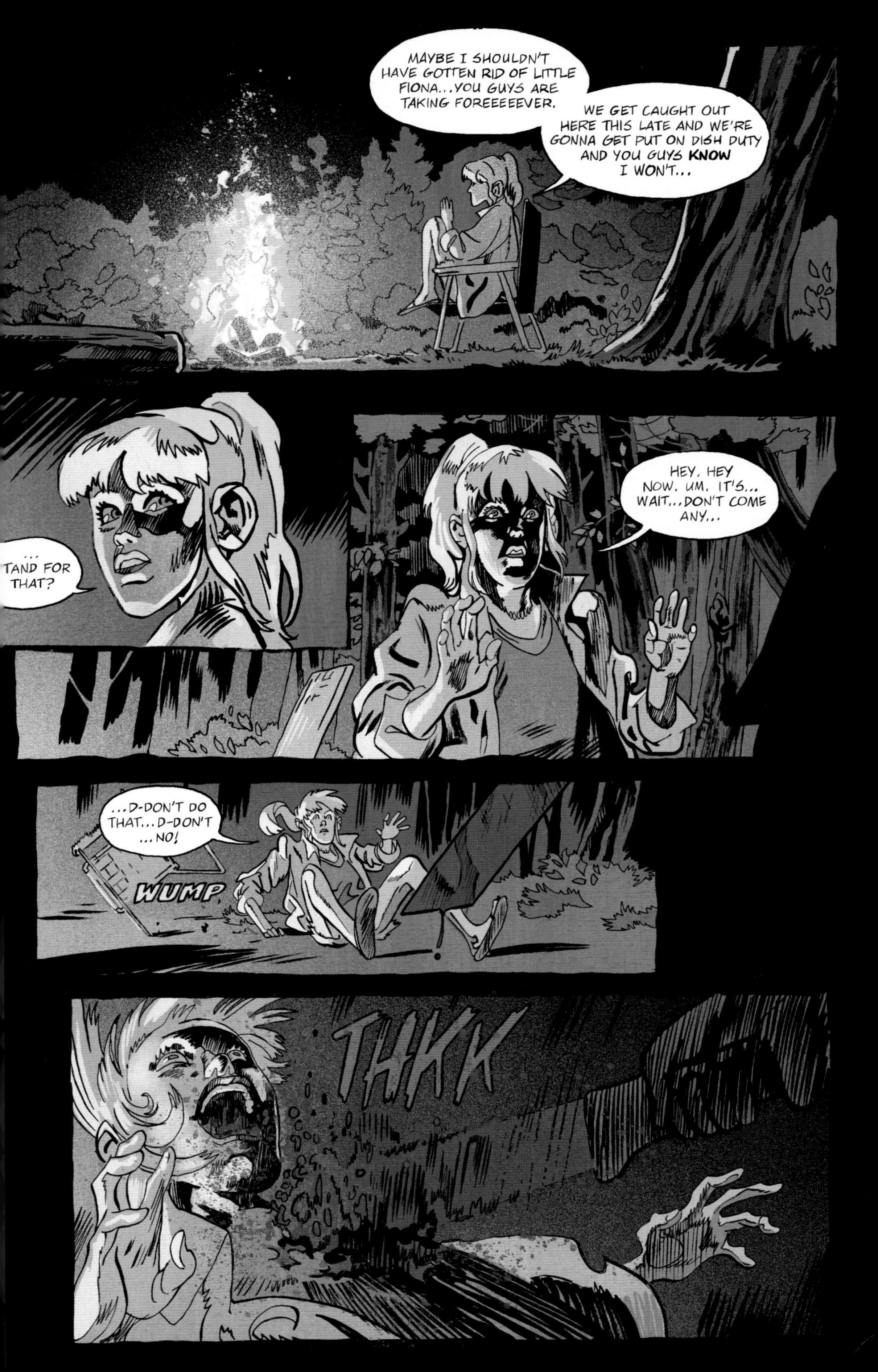
MAYBE I SHOULDN'T HAVE GOTTEN RID OF LITTLE FIONA...YOU GUYS ARE TAKING FOREEEEEVER.
WE GET CAUGHT OUT HERE THIS LATE AND WE'RE GONNA GET PUT ON DISH DUTY AND YOU GUYS KNOW I WON'T...
...TAND FOR THAT?
HEY, HEY NOW. UM, IT'S... WAIT...DON'T COME ANY...
...D-DON'T DO THAT...D-DON'T ...NO!
WUMP
THKK

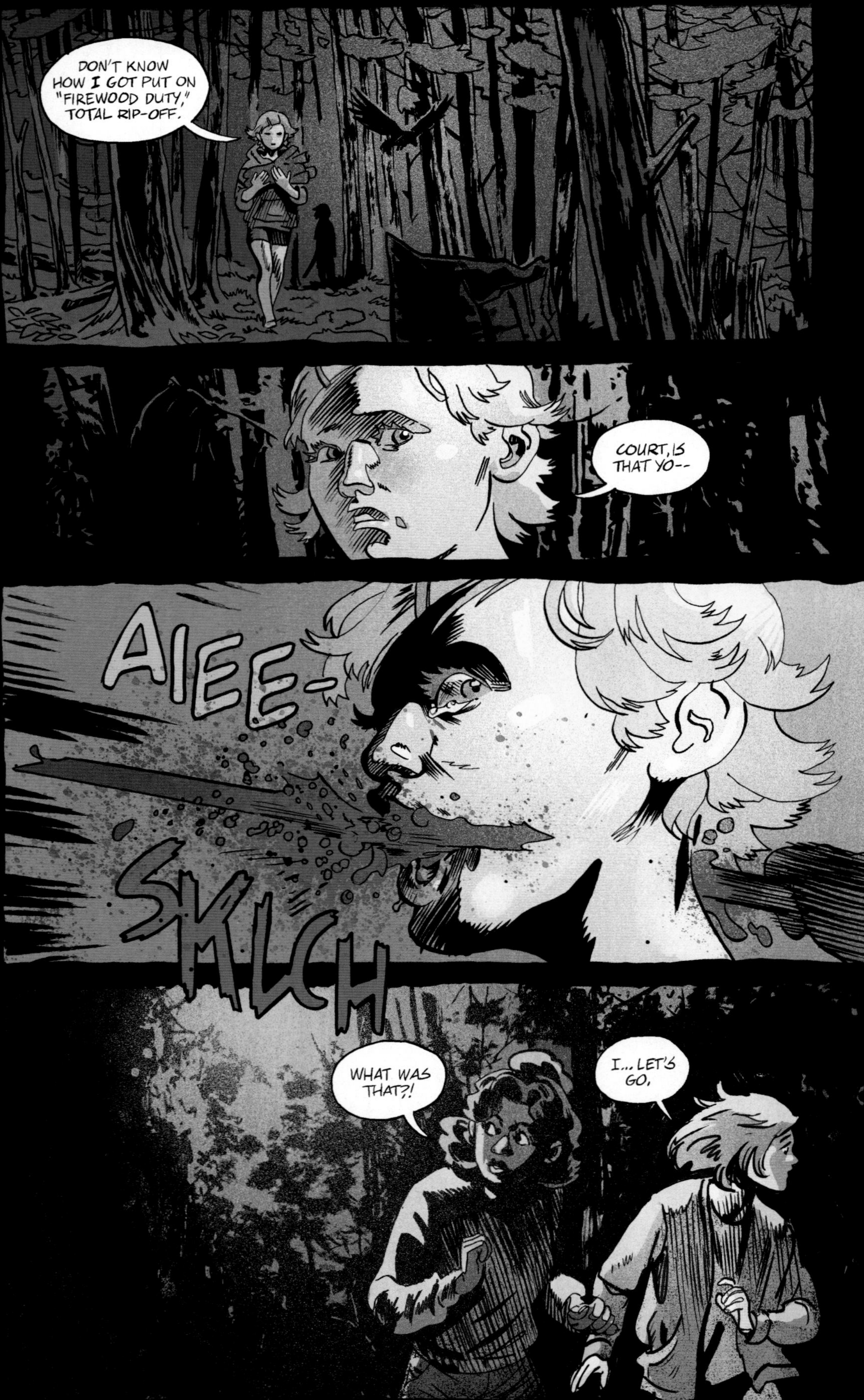

DON'T KNOW HOW I GOT PUT ON "FIREWOOD DUTY," TOTAL RIP-OFF.
COURT, IS THAT YO--
AIEE-
SKLCH
WHAT WAS THAT?!
I... LET'S GO.

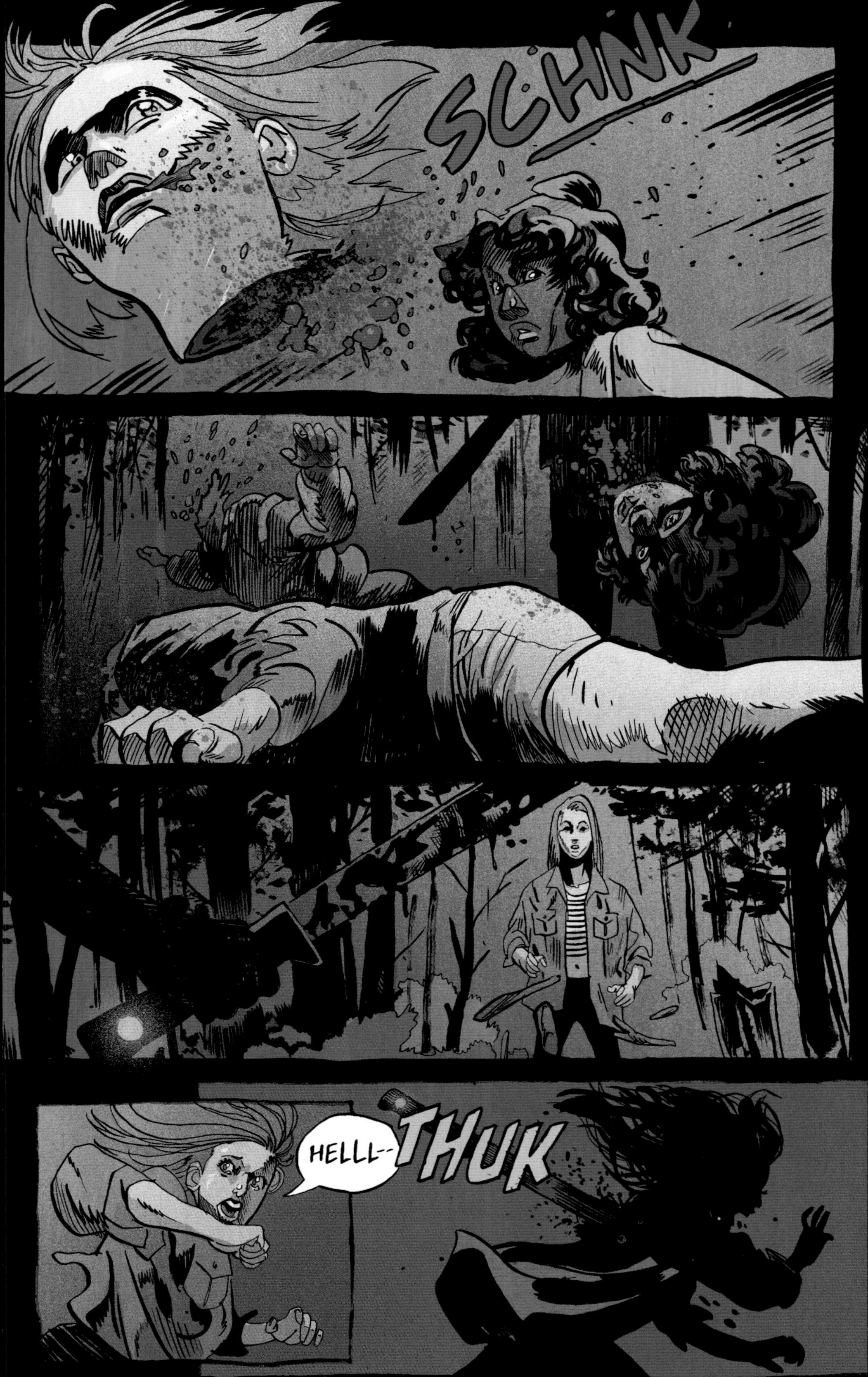
SCHNK
HELLL--
THUK

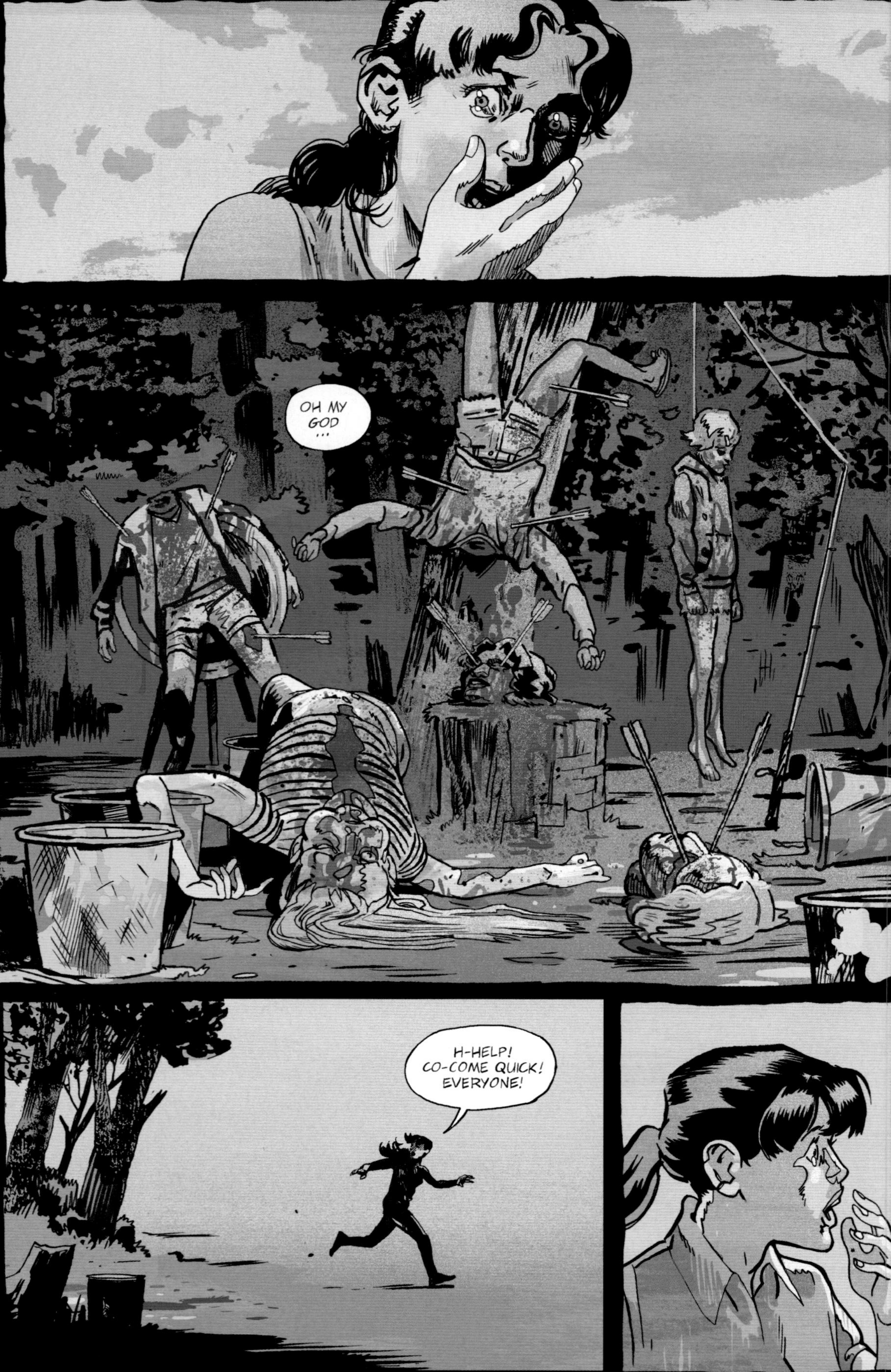
OH MY GOD ...
H-HELP! CO-COME QUICK! EVERYONE!

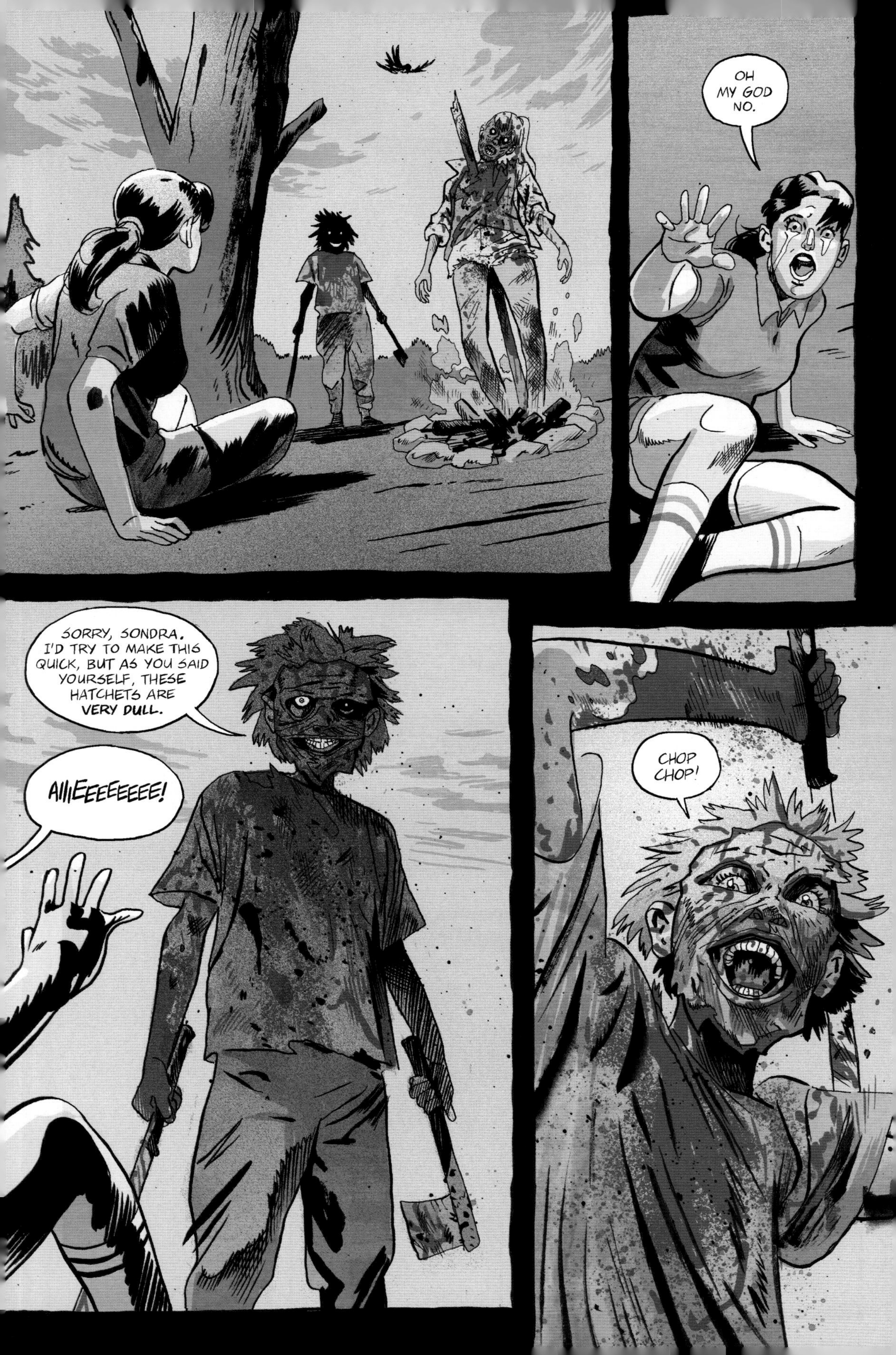
OH MY GOD NO.
SORRY, SONDRA. I'D TRY TO MAKE THIS QUICK, BUT AS YOU SAID YOURSELF, THESE HATCHETS ARE **VERY DULL.**
AIIIEEEEEEEE!
CHOP CHOP!

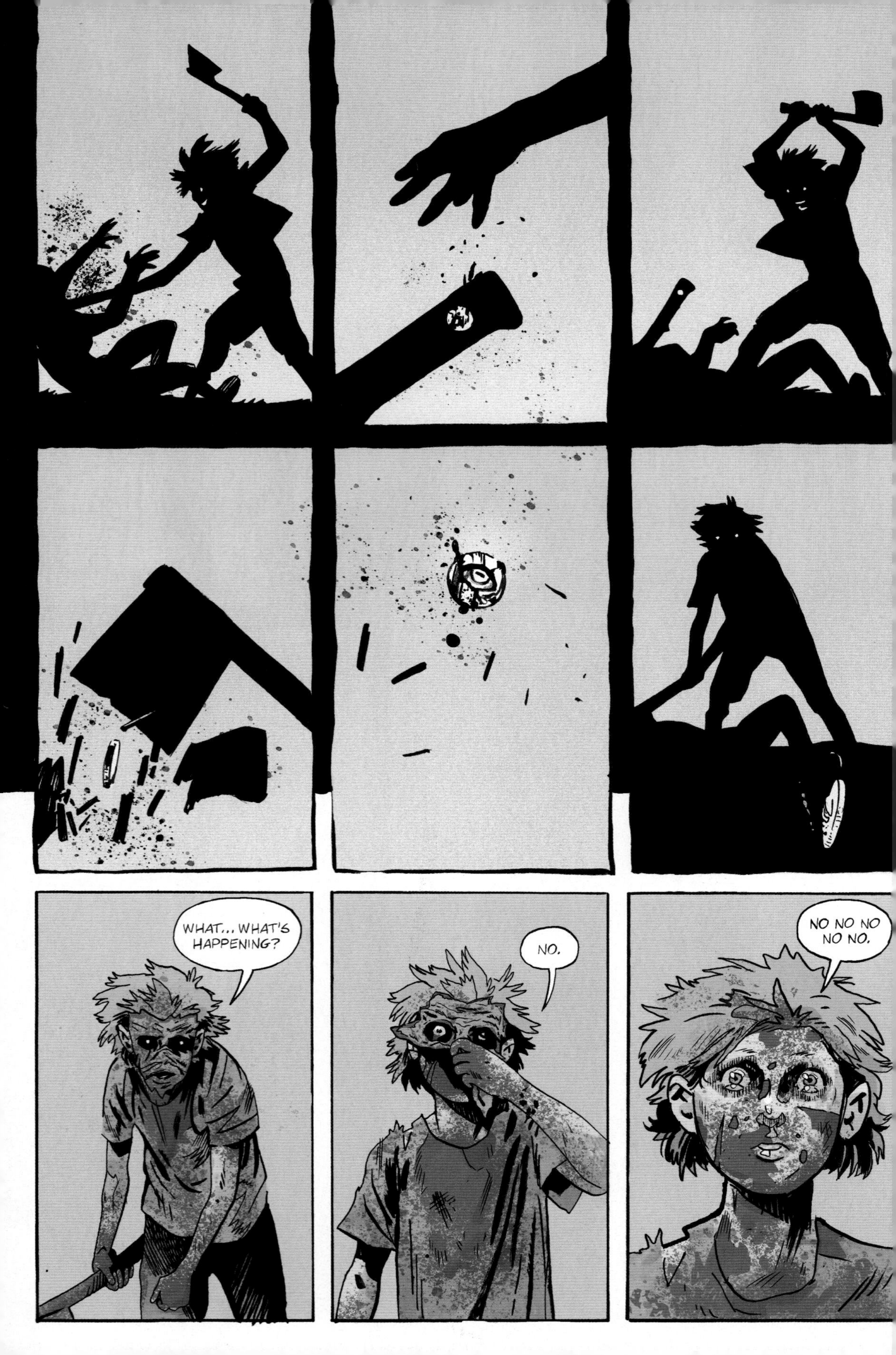
WHAT... WHAT'S HAPPENING?
NO.
NO NO NO NO NO.

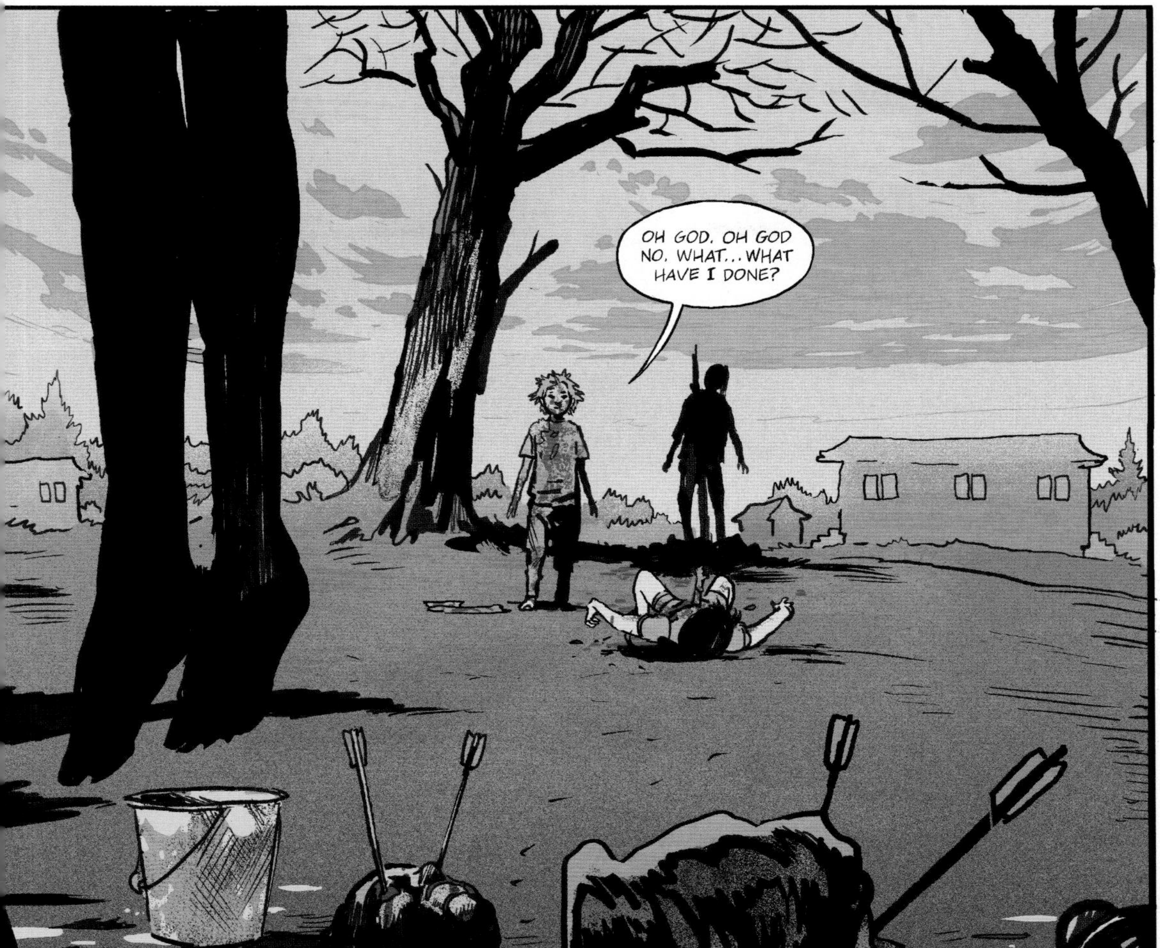
OH GOD. OH GOD NO. WHAT... WHAT HAVE I DONE?

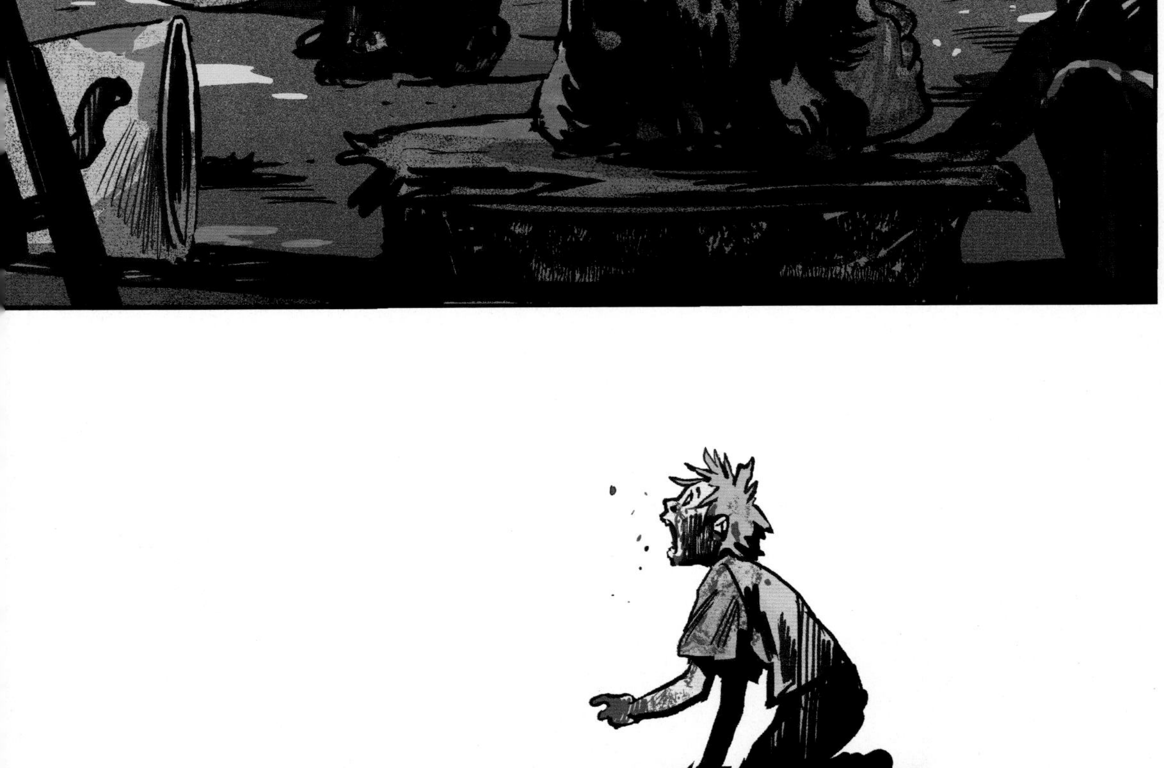

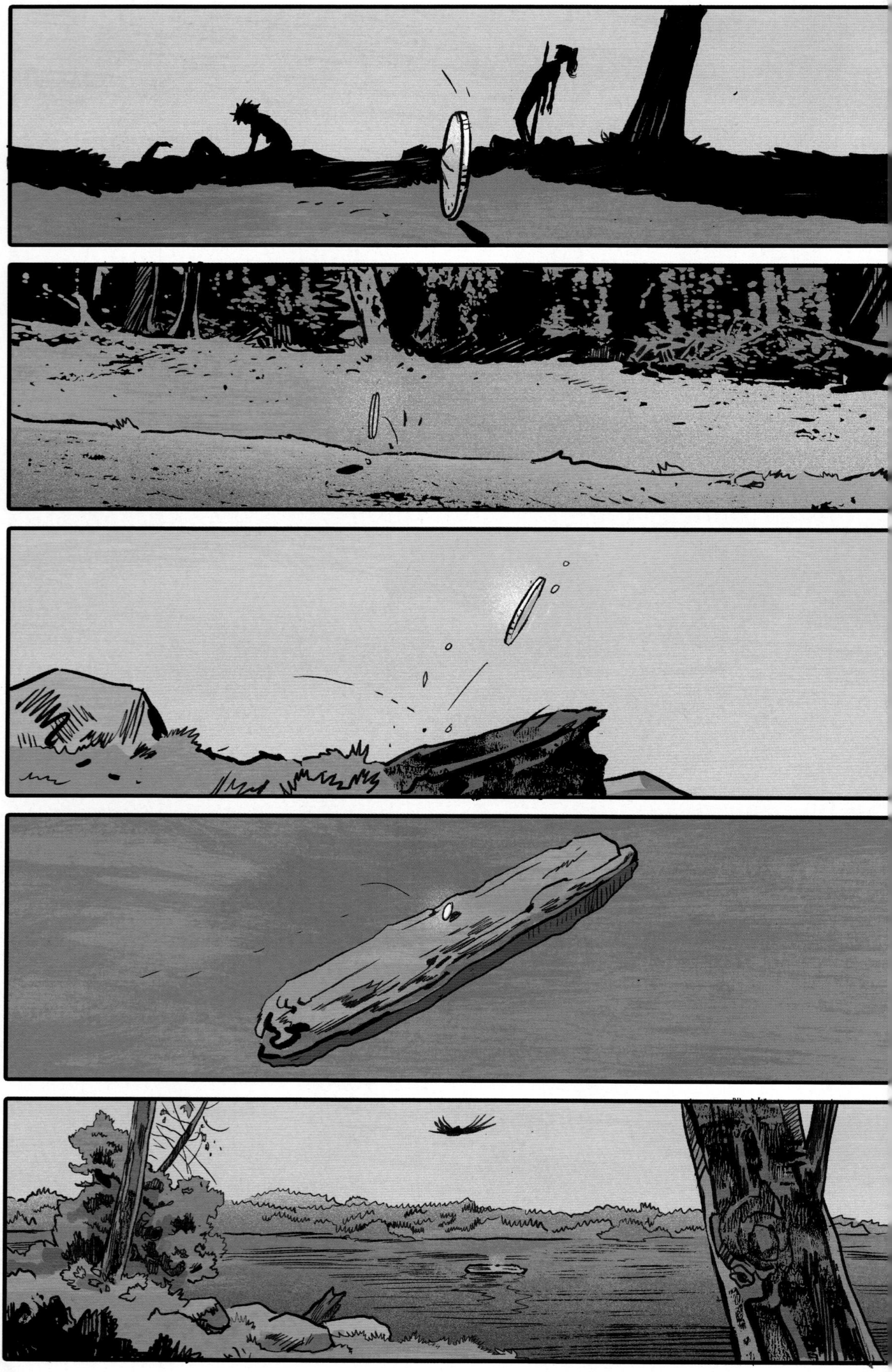

"I think I might be lost..."

3 Death Rattle

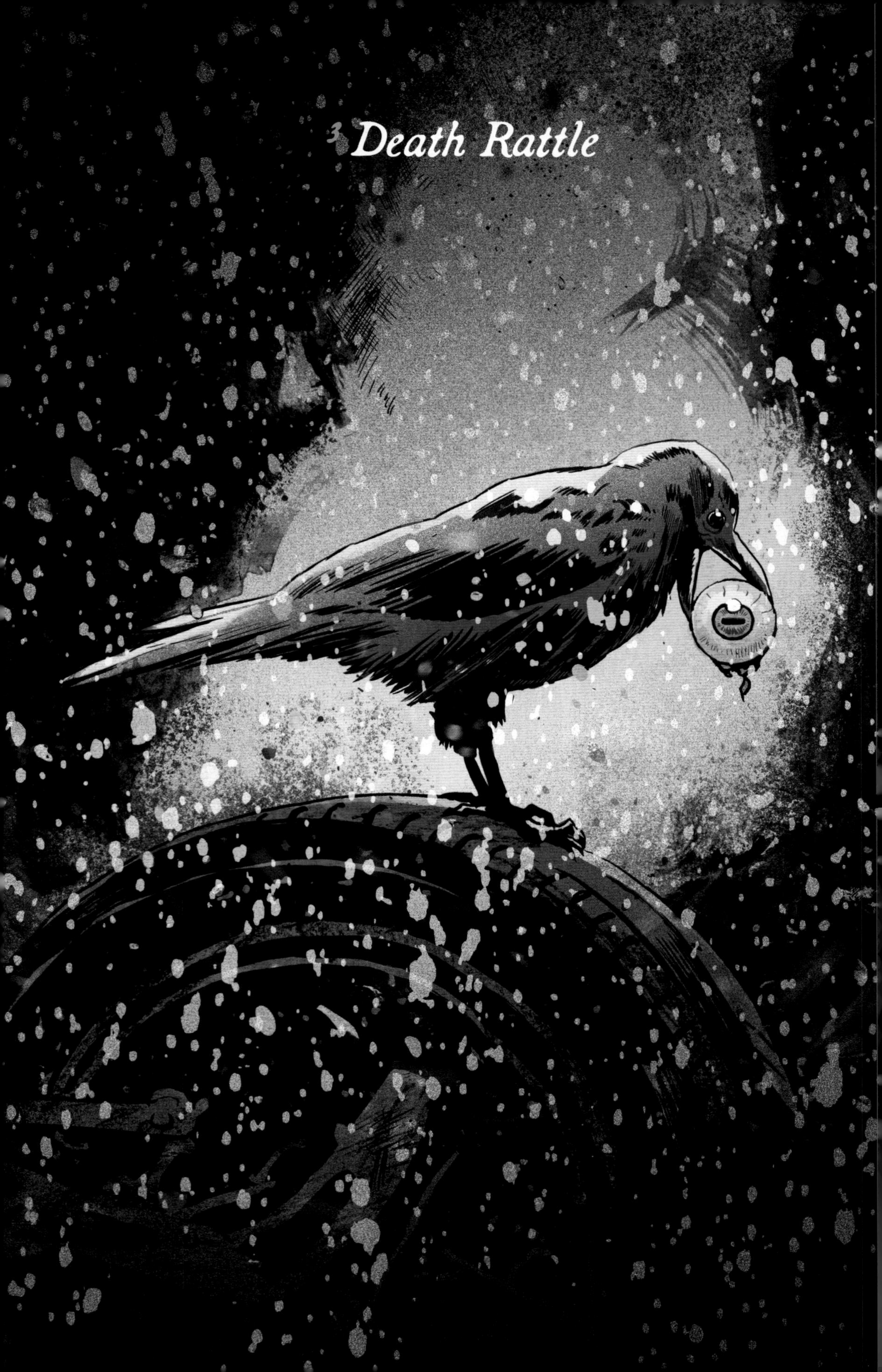

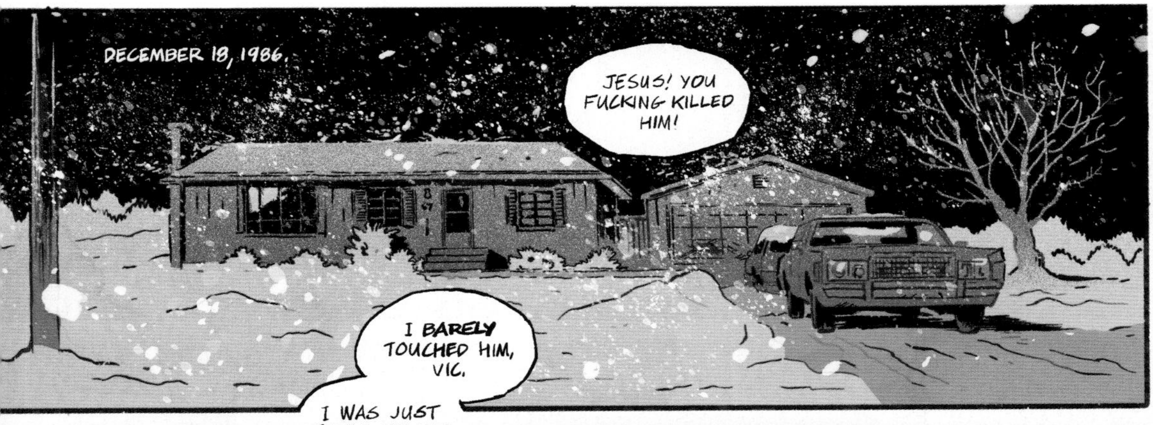
DECEMBER 18, 1986.
JESUS! YOU FUCKING KILLED HIM!
I BARELY TOUCHED HIM, VIC.
I WAS JUST GONNA TIE HIM UP AND...
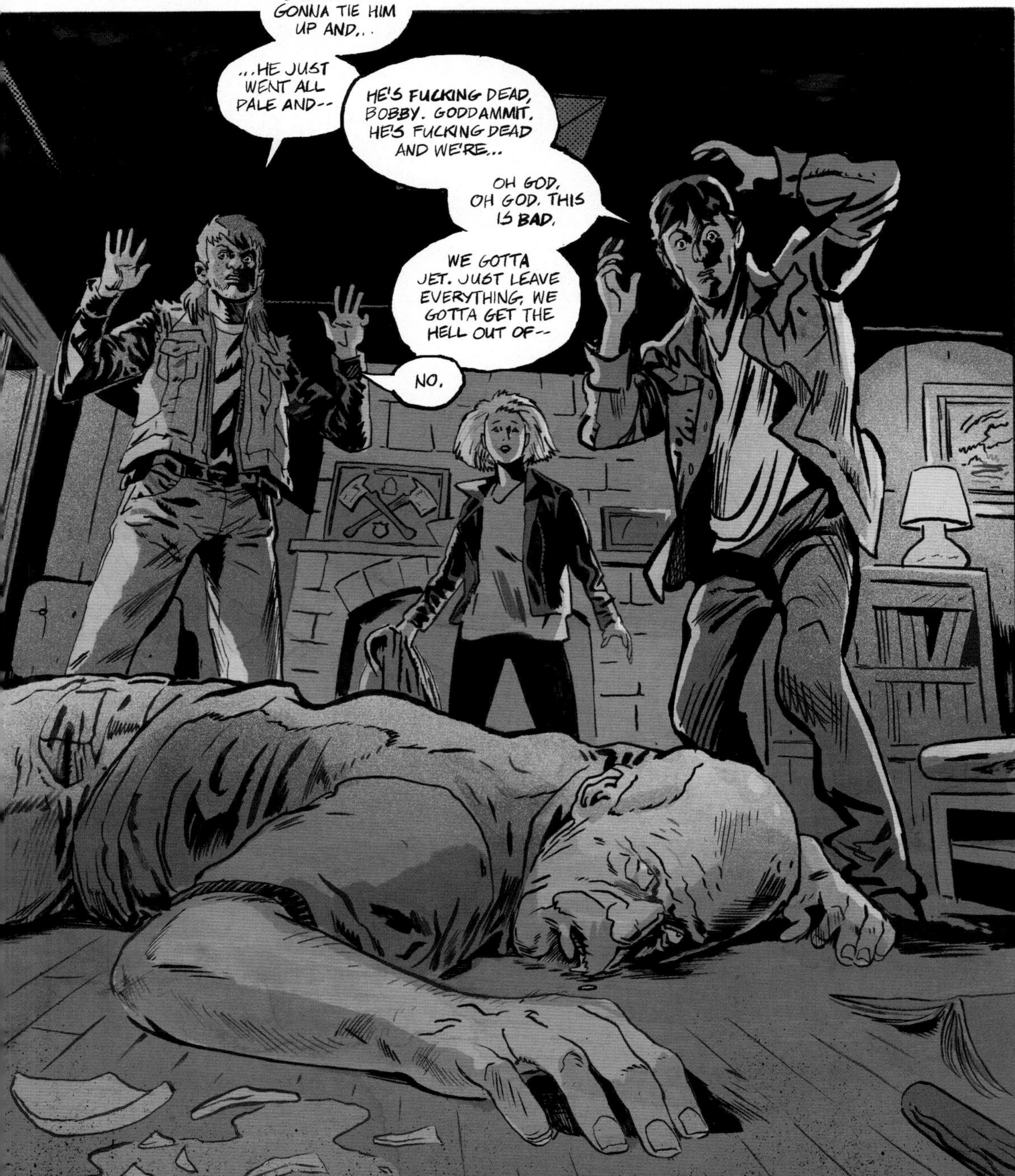
...HE JUST WENT ALL PALE AND--
HE'S FUCKING DEAD, BOBBY. GODDAMMIT. HE'S FUCKING DEAD AND WE'RE...
OH GOD. OH GOD. THIS IS BAD.
WE GOTTA JET. JUST LEAVE EVERYTHING. WE GOTTA GET THE HELL OUT OF--
NO.

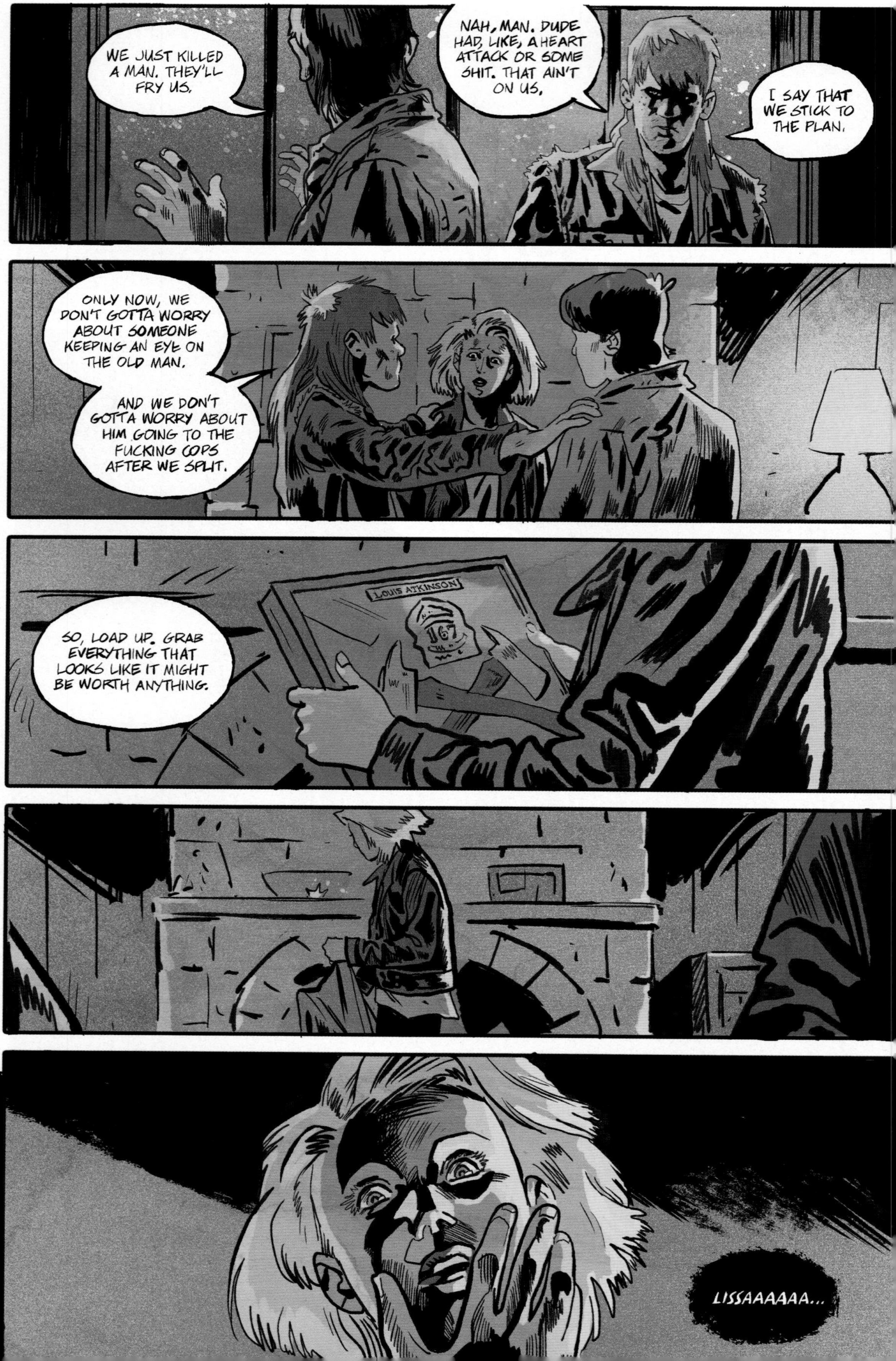
WE JUST KILLED A MAN. THEY'LL FRY US.
NAH, MAN. DUDE HAD, LIKE, A HEART ATTACK OR SOME SHIT. THAT AIN'T ON US.
I SAY THAT WE STICK TO THE PLAN.
ONLY NOW, WE DON'T GOTTA WORRY ABOUT SOMEONE KEEPING AN EYE ON THE OLD MAN.
AND WE DON'T GOTTA WORRY ABOUT HIM GOING TO THE FUCKING COPS AFTER WE SPLIT.
LOUIS ATKINSON
167
SO, LOAD UP. GRAB EVERYTHING THAT LOOKS LIKE IT MIGHT BE WORTH ANYTHING.
LISSAAAAAA...

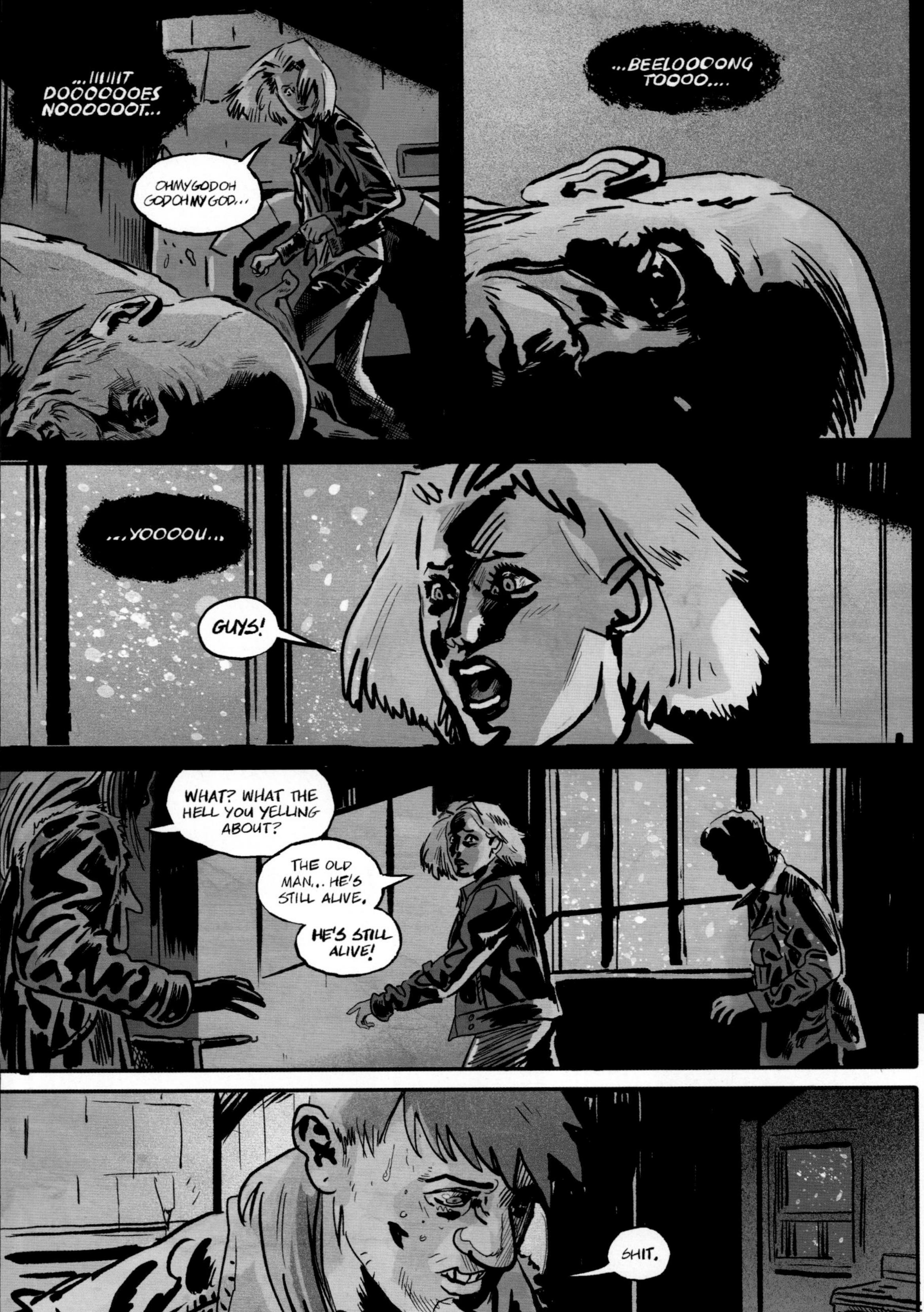
...IIIIIIT DOOOOOOES NOOOOOOT...
OHMYGODOH GODOHMYGOD...
...BEELOOOONG TOOOO....
...YOOOOU...
GUYS!
WHAT? WHAT THE HELL YOU YELLING ABOUT?
THE OLD MAN... HE'S STILL ALIVE.
HE'S STILL ALIVE!
SHIT.

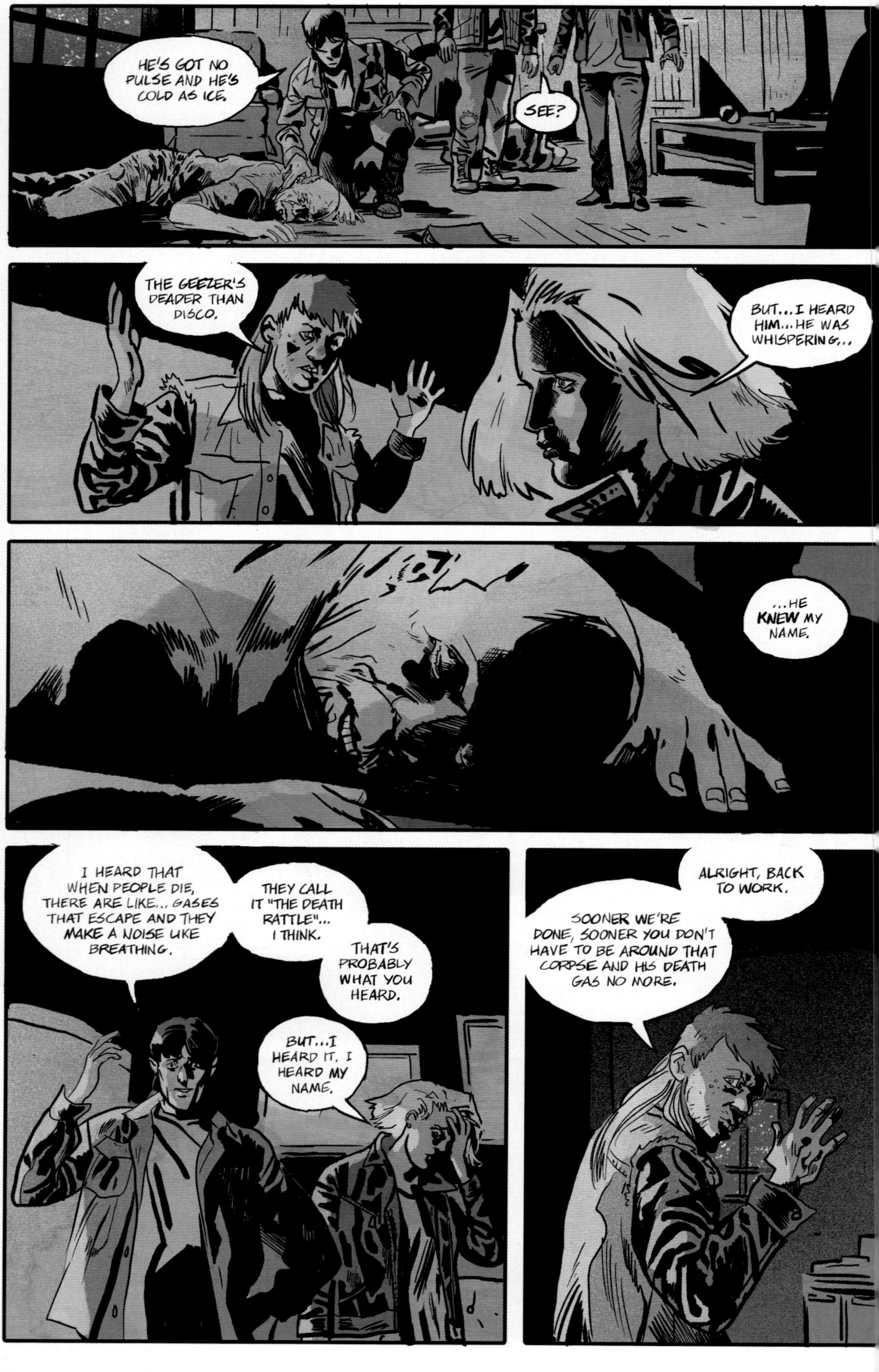
HE'S GOT NO PULSE AND HE'S COLD AS ICE.
SEE?
THE GEEZER'S DEADER THAN DISCO.
BUT... I HEARD HIM... HE WAS WHISPERING...
...HE KNEW MY NAME.
I HEARD THAT WHEN PEOPLE DIE, THERE ARE LIKE... GASES THAT ESCAPE AND THEY MAKE A NOISE LIKE BREATHING.
THEY CALL IT "THE DEATH RATTLE"... I THINK.
THAT'S PROBABLY WHAT YOU HEARD.
BUT...I HEARD IT. I HEARD MY NAME.
ALRIGHT, BACK TO WORK.
SOONER WE'RE DONE, SOONER YOU DON'T HAVE TO BE AROUND THAT CORPSE AND HIS DEATH GAS NO MORE.

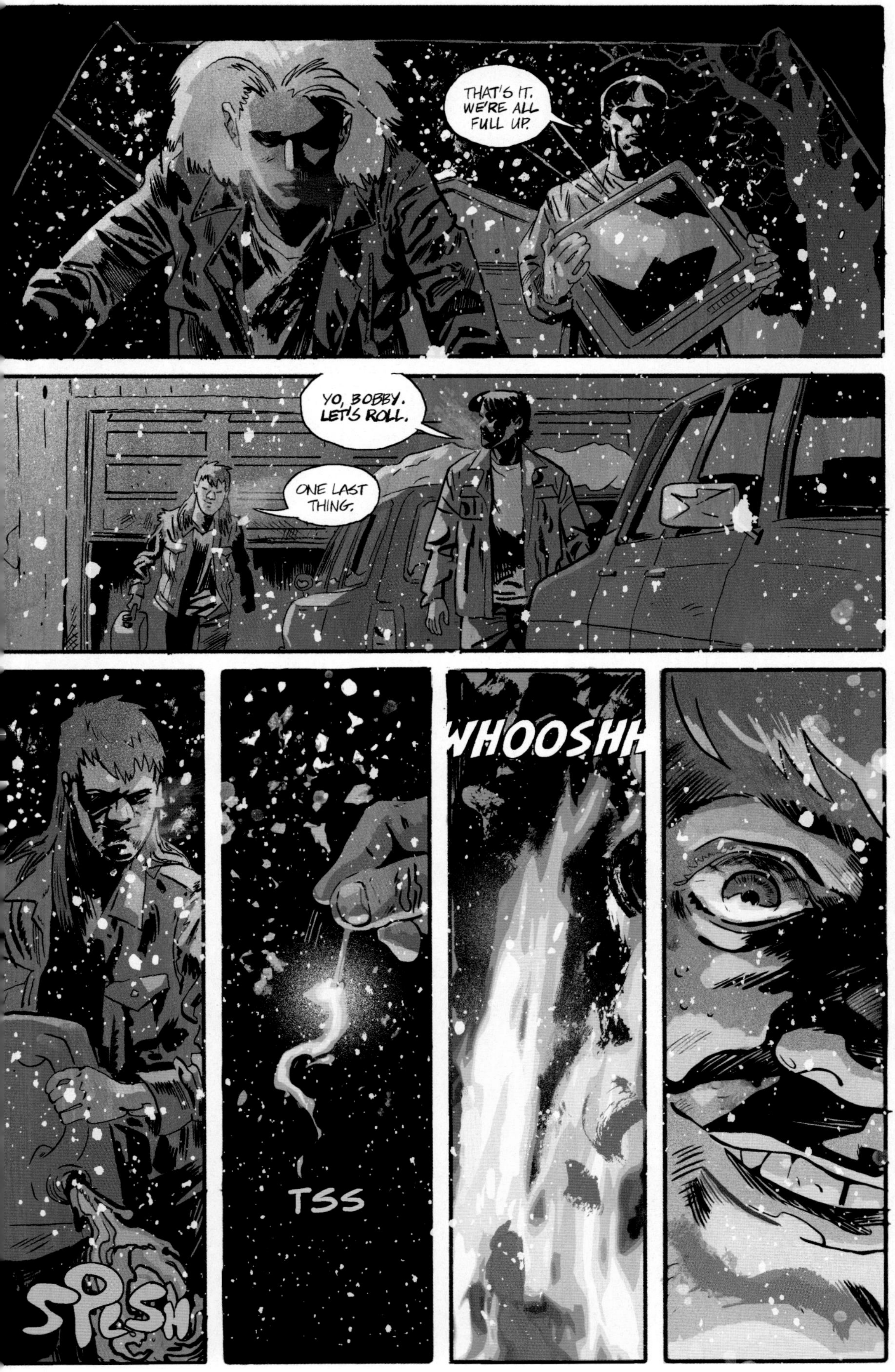
THAT'S IT. WE'RE ALL FULL UP.
YO, BOBBY. LET'S ROLL.
ONE LAST THING.
SPLSH
TSS
WHOOSHH

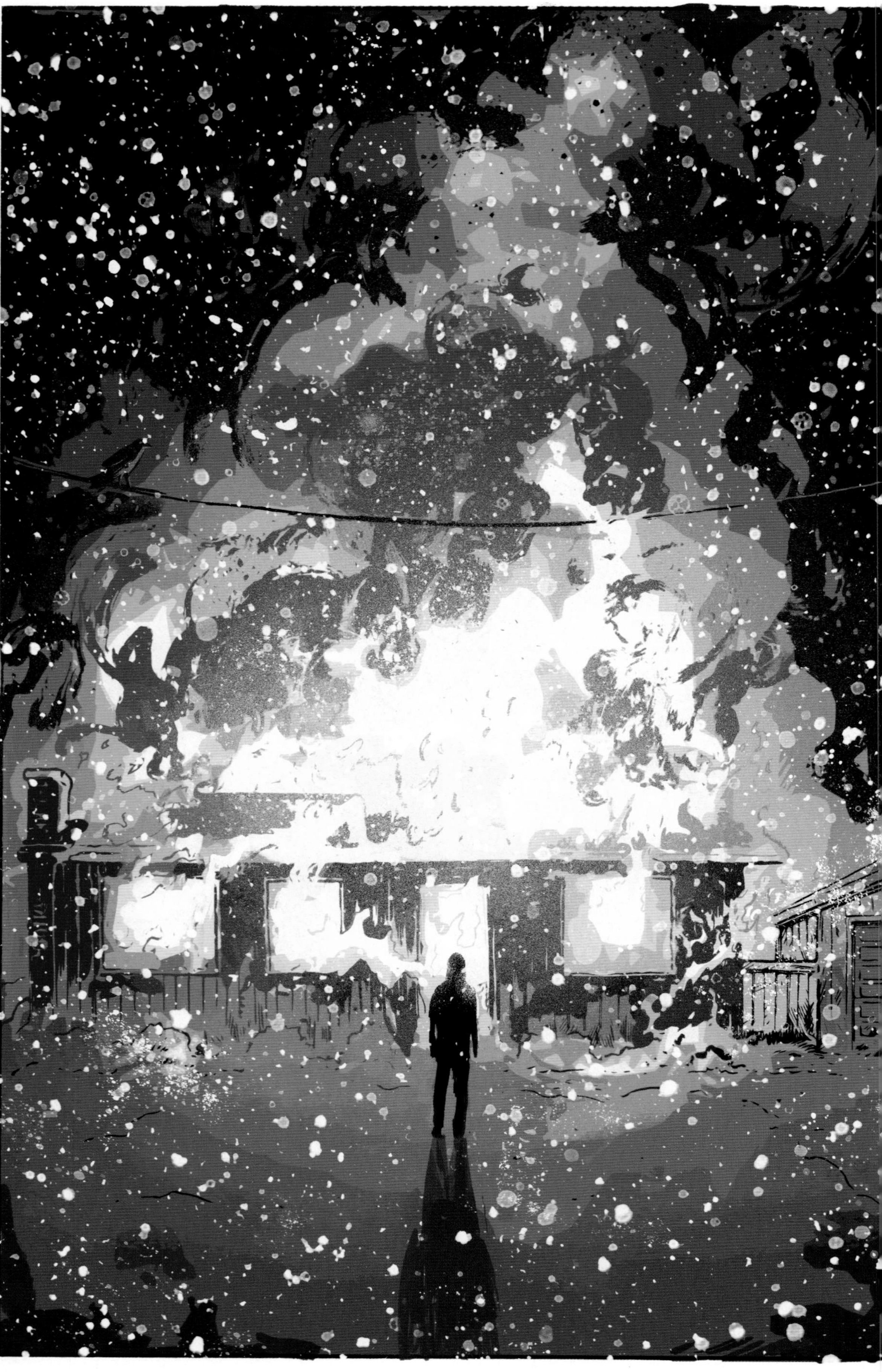

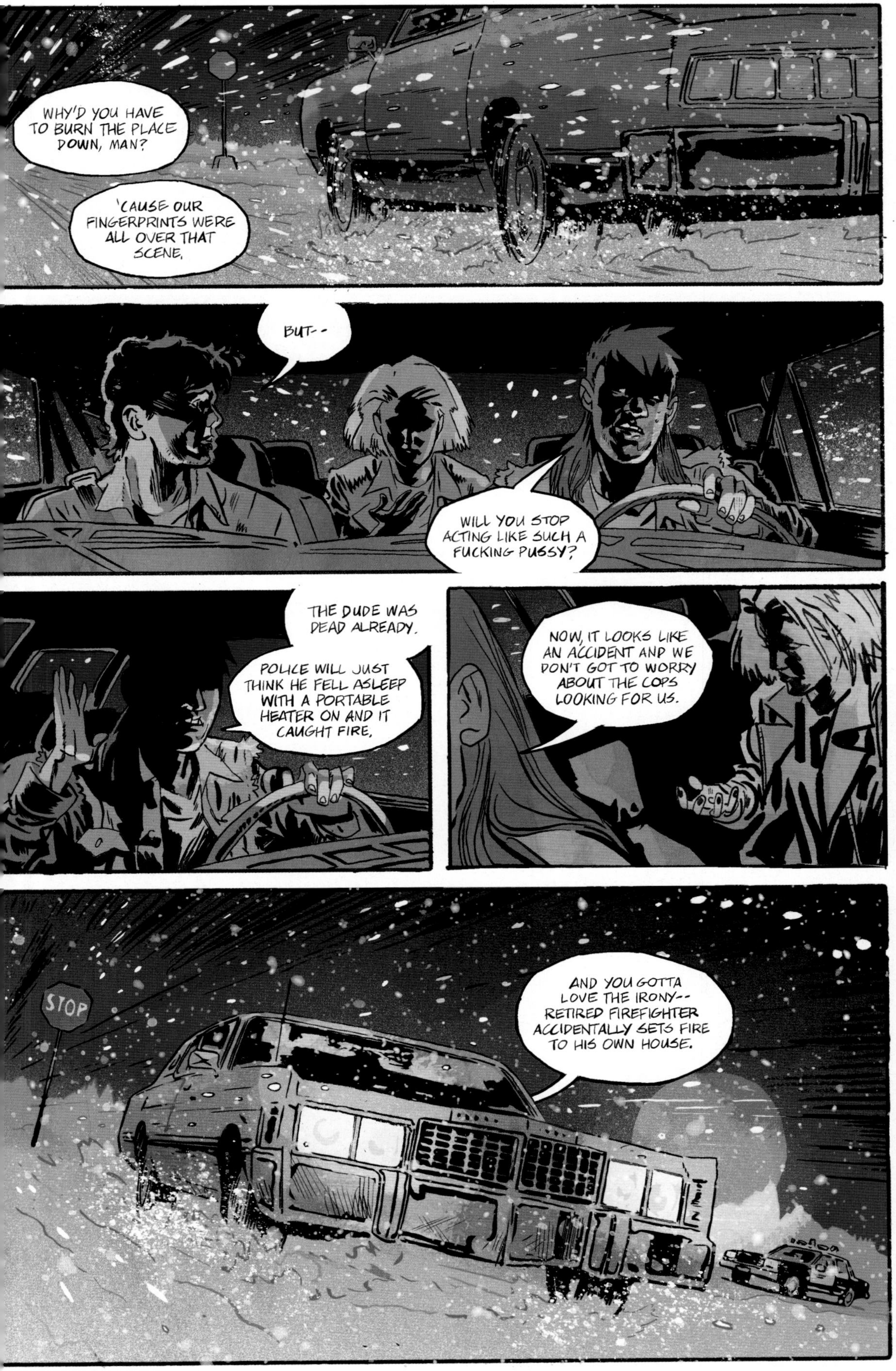

WHY'D YOU HAVE TO BURN THE PLACE DOWN, MAN?
'CAUSE OUR FINGERPRINTS WERE ALL OVER THAT SCENE.
BUT--
WILL YOU STOP ACTING LIKE SUCH A FUCKING PUSSY?
THE DUDE WAS DEAD ALREADY.
POLICE WILL JUST THINK HE FELL ASLEEP WITH A PORTABLE HEATER ON AND IT CAUGHT FIRE.
NOW, IT LOOKS LIKE AN ACCIDENT AND WE DON'T GOT TO WORRY ABOUT THE COPS LOOKING FOR US.
STOP
AND YOU GOTTA LOVE THE IRONY-- RETIRED FIREFIGHTER ACCIDENTALLY SETS FIRE TO HIS OWN HOUSE.

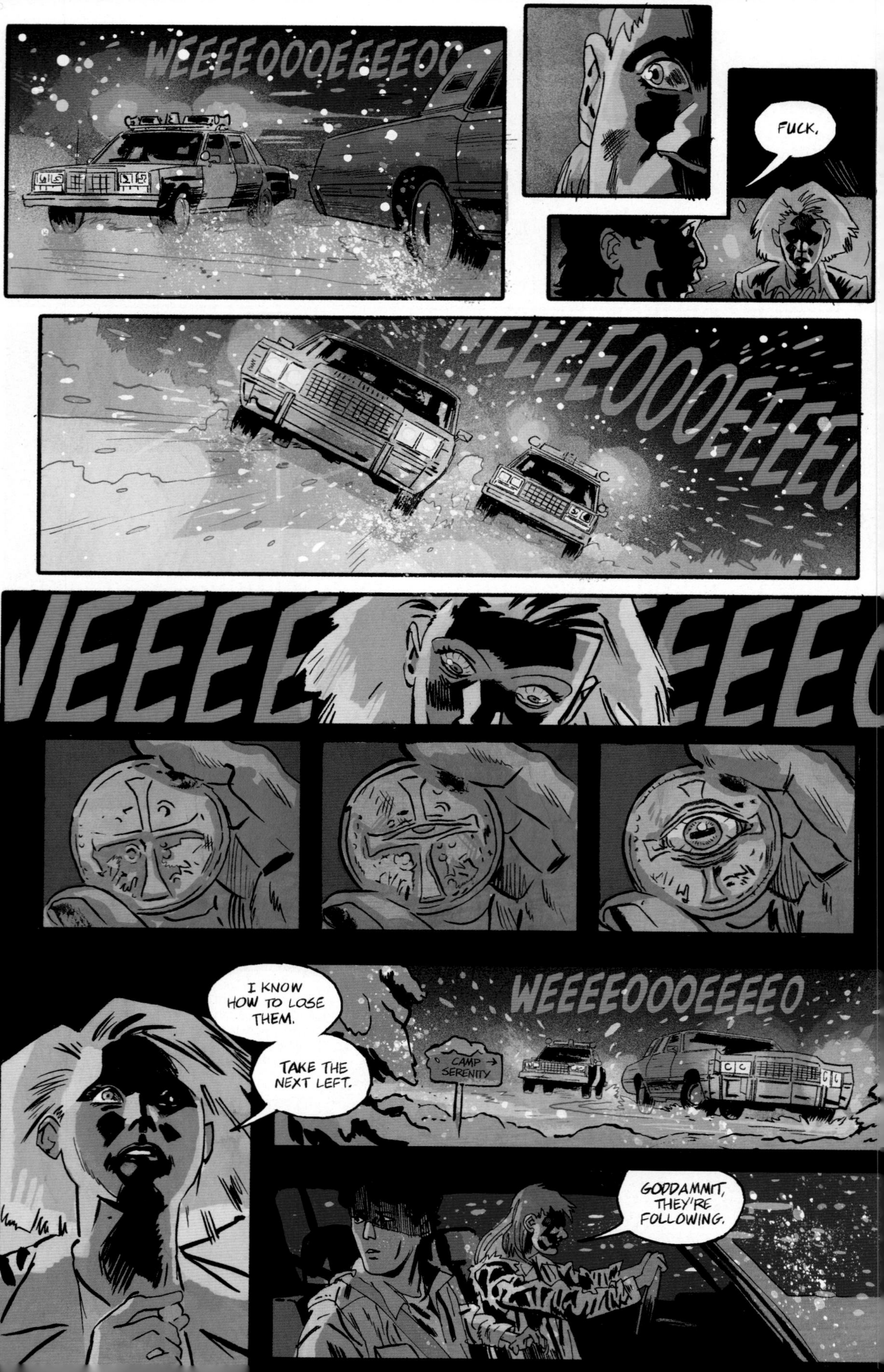
WEEEEOOOEEEEOO
FUCK.
WEEEEOOOEEEEO
WEEEE
EEEO
I KNOW HOW TO LOSE THEM.
TAKE THE NEXT LEFT.
WEEEEOOOEEEEO
CAMP SERENITY
GODDAMMIT, THEY'RE FOLLOWING.

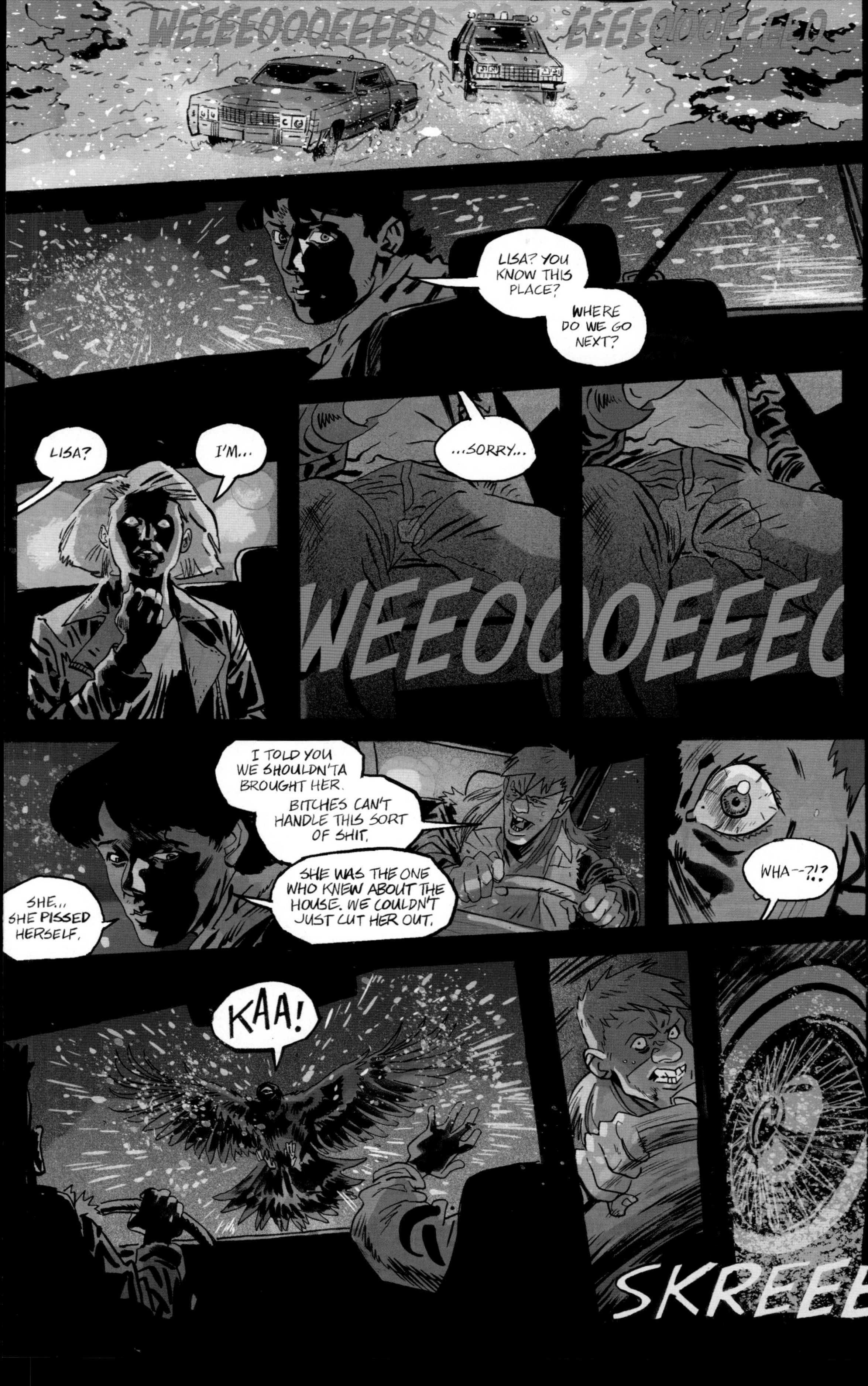
WEEEEOOOEEEEO
EEEEOOOEEEEO
LISA? YOU KNOW THIS PLACE?
WHERE DO WE GO NEXT?
LISA?
I'M...
...SORRY...
WEEOOOEEEC
I TOLD YOU WE SHOULDN'TA BROUGHT HER.
BITCHES CAN'T HANDLE THIS SORT OF SHIT.
SHE WAS THE ONE WHO KNEW ABOUT THE HOUSE. WE COULDN'T JUST CUT HER OUT.
SHE... SHE PISSED HERSELF.
WHA--?!?
KAA!
SKREEE

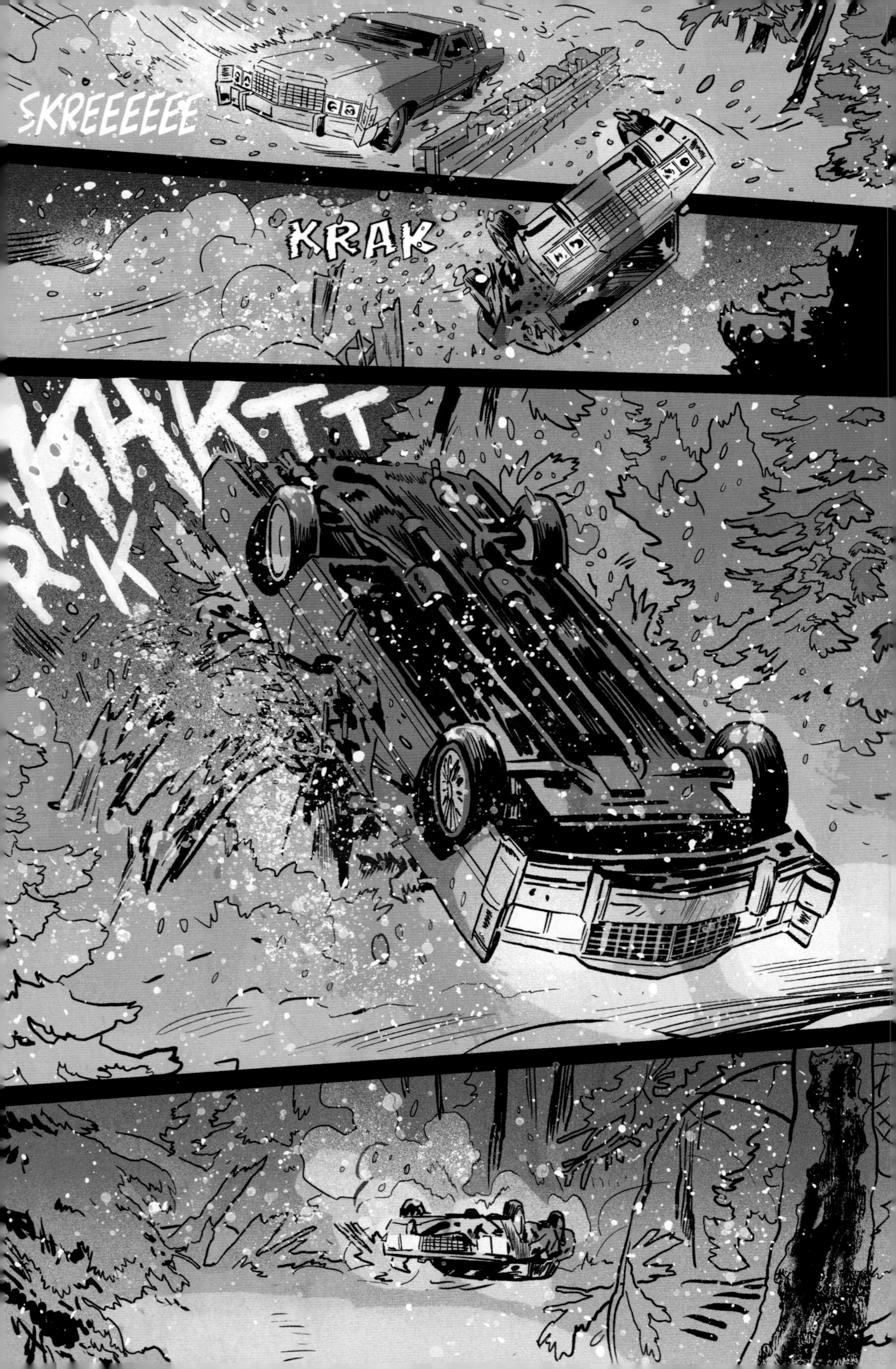
SKREEEEEEE
KRAK

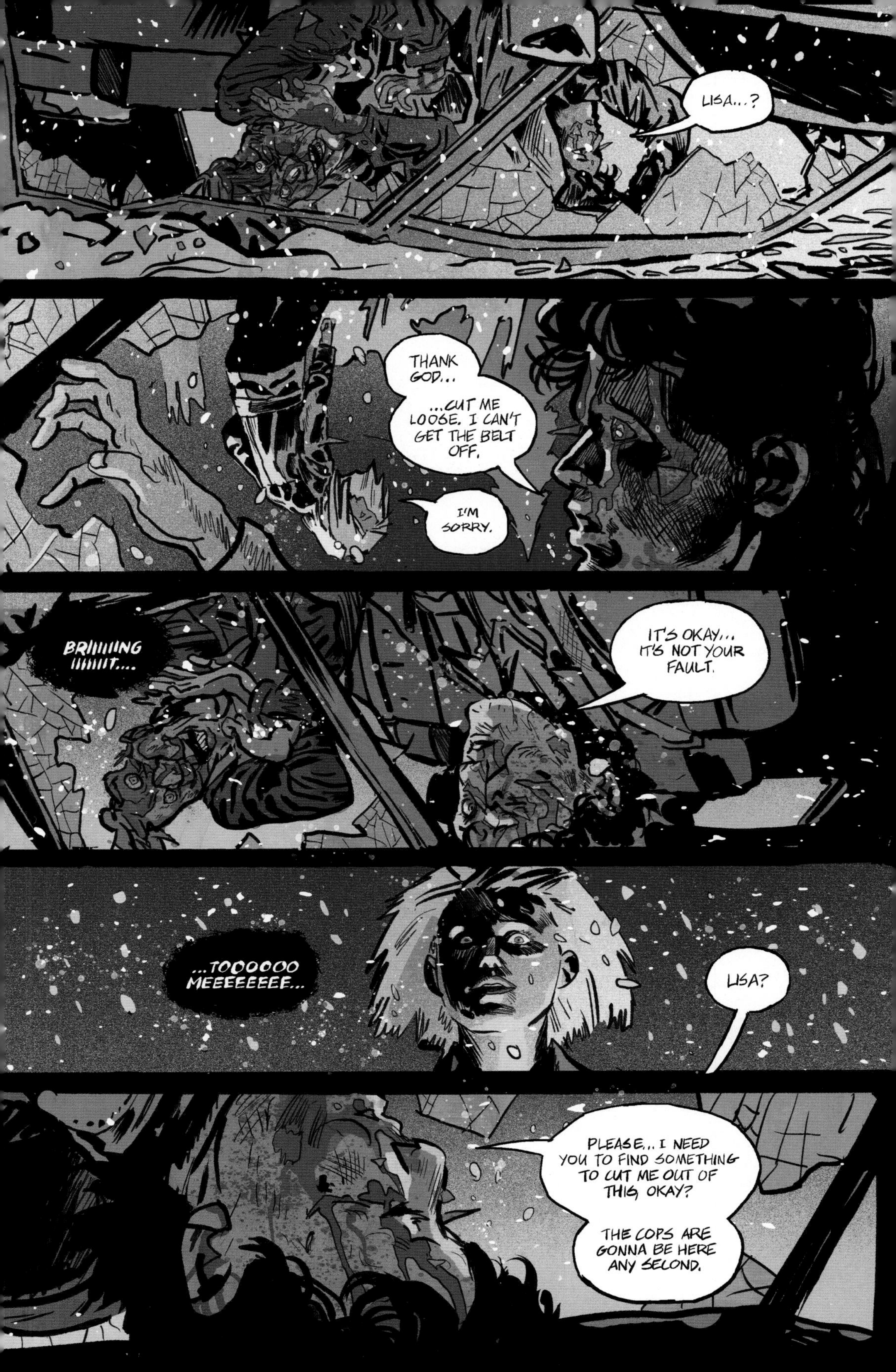
LISA...?
THANK GOD...
...CUT ME LOOSE. I CAN'T GET THE BELT OFF.
I'M SORRY.
BRIIIIING IIIIIIT....
IT'S OKAY... IT'S NOT YOUR FAULT.
...TOOOOOO MEEEEEEEE...
LISA?
PLEASE... I NEED YOU TO FIND SOMETHING TO CUT ME OUT OF THIS, OKAY?
THE COPS ARE GONNA BE HERE ANY SECOND.

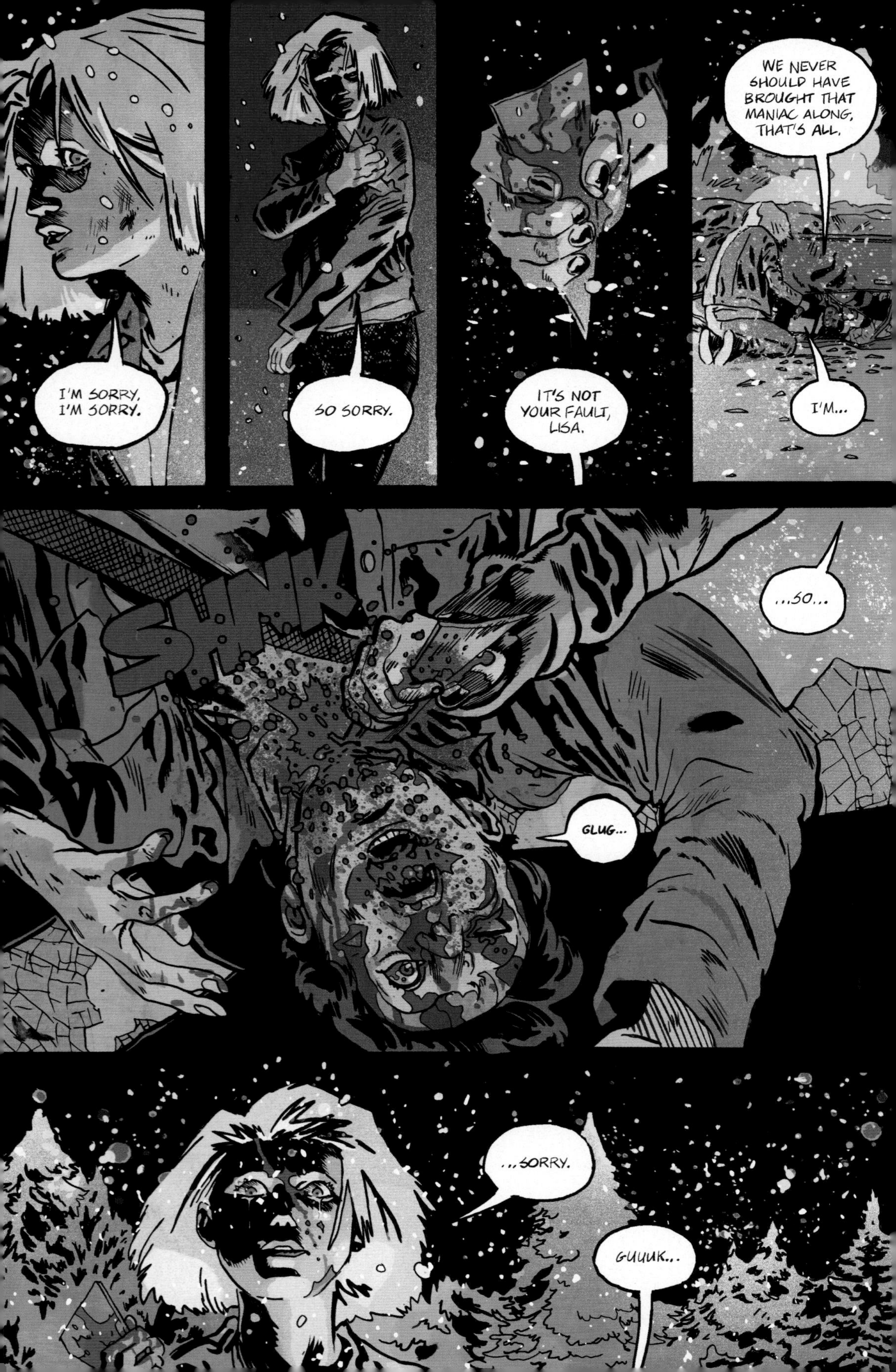
I'M SORRY, I'M SORRY.
SO SORRY.
IT'S NOT YOUR FAULT, LISA.
WE NEVER SHOULD HAVE BROUGHT THAT MANIAC ALONG, THAT'S ALL.
I'M...
...SO...
GLUG...
...SORRY.
GUUUK...

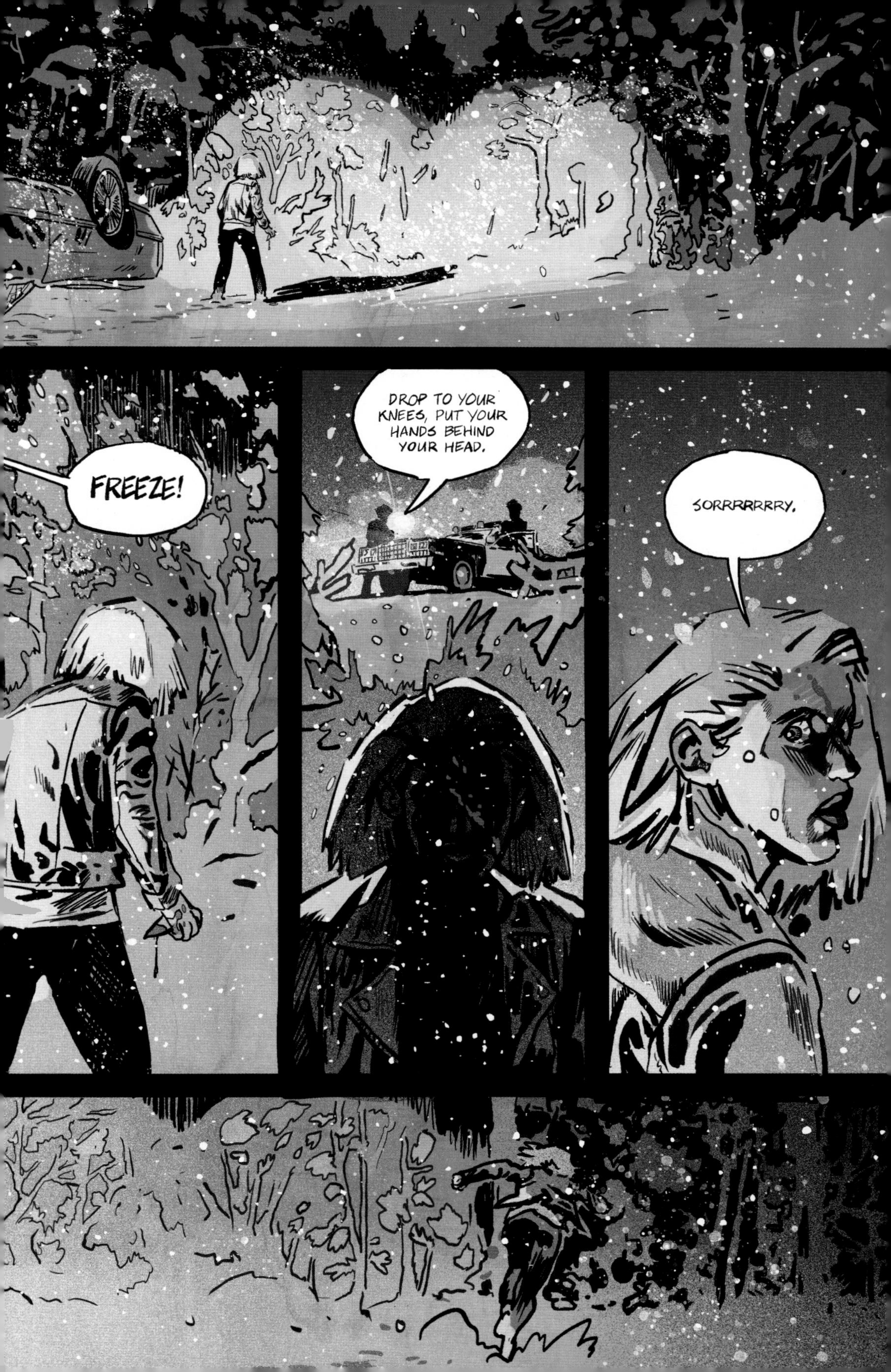
FREEZE!
DROP TO YOUR KNEES, PUT YOUR HANDS BEHIND YOUR HEAD.
SORRRRRRRY.

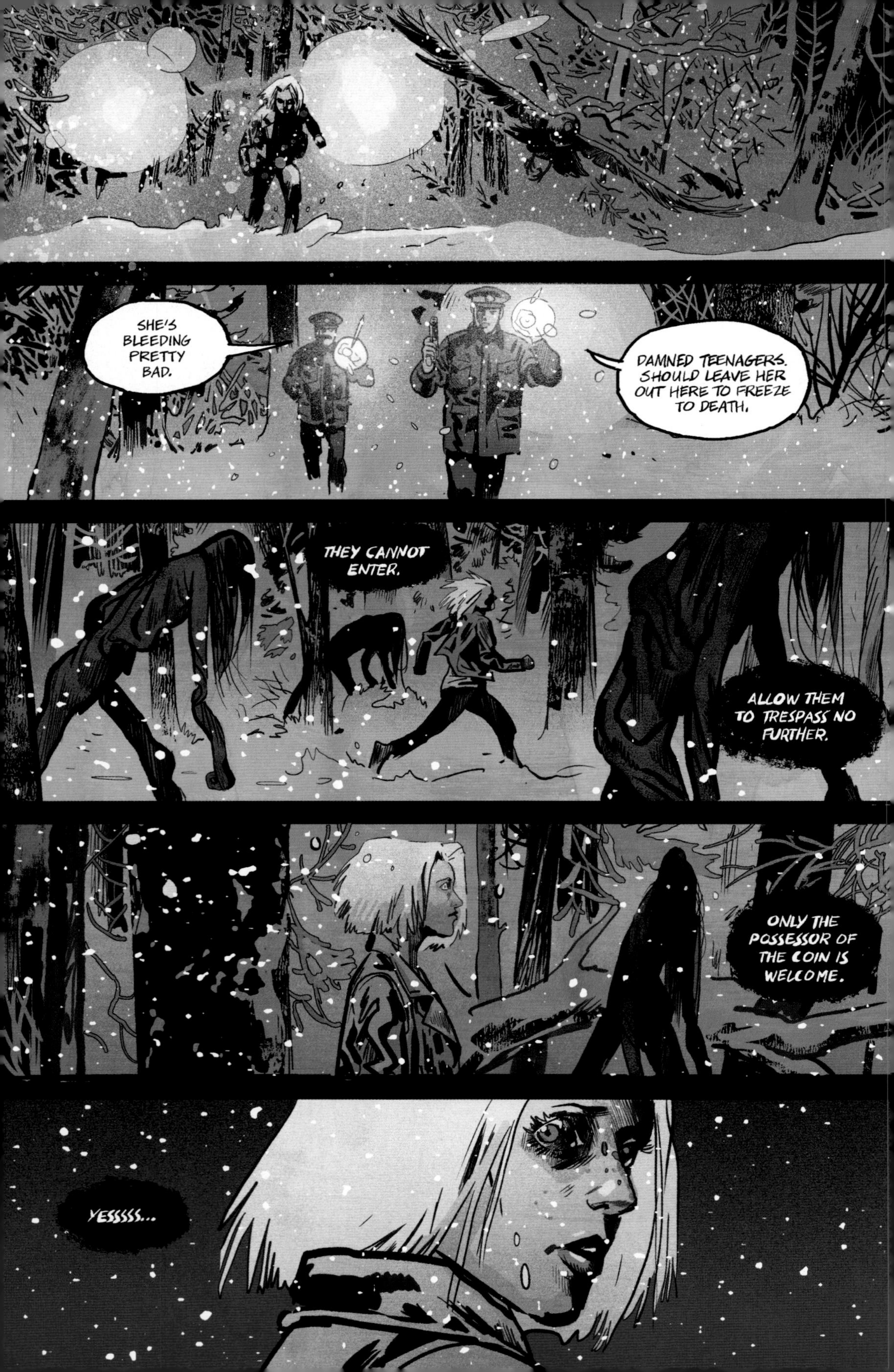
SHE'S BLEEDING PRETTY BAD.
DAMNED TEENAGERS. SHOULD LEAVE HER OUT HERE TO FREEZE TO DEATH.
THEY CANNOT ENTER.
ALLOW THEM TO TRESPASS NO FURTHER.
ONLY THE POSSESSOR OF THE COIN IS WELCOME.
YESSSSS...

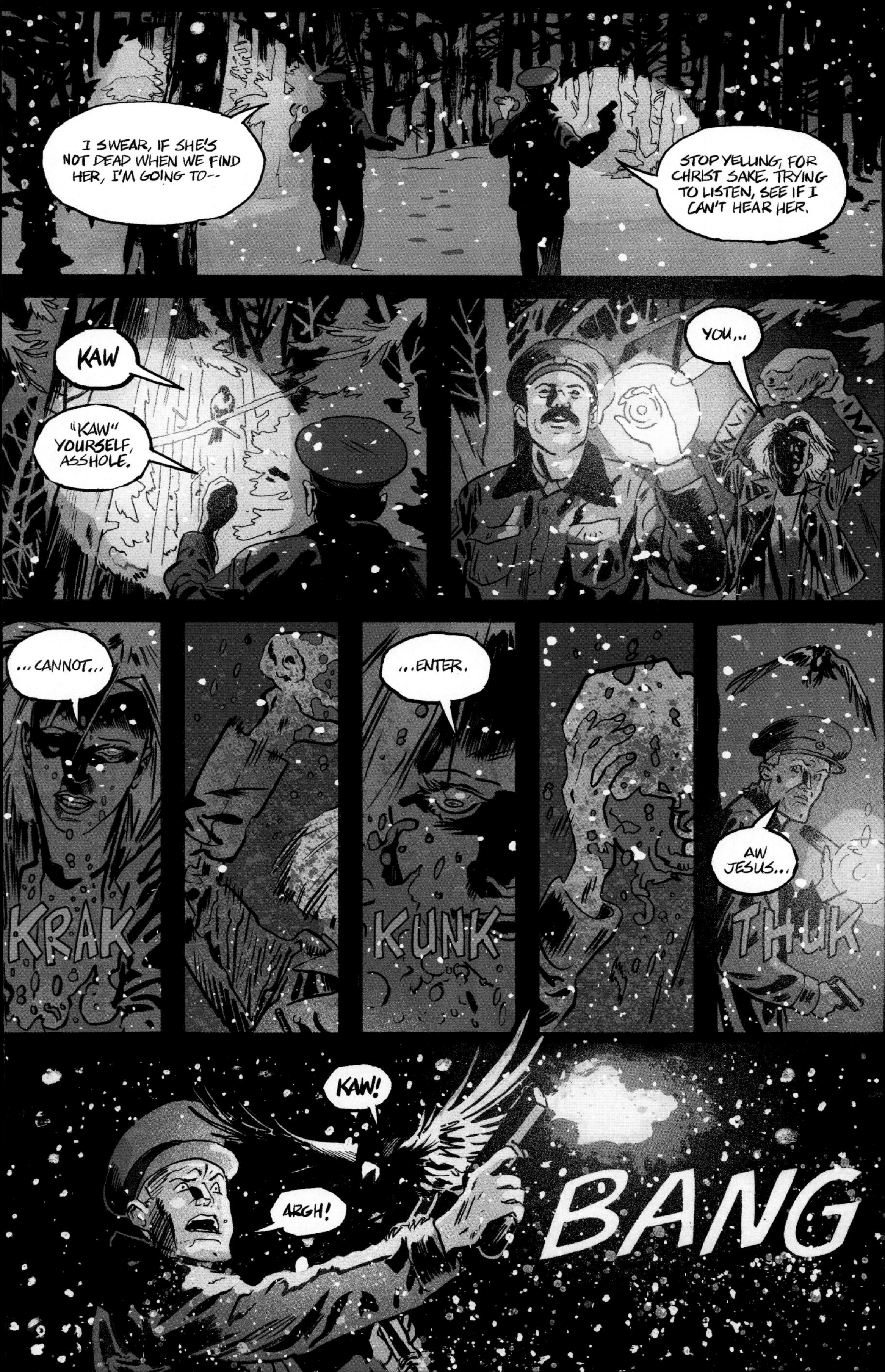
I SWEAR, IF SHE'S NOT DEAD WHEN WE FIND HER, I'M GOING TO--
STOP YELLING, FOR CHRIST SAKE. TRYING TO LISTEN, SEE IF I CAN'T HEAR HER.
KAW
"KAW" YOURSELF, ASSHOLE.
YOU...
...CANNOT...
KRAK
...ENTER.
KUNK
AW JESUS...
THUK
KAW!
ARGH!
BANG

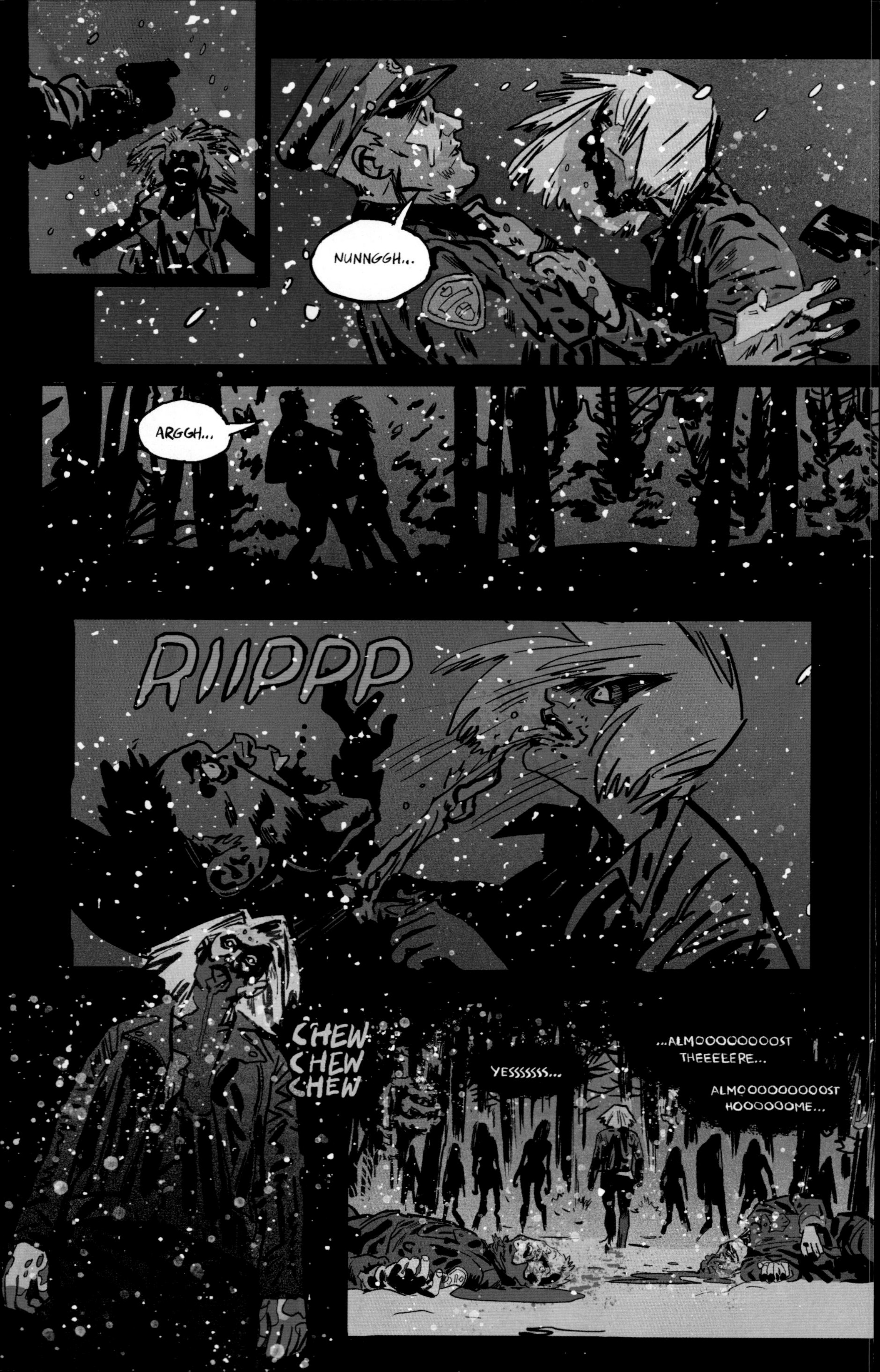
NUNNGGH...
ARGGH...
RIIPPP
CHEW CHEW CHEW
YESSSSSSS...
...ALMOOOOOOOOOST THEEEEERE...
ALMOOOOOOOOOST HOOOOOOME...

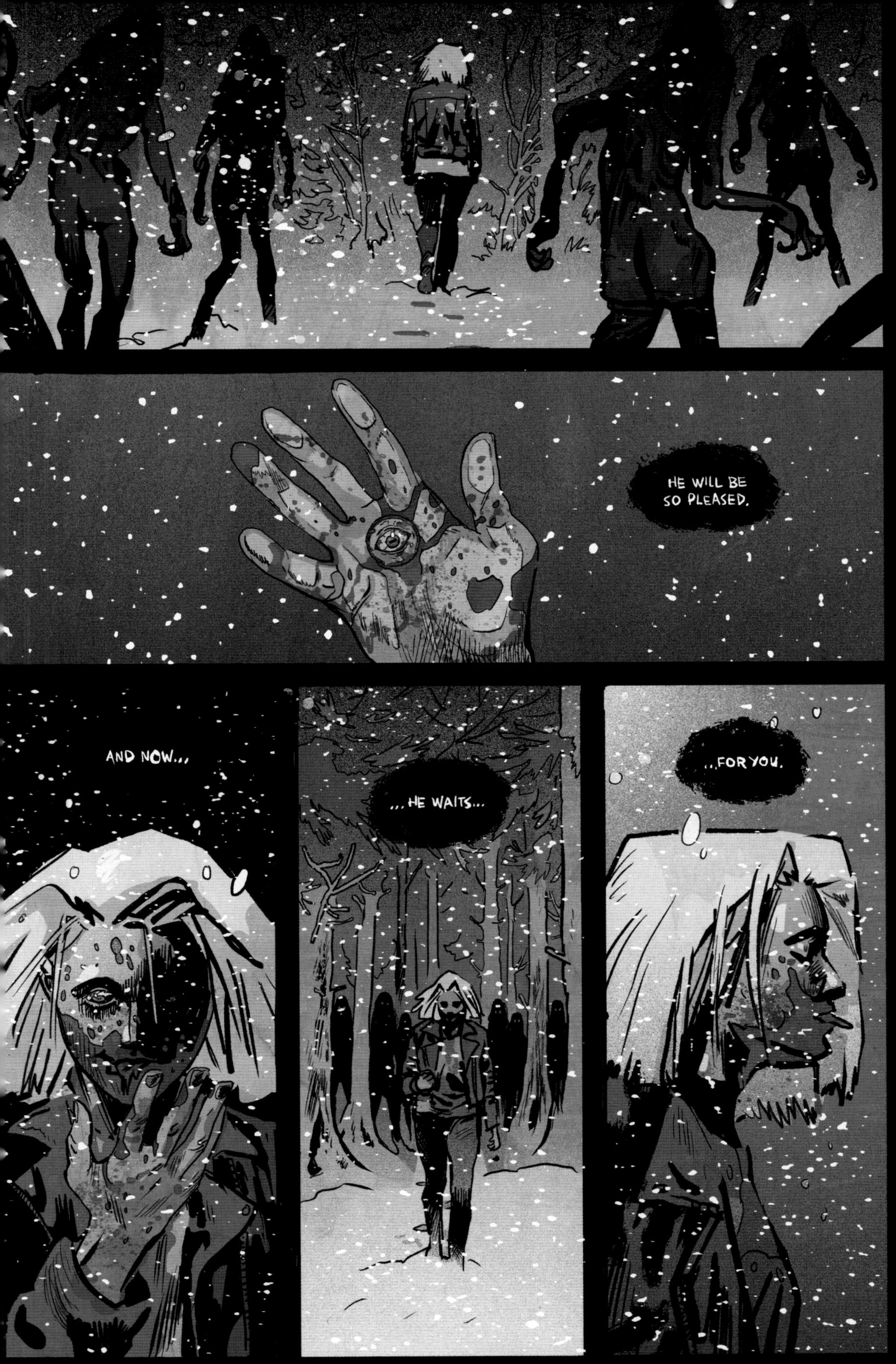
HE WILL BE SO PLEASED.
AND NOW...
...HE WAITS...
...FOR YOU.

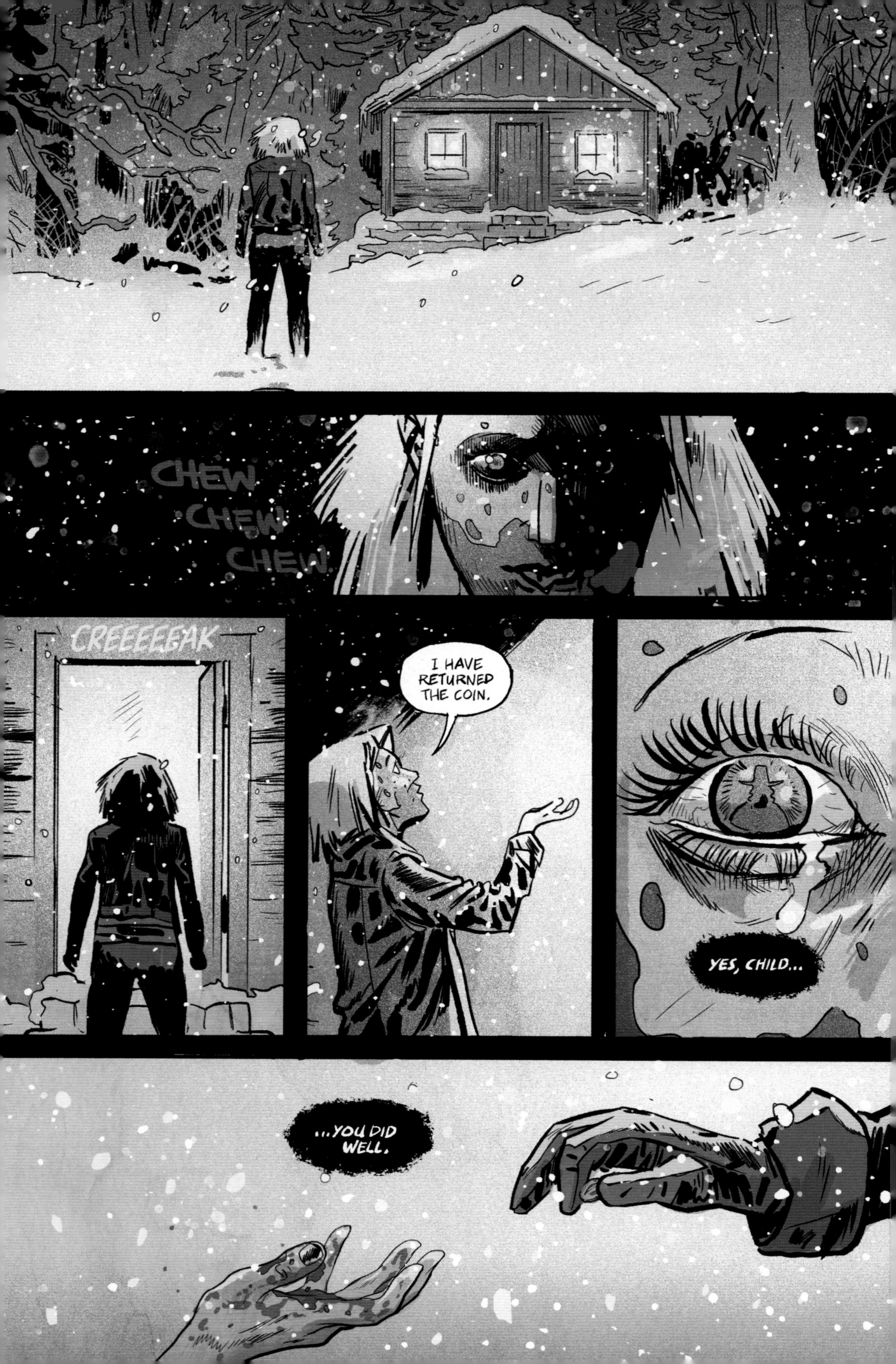
CHEW
CHEW
CHEW
CREEEEEEAK
I HAVE RETURNED THE COIN.
YES, CHILD...
...YOU DID WELL.

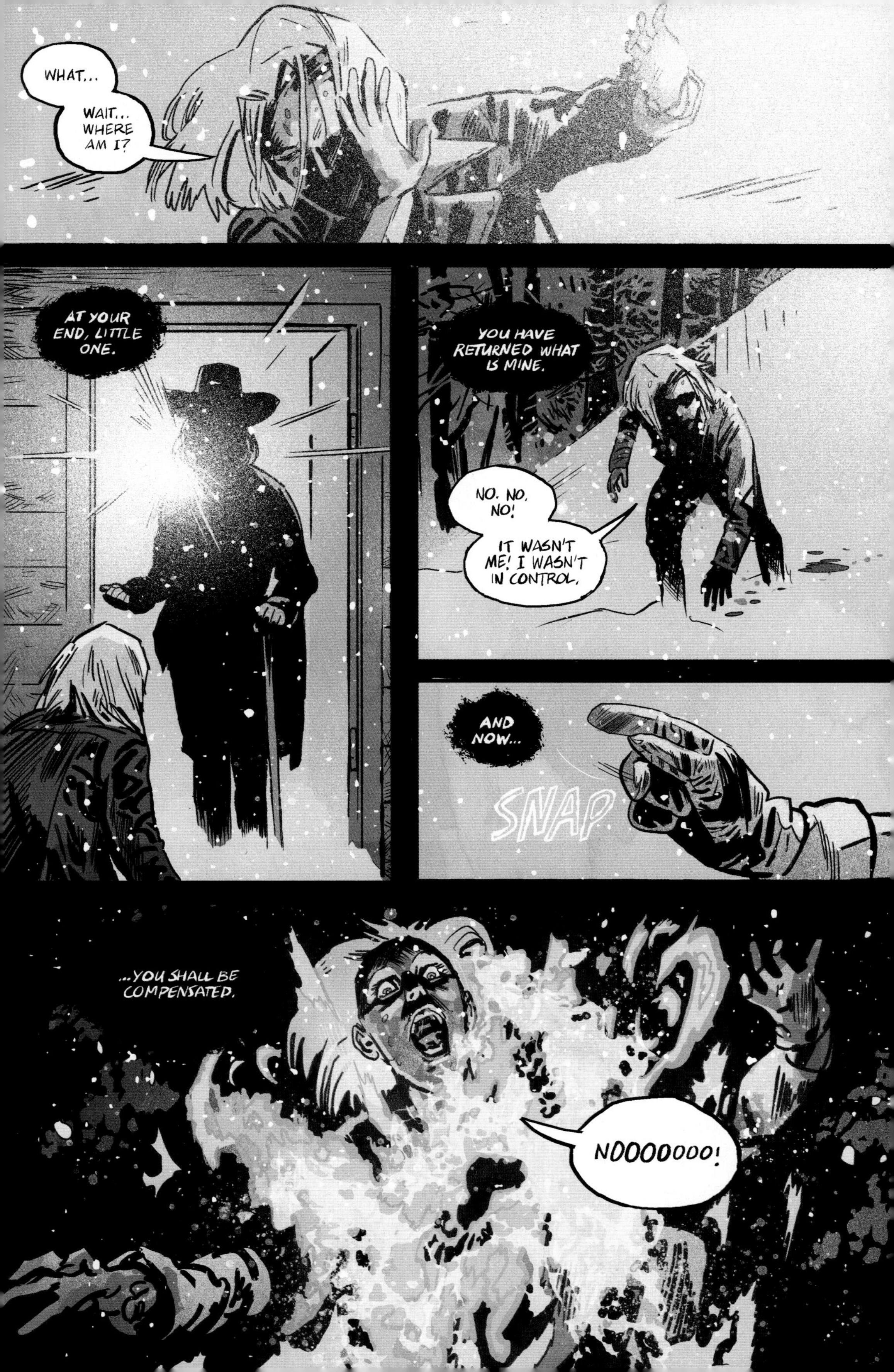
WHAT...
WAIT... WHERE AM I?
AT YOUR END, LITTLE ONE.
YOU HAVE RETURNED WHAT IS MINE.
NO. NO, NO!
IT WASN'T ME! I WASN'T IN CONTROL.
AND NOW...
SNAP
...YOU SHALL BE COMPENSATED.
NOOOOOOO!

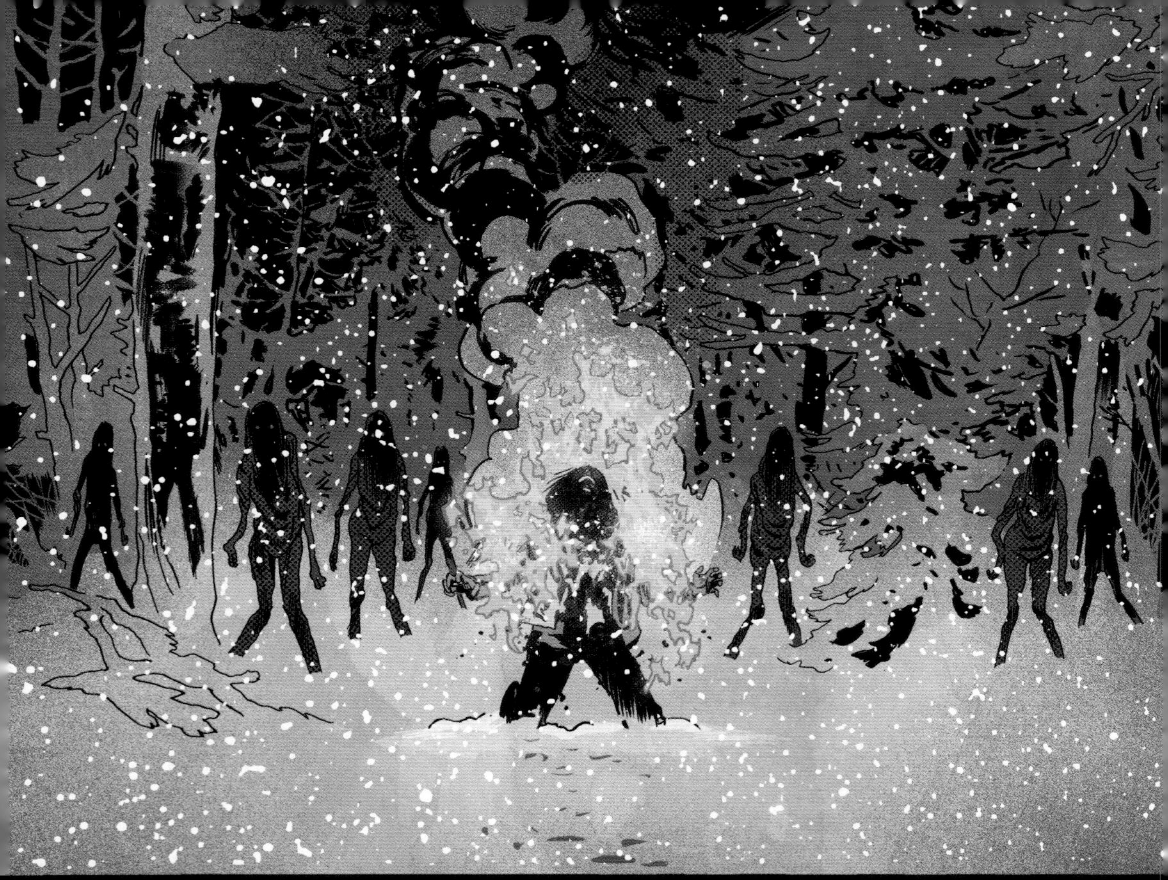

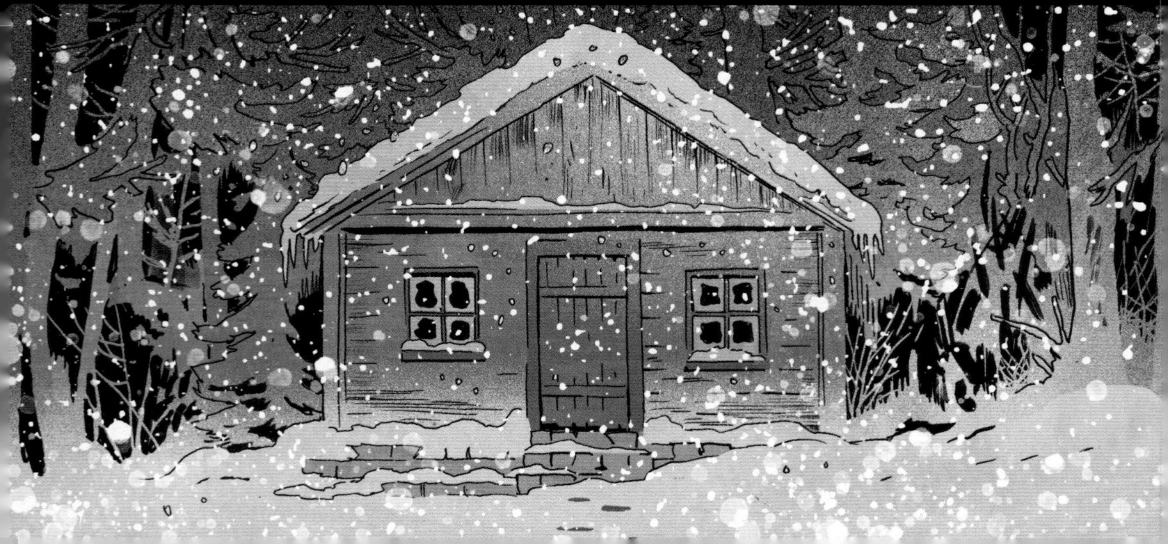

"You shall be compensated."

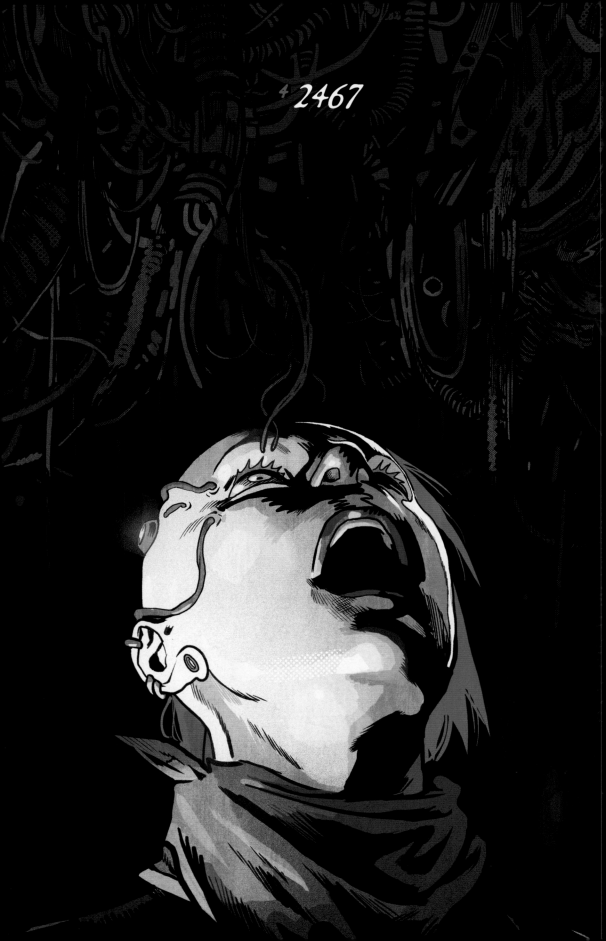

UPLINK
REQUESTED_

INITIATING_
PLEASE WAIT_

LINK MADE_
UPLOADING_

ONLINE_

BIRD IS IN THE AIR.
THIS IS OFFICER COLTEN
DUDLEY REQUESTING
OPEN CASES.

REQUEST RECEIVED_
REROUTING_

OFFICER DUDLEY, PLEASE
PROCEED TO OUTER ZONE
6F_ WE HAVE A 413 IN PROGRESS_

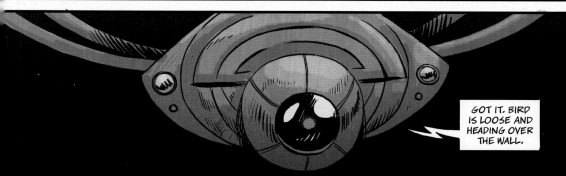

GOT IT. BIRD
IS LOOSE AND
HEADING OVER
THE WALL.

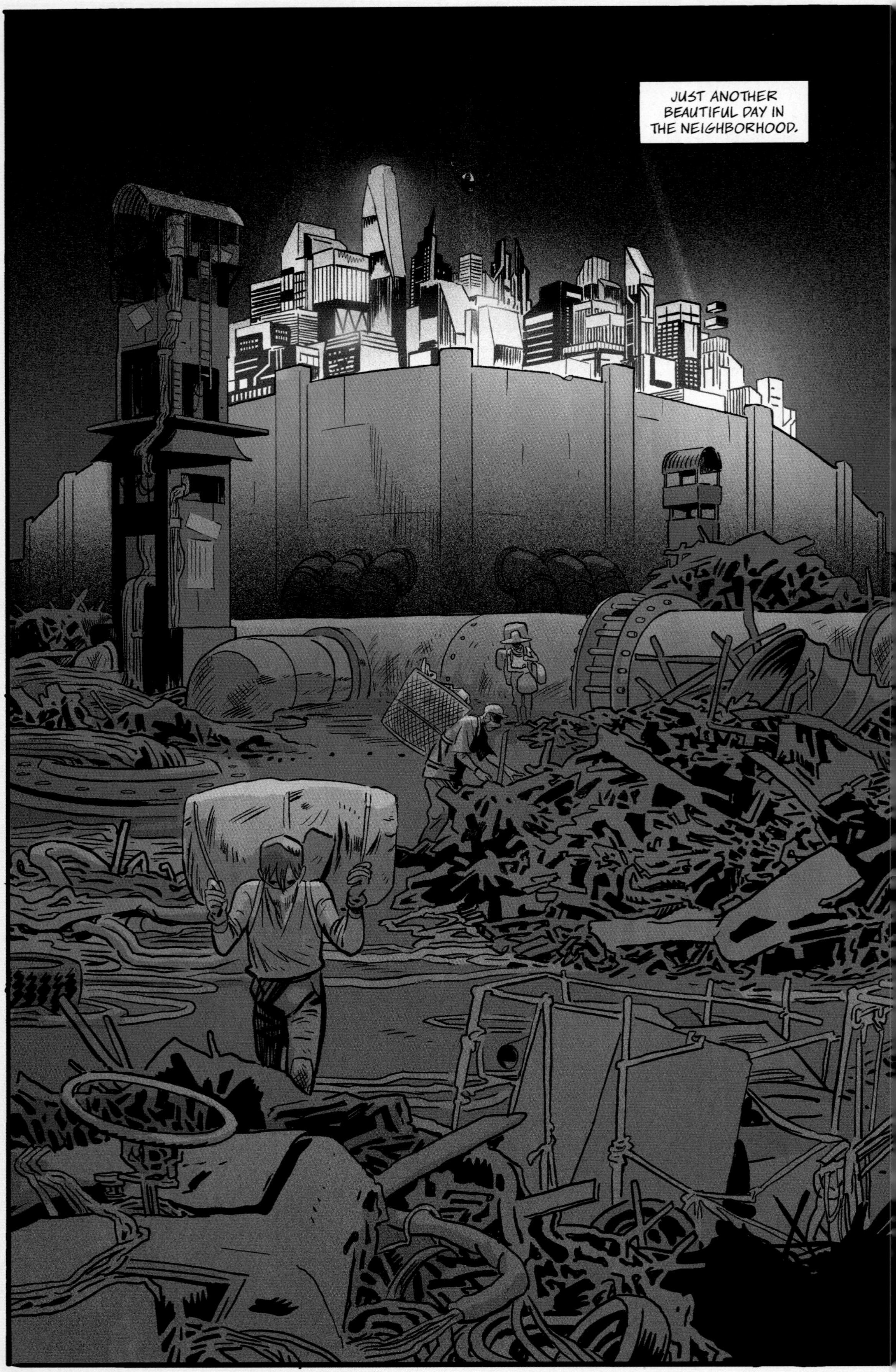
JUST ANOTHER BEAUTIFUL DAY IN THE NEIGHBORHOOD.

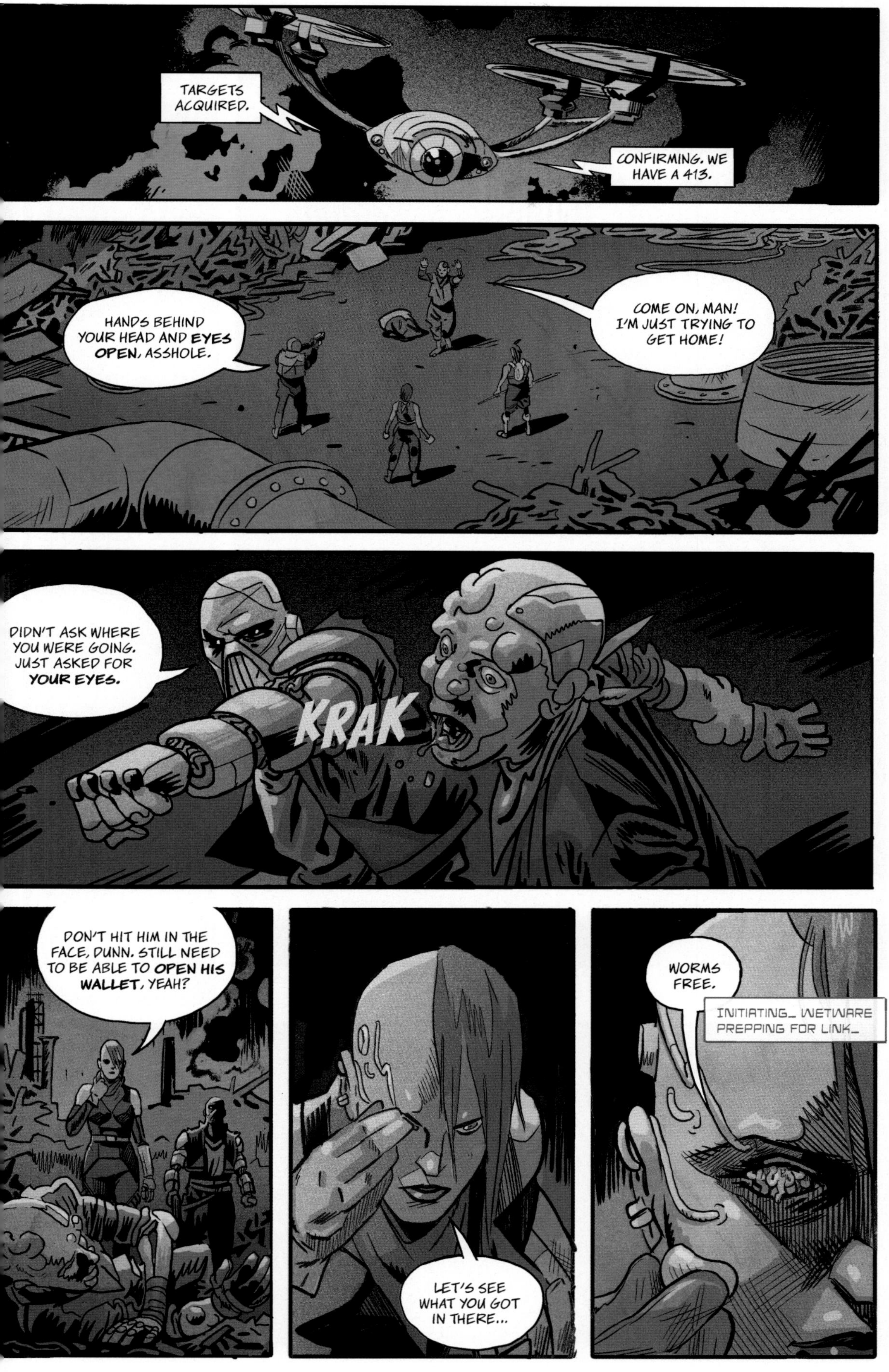
TARGETS ACQUIRED.
CONFIRMING. WE HAVE A 413.
HANDS BEHIND YOUR HEAD AND EYES OPEN, ASSHOLE.
COME ON, MAN! I'M JUST TRYING TO GET HOME!
DIDN'T ASK WHERE YOU WERE GOING. JUST ASKED FOR YOUR EYES.
KRAK
DON'T HIT HIM IN THE FACE, DUNN. STILL NEED TO BE ABLE TO OPEN HIS WALLET, YEAH?
LET'S SEE WHAT YOU GOT IN THERE...
WORMS FREE.
INITIATING_ WETWARE
PREPPING FOR LINK_

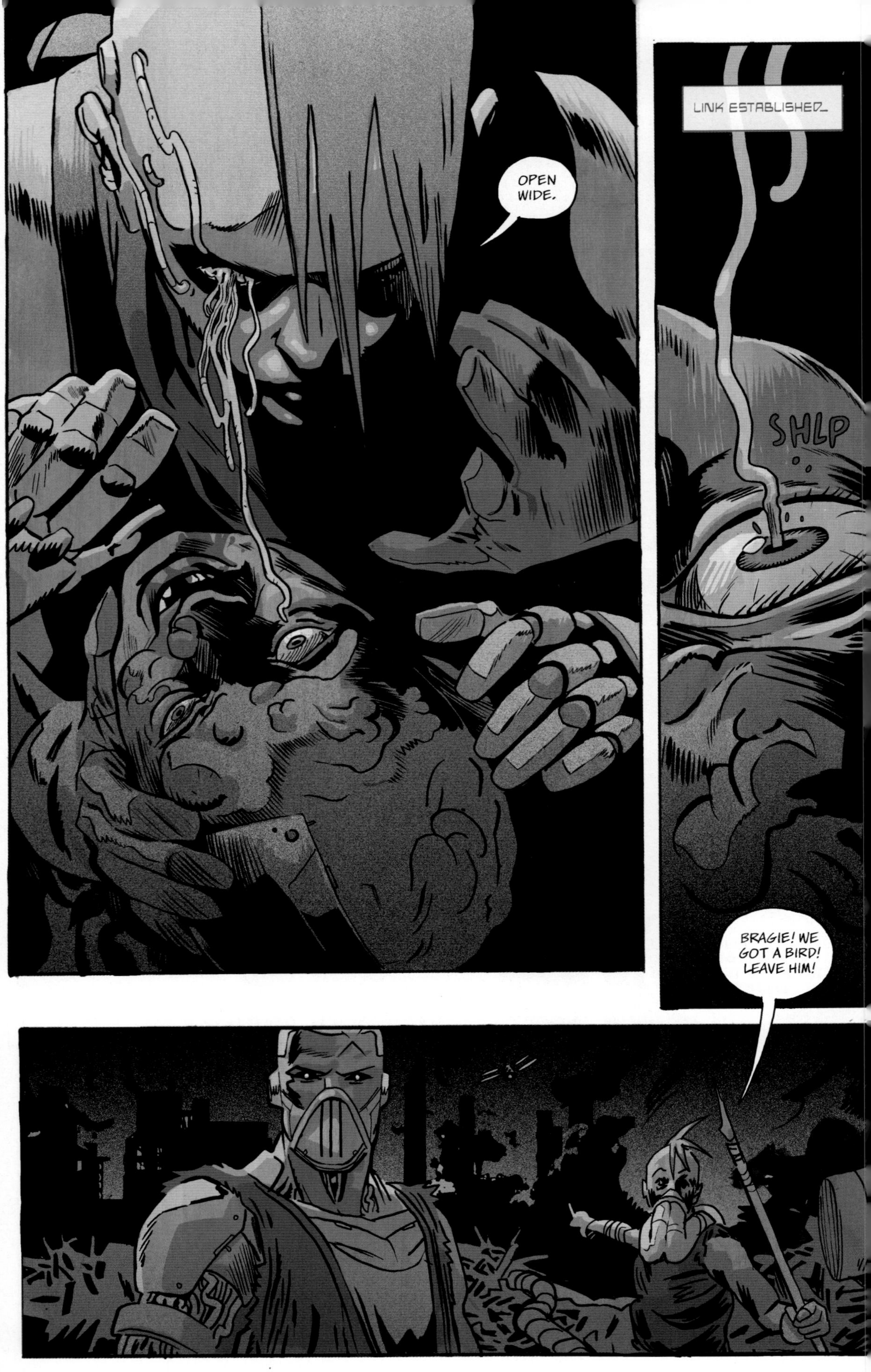
OPEN WIDE.
LINK ESTABLISHED_
SHLP
BRAGIE! WE GOT A BIRD! LEAVE HIM!

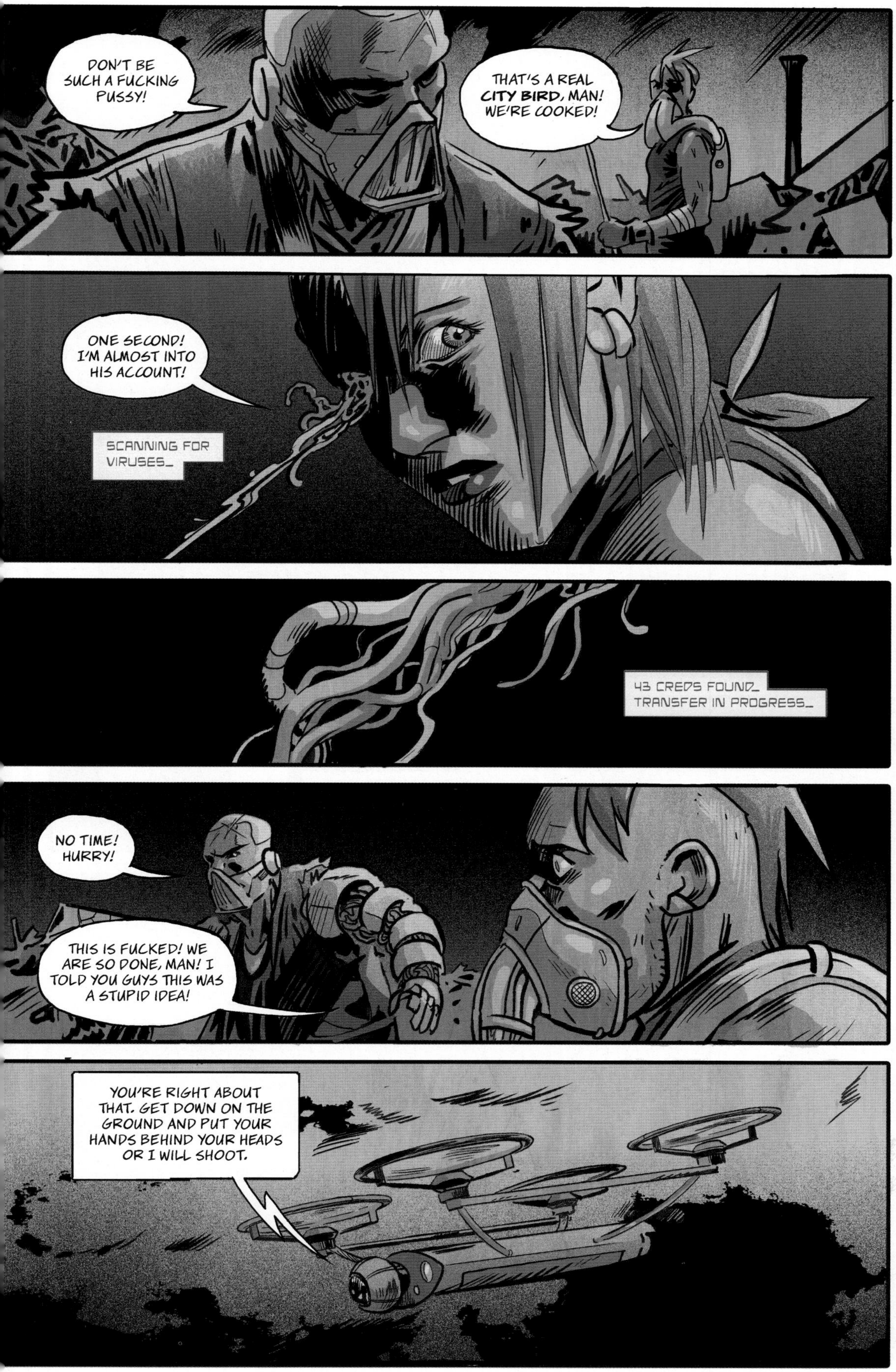
DON'T BE SUCH A FUCKING PUSSY!
THAT'S A REAL CITY BIRD, MAN! WE'RE COOKED!
ONE SECOND! I'M ALMOST INTO HIS ACCOUNT!
SCANNING FOR VIRUSES_
43 CREDS FOUND_ TRANSFER IN PROGRESS_
NO TIME! HURRY!
THIS IS FUCKED! WE ARE SO DONE, MAN! I TOLD YOU GUYS THIS WAS A STUPID IDEA!
YOU'RE RIGHT ABOUT THAT. GET DOWN ON THE GROUND AND PUT YOUR HANDS BEHIND YOUR HEADS OR I WILL SHOOT.

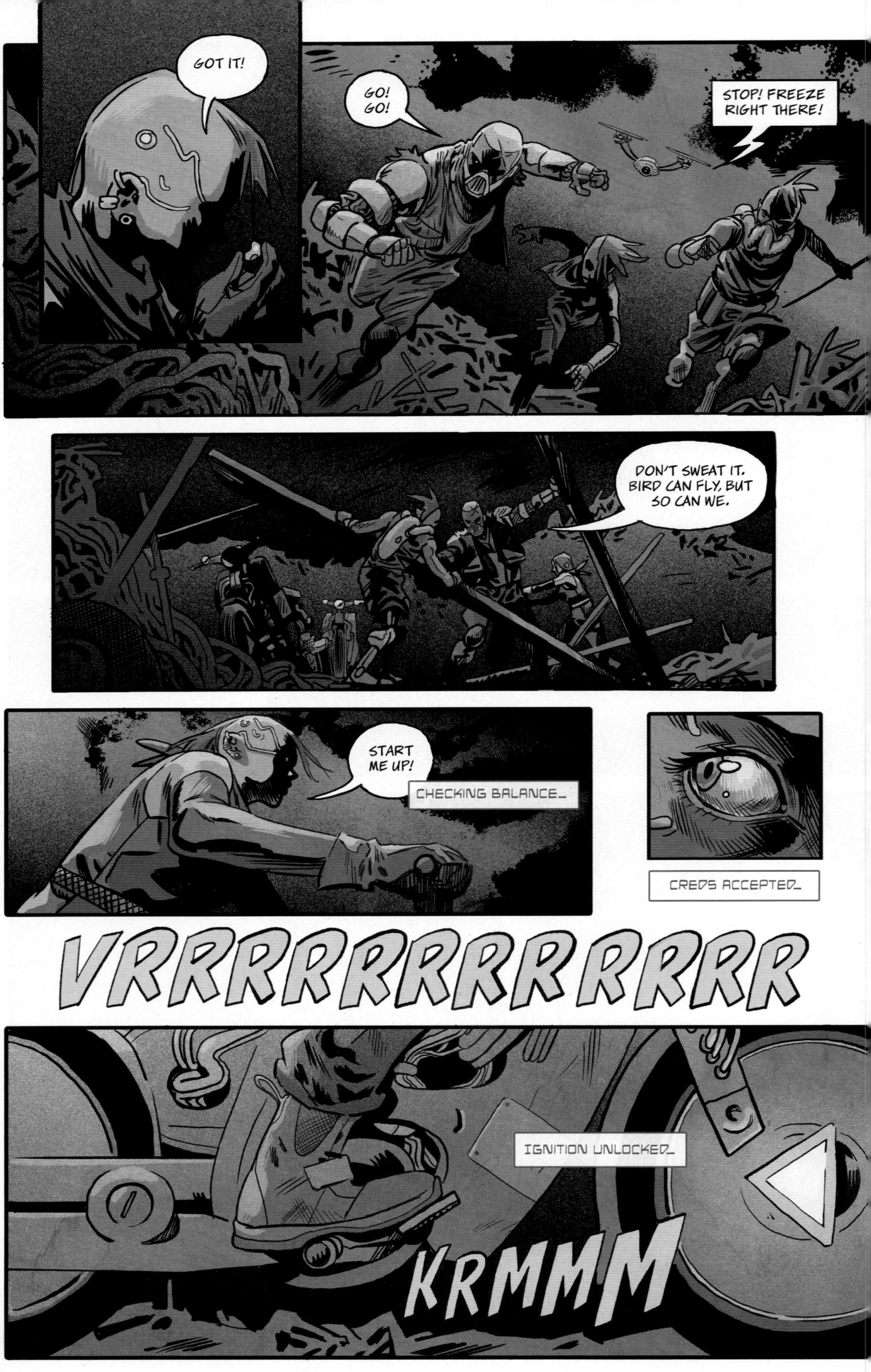
GOT IT!
GO! GO!
STOP! FREEZE RIGHT THERE!
DON'T SWEAT IT. BIRD CAN FLY, BUT SO CAN WE.
START ME UP!
CHECKING BALANCE_
CREDS ACCEPTED_
VRRRRRRRRRRRRR
IGNITION UNLOCKED_
KRMMM

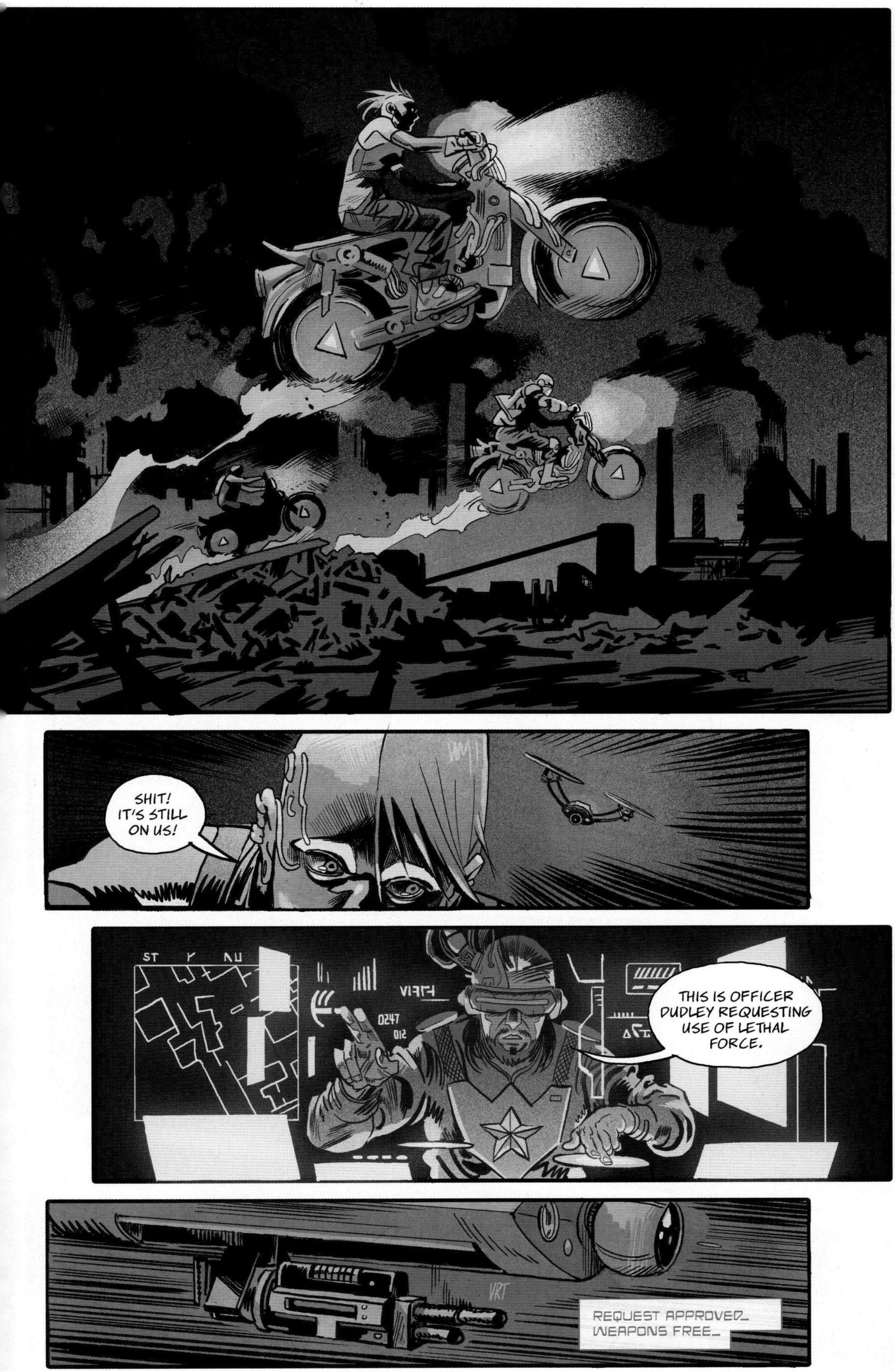
SHIT! IT'S STILL ON US!
THIS IS OFFICER DUDLEY REQUESTING USE OF LETHAL FORCE.
REQUEST APPROVED_
WEAPONS FREE_

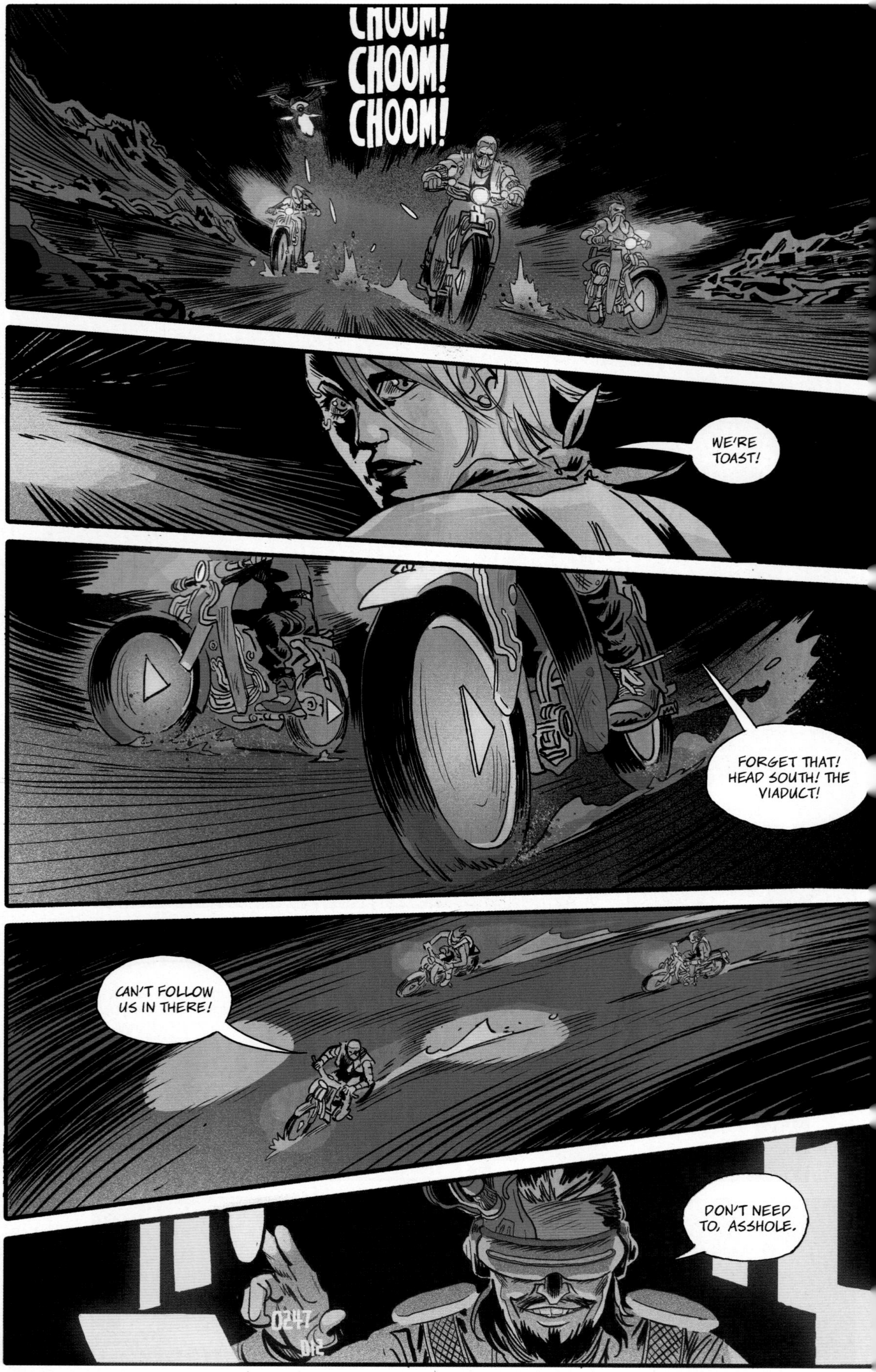
CHOOM!
CHOOM!
CHOOM!
WE'RE TOAST!
FORGET THAT! HEAD SOUTH! THE VIADUCT!
CAN'T FOLLOW US IN THERE!
DON'T NEED TO, ASSHOLE.
0247

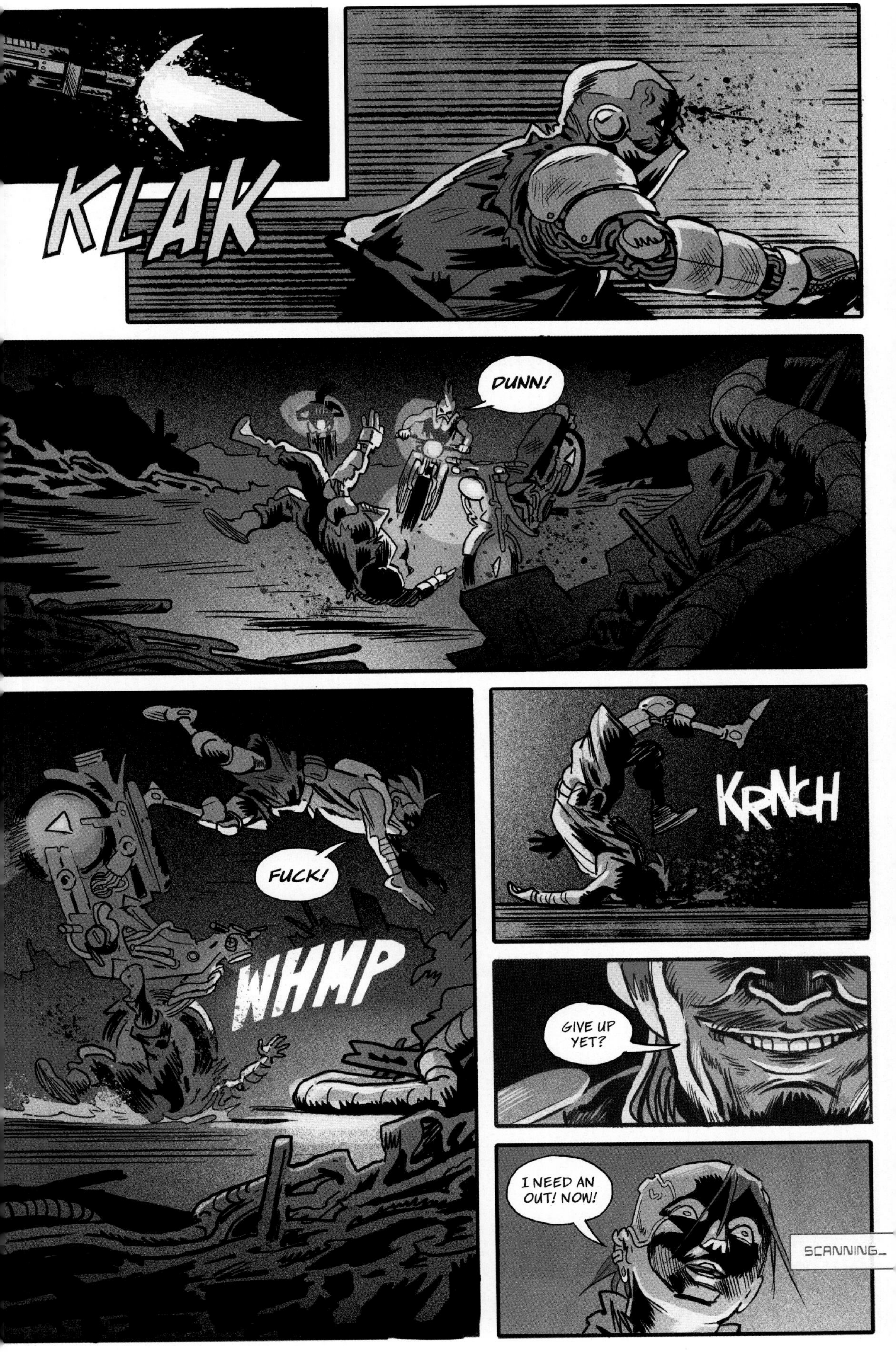
KLAK
DUNN!
FUCK!
WHMP
KRNCH
GIVE UP YET?
I NEED AN OUT! NOW!
SCANNING_

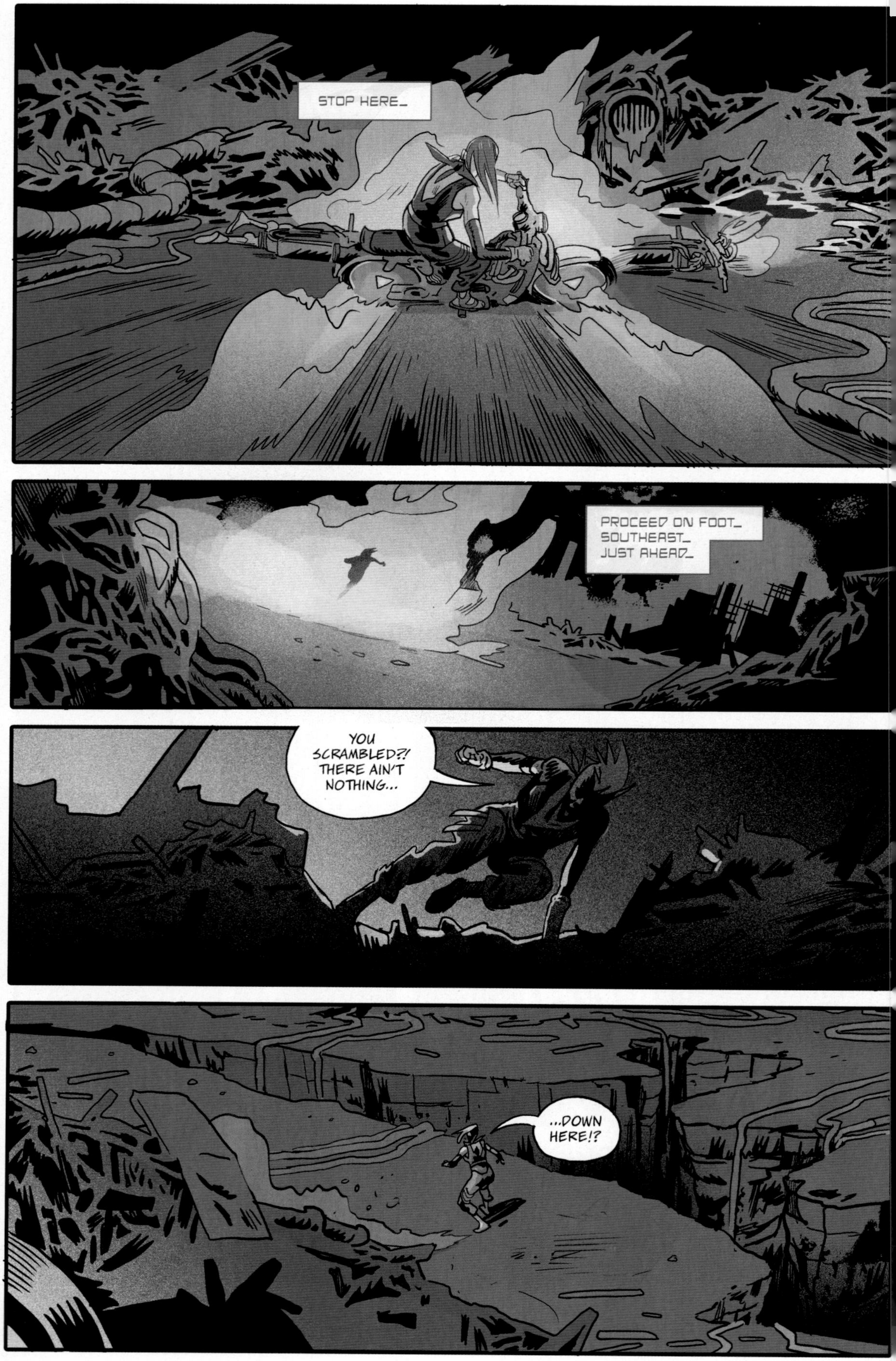
STOP HERE_
PROCEED ON FOOT_
SOUTHEAST_
JUST AHEAD_
YOU SCRAMBLED?! THERE AIN'T NOTHING...
...DOWN HERE!?

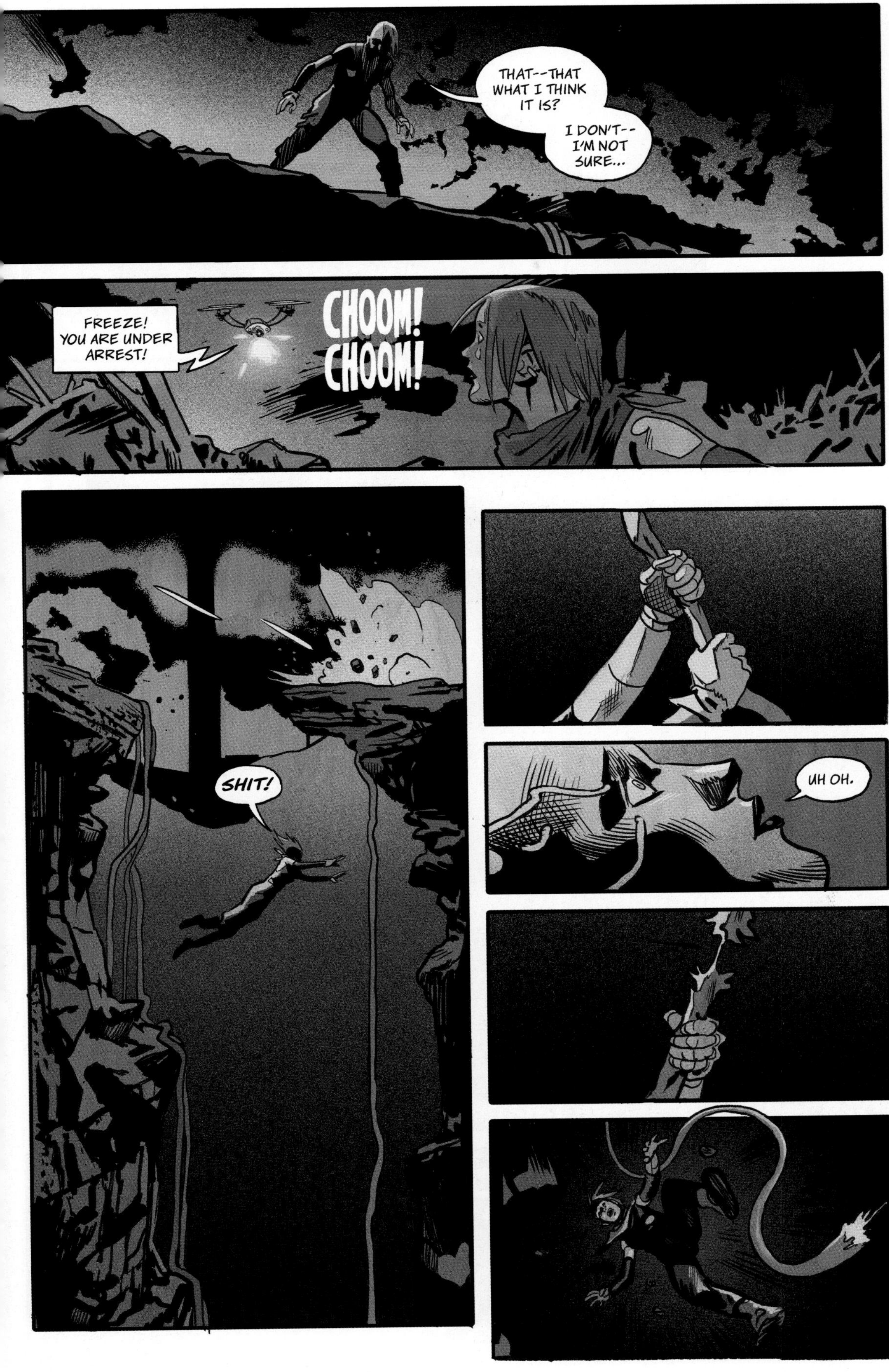
THAT--THAT WHAT I THINK IT IS?
I DON'T-- I'M NOT SURE...
FREEZE! YOU ARE UNDER ARREST!
CHOOM! CHOOM!
SHIT!
UH OH.

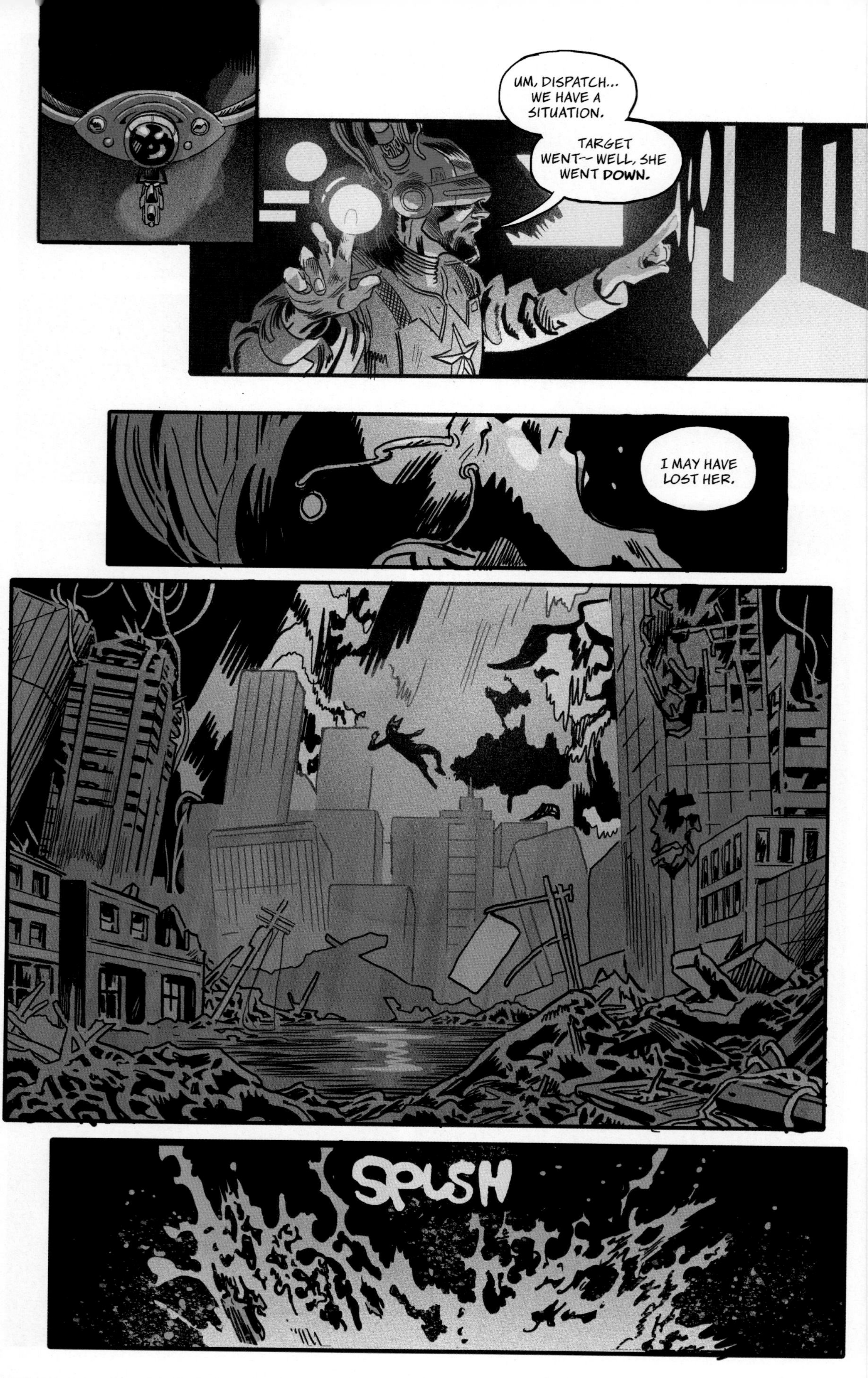
UM, DISPATCH...
WE HAVE A
SITUATION.
TARGET
WENT-- WELL, SHE
WENT **DOWN.**
I MAY HAVE
LOST HER.
SPLSH

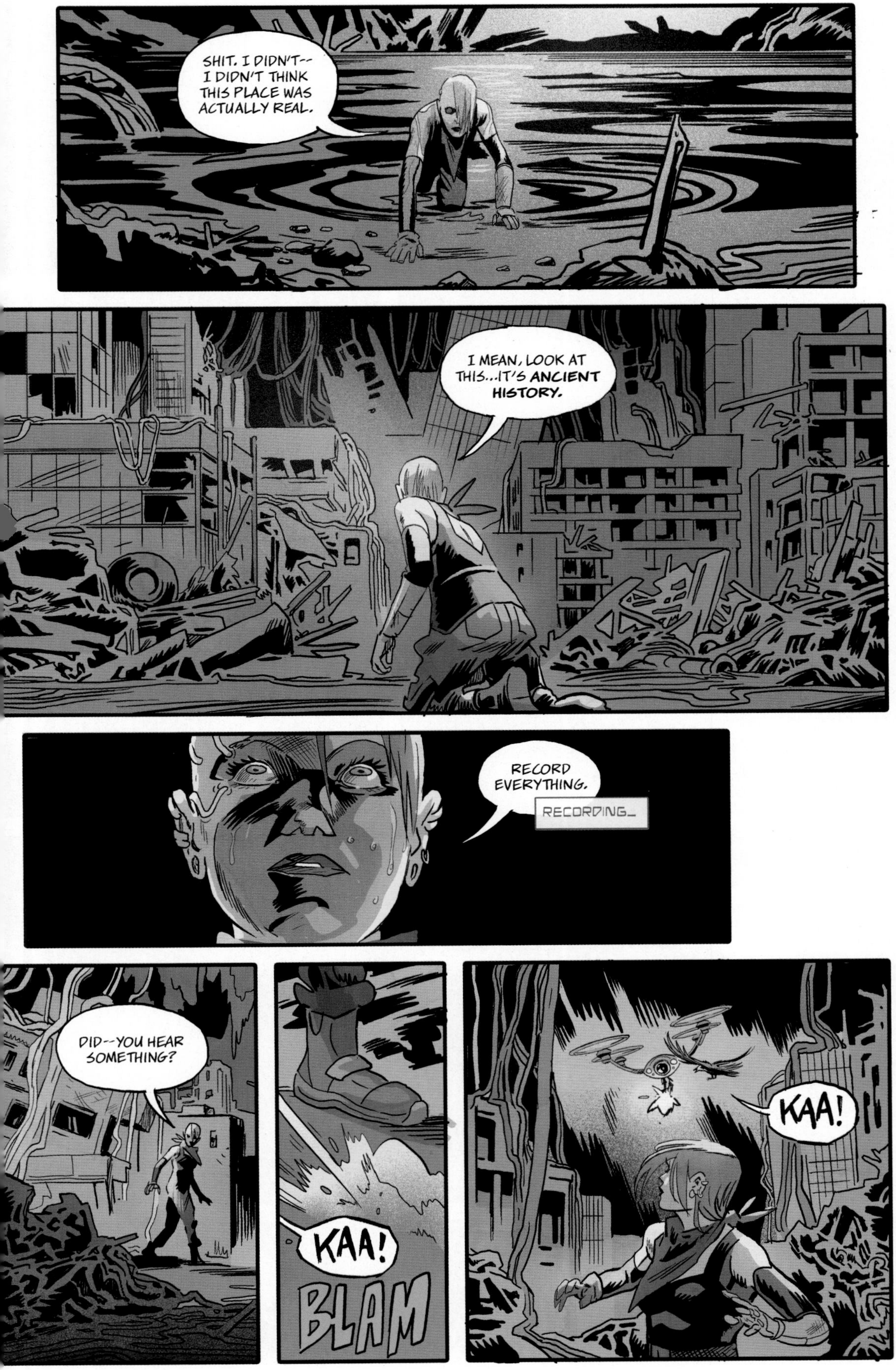
SHIT. I DIDN'T-- I DIDN'T THINK THIS PLACE WAS ACTUALLY REAL.
I MEAN, LOOK AT THIS...IT'S **ANCIENT HISTORY.**
RECORD EVERYTHING.
RECORDING_
DID--YOU HEAR SOMETHING?
KAA!
BLAM
KAA!

SHIT! SHIT! SHIT!
THINK--THINK I LOST IT.
HEY! YOU STILL WITH ME?
COMPUTER?

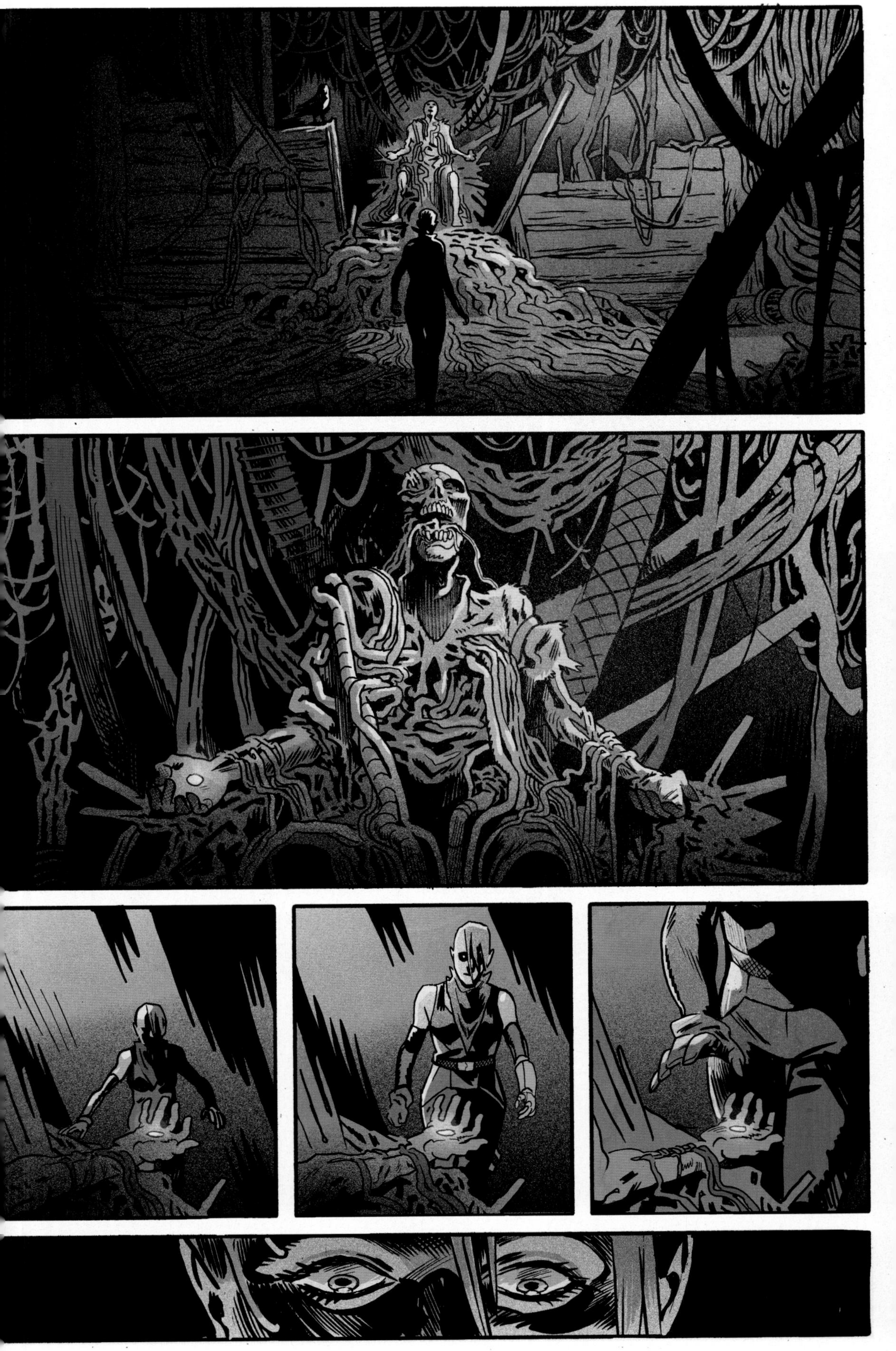

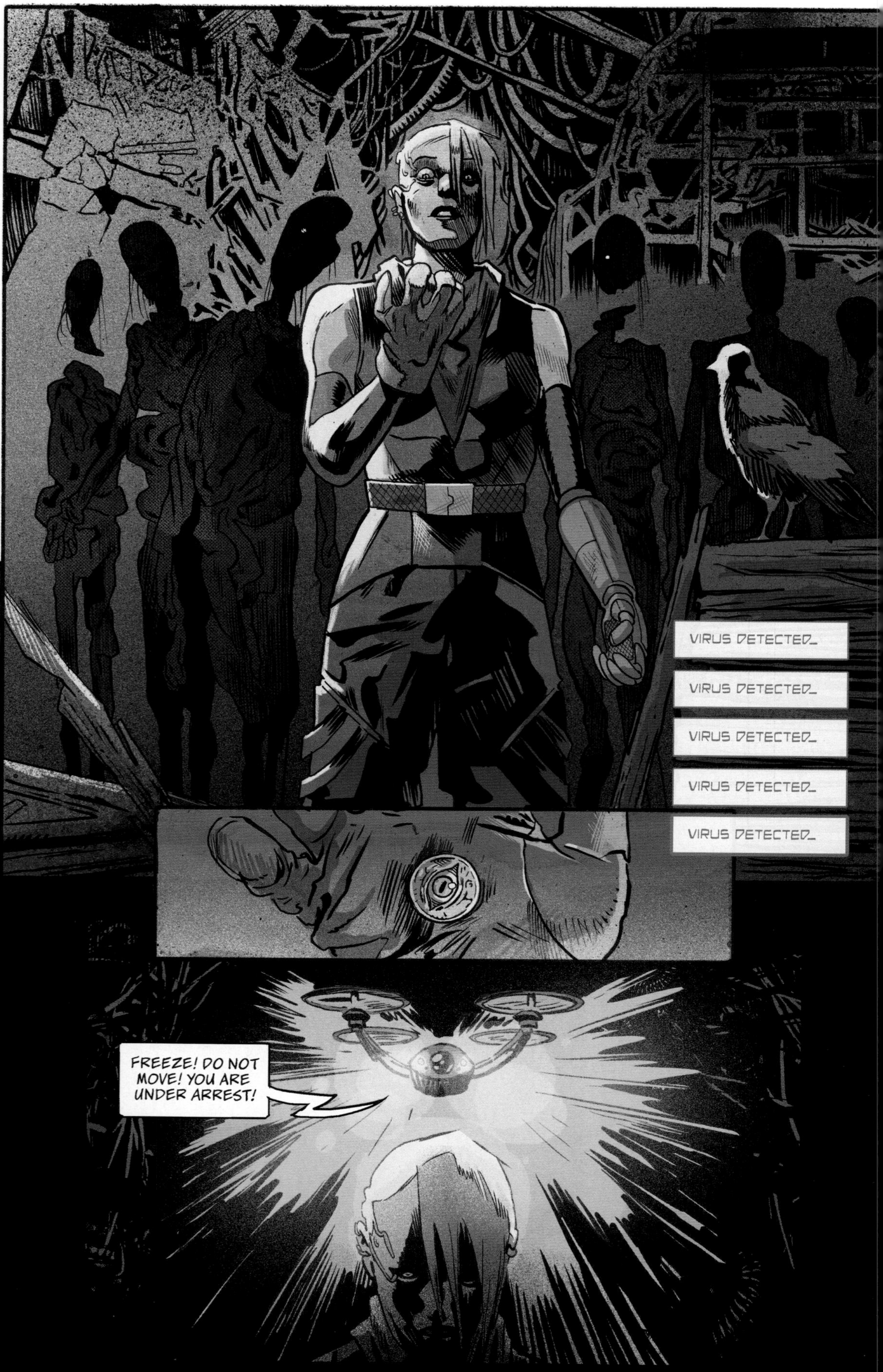
VIRUS DETECTED_
VIRUS DETECTED_
VIRUS DETECTED_
VIRUS DETECTED_
VIRUS DETECTED_
FREEZE! DO NOT MOVE! YOU ARE UNDER ARREST!

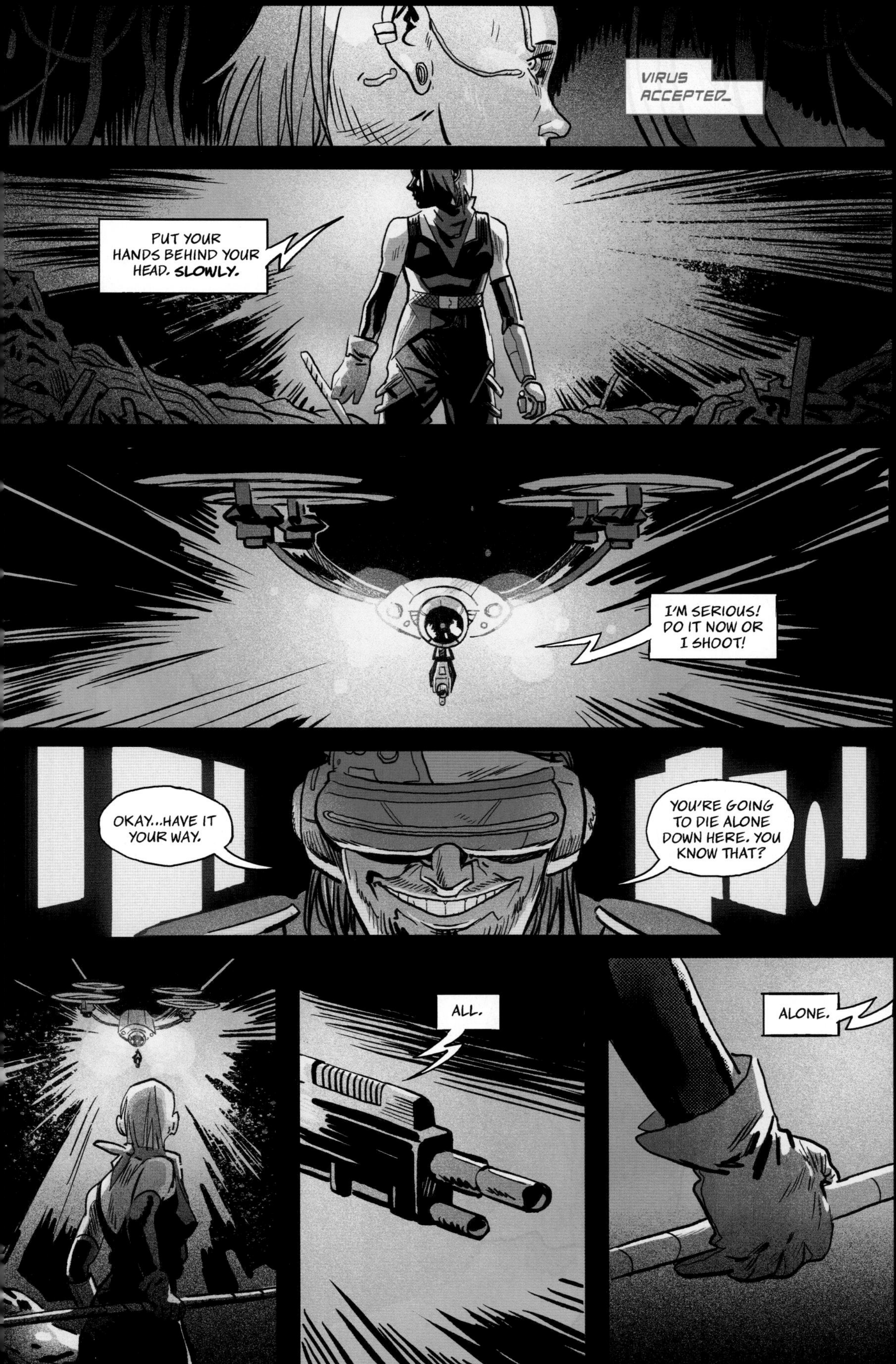
VIRUS ACCEPTED_
PUT YOUR HANDS BEHIND YOUR HEAD. **SLOWLY.**
I'M SERIOUS! DO IT NOW OR I SHOOT!
OKAY...HAVE IT YOUR WAY.
YOU'RE GOING TO DIE ALONE DOWN HERE. YOU KNOW THAT?
ALL.
ALONE.

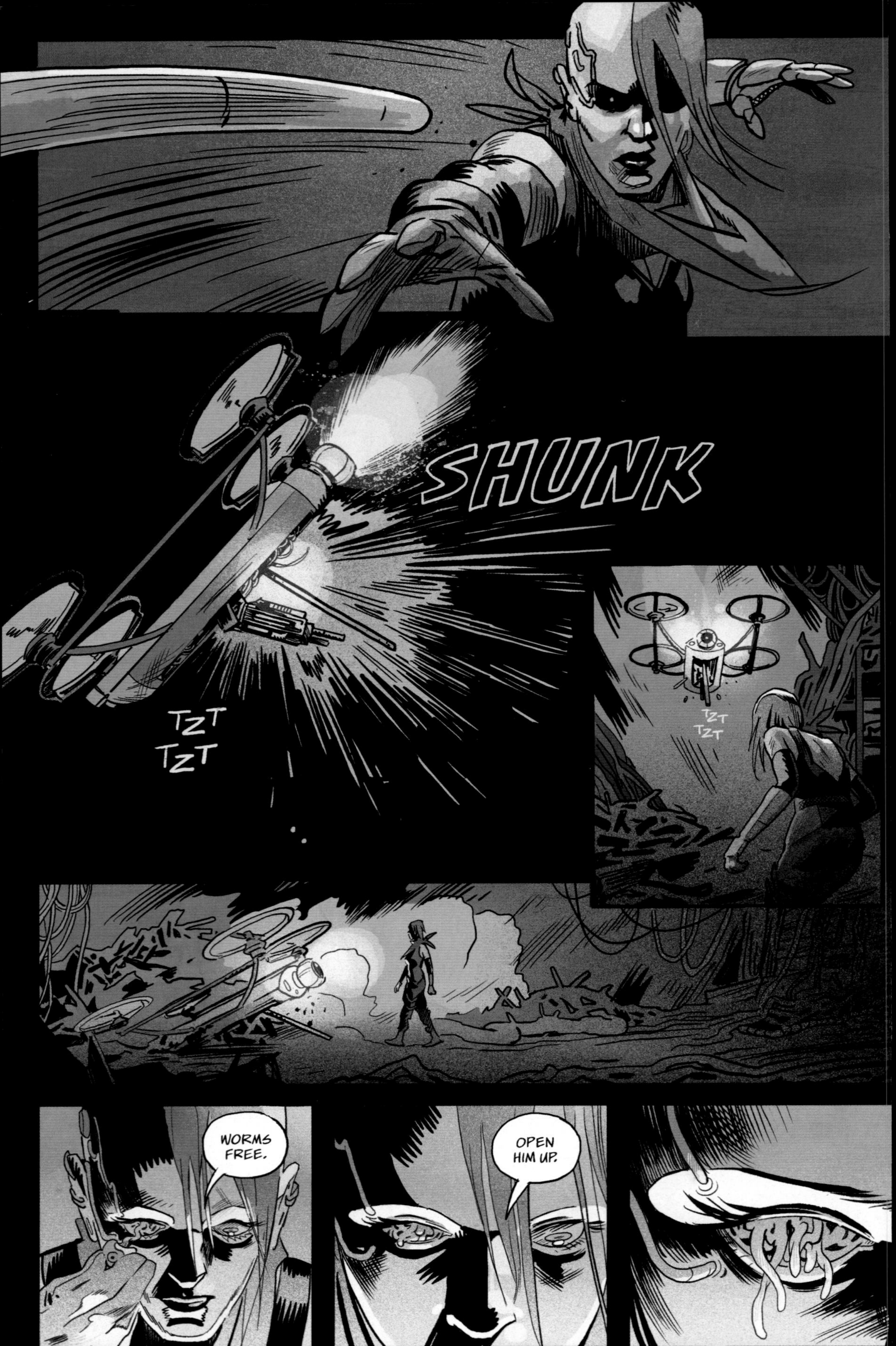
SHUNK
TZT
TZT
TZT
TZT
WORMS FREE.
OPEN HIM UP.

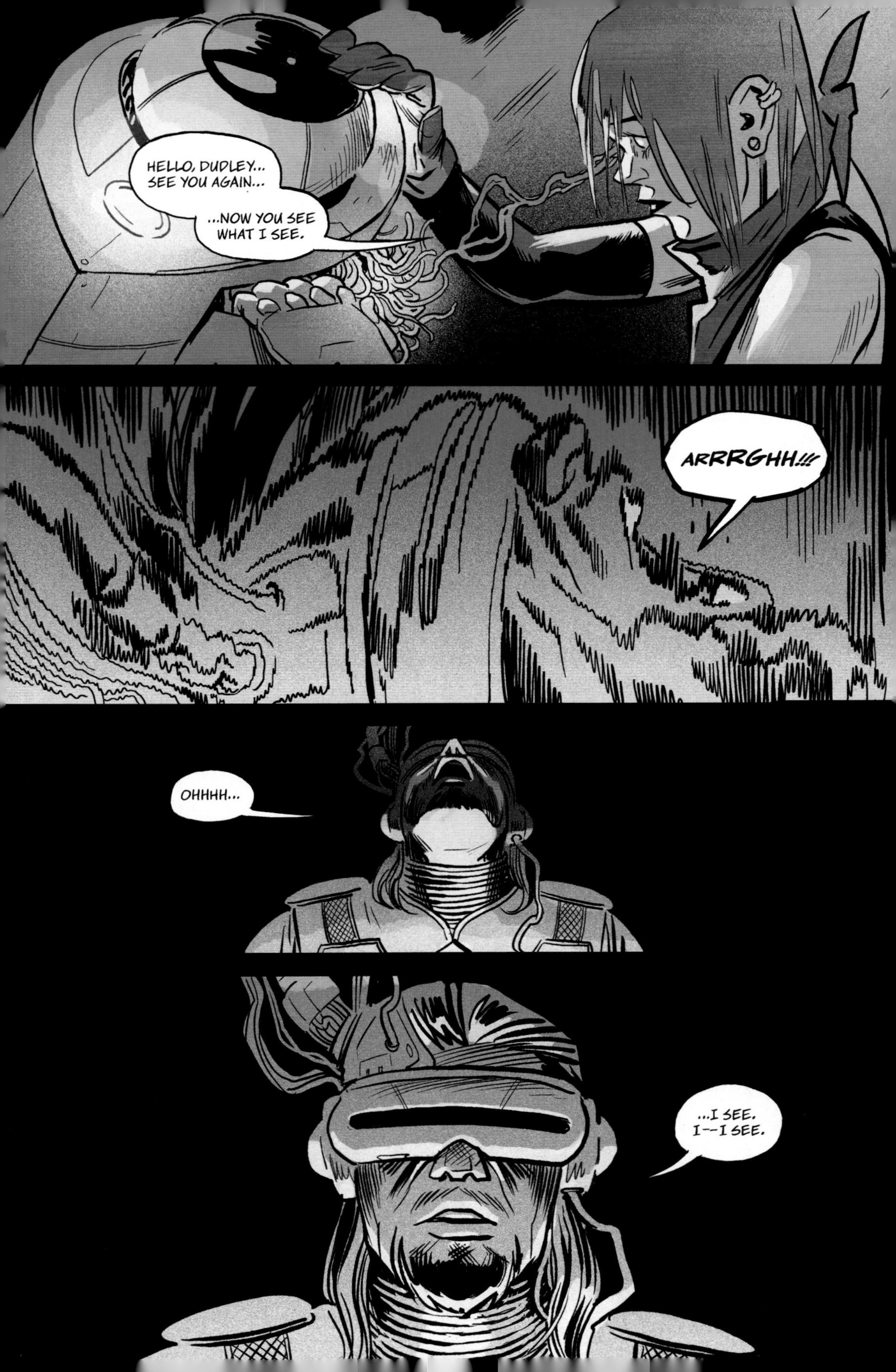
HELLO, DUDLEY... SEE YOU AGAIN...
...NOW YOU SEE WHAT I SEE.
ARRRGHH!!!
OHHHH...
...I SEE. I--I SEE.

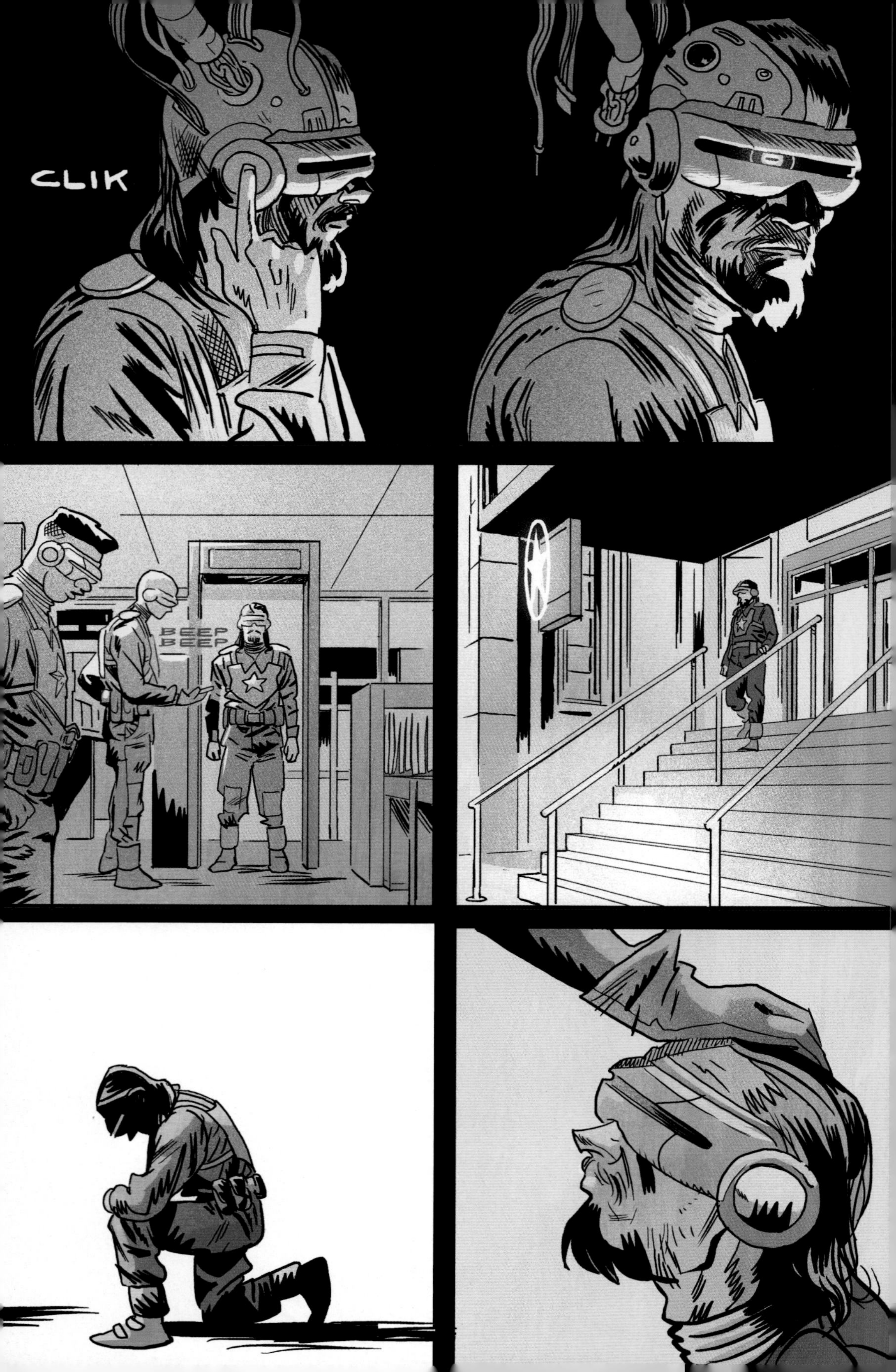
CLIK
BEEP
BEEP

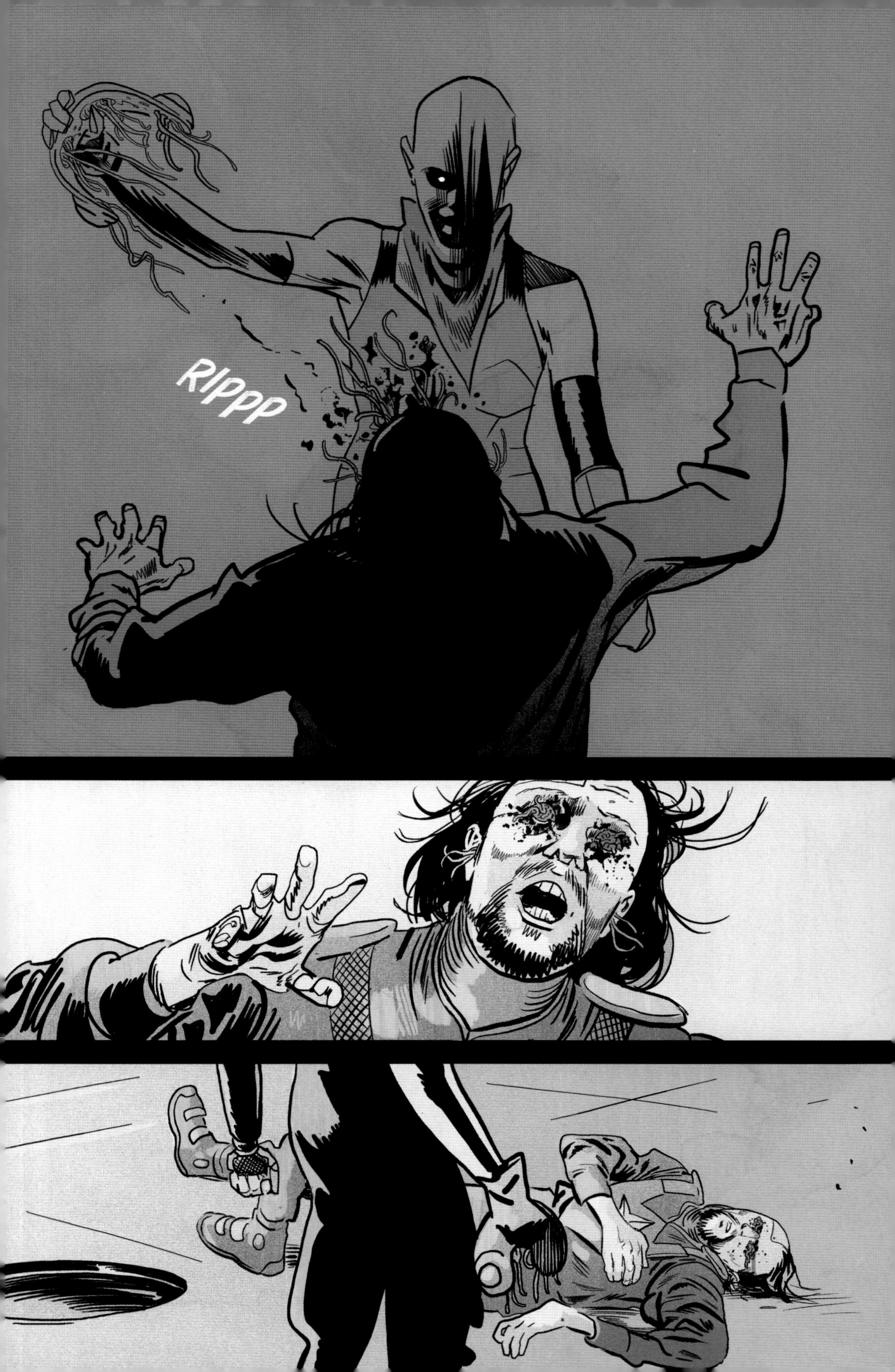
RIPPP

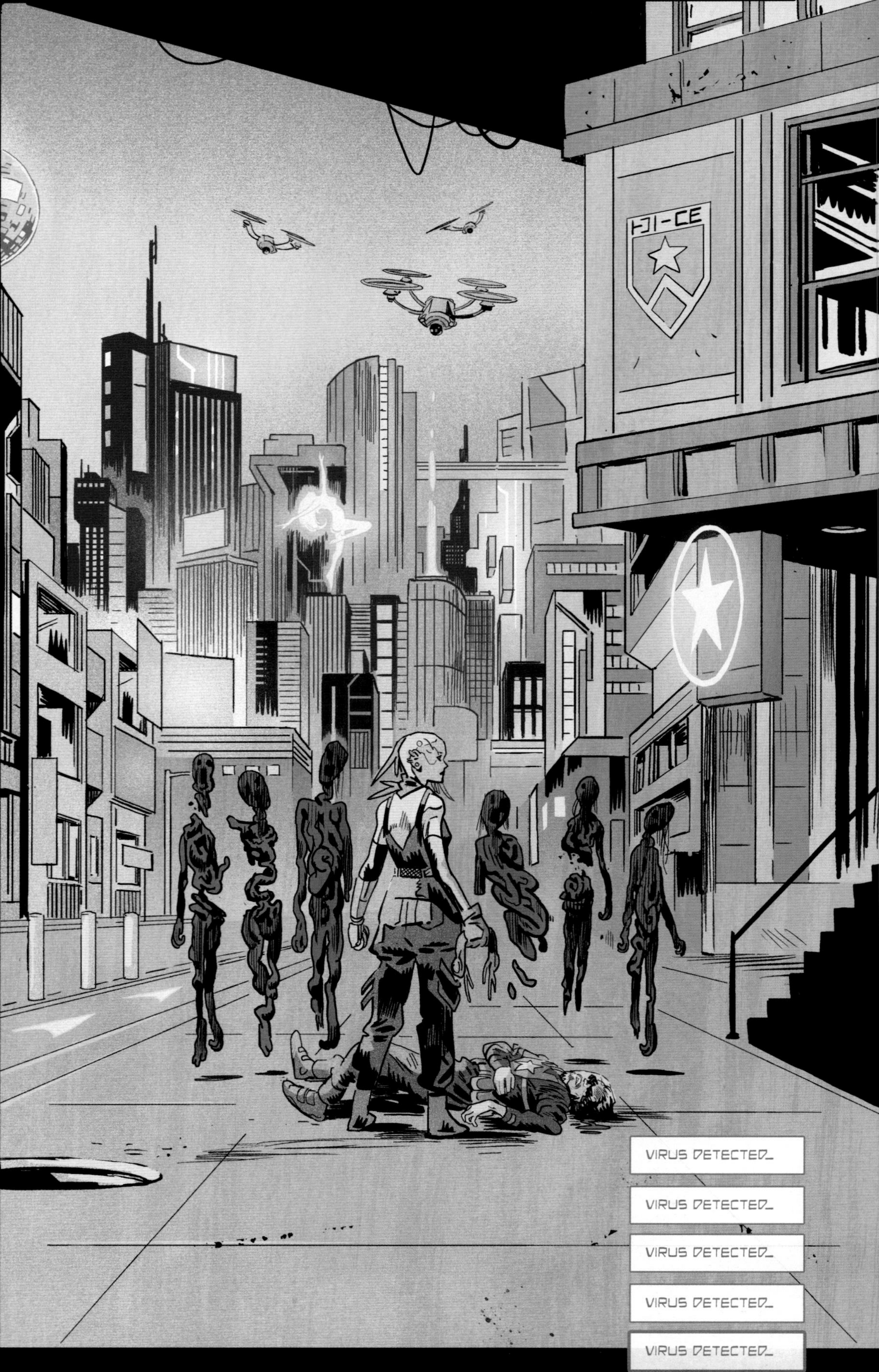
HJI-CE
VIRUS DETECTED_
VIRUS DETECTED_
VIRUS DETECTED_
VIRUS DETECTED_
VIRUS DETECTED_

"Now you see what I see."

5 Covenant

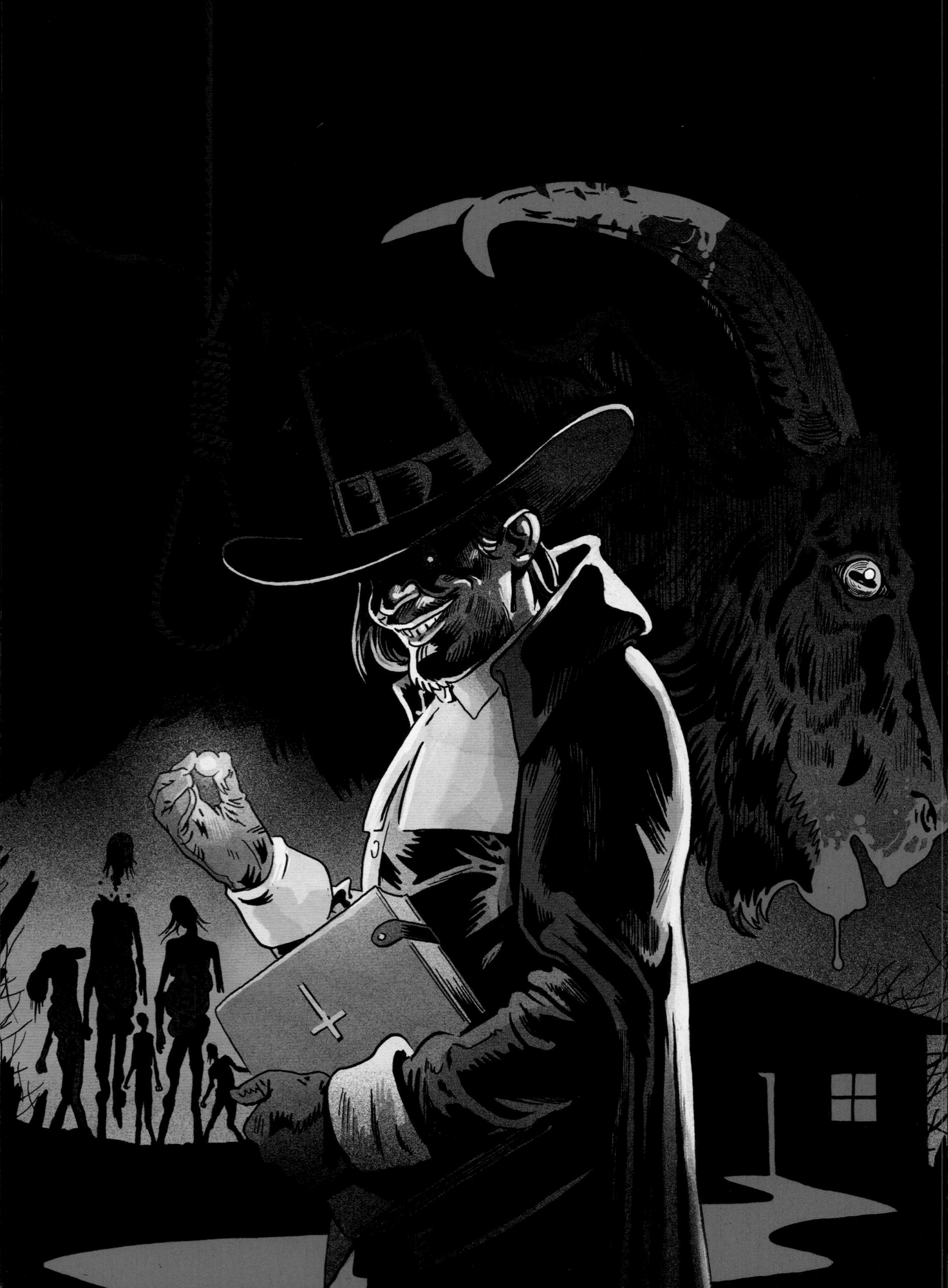

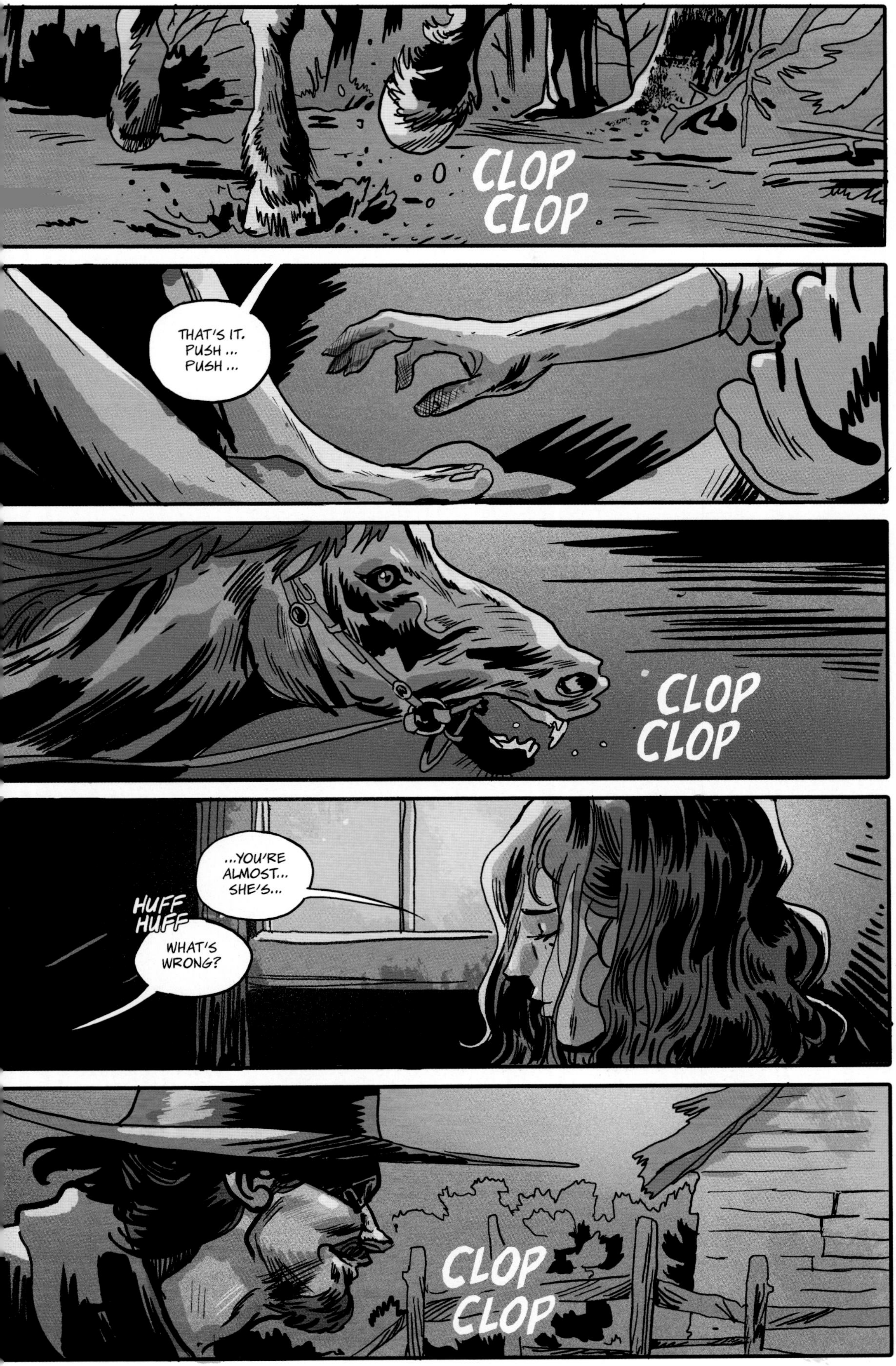
CLOP
CLOP
THAT'S IT. PUSH... PUSH...
CLOP
CLOP
...YOU'RE ALMOST... SHE'S...
HUFF
HUFF
WHAT'S WRONG?
CLOP
CLOP

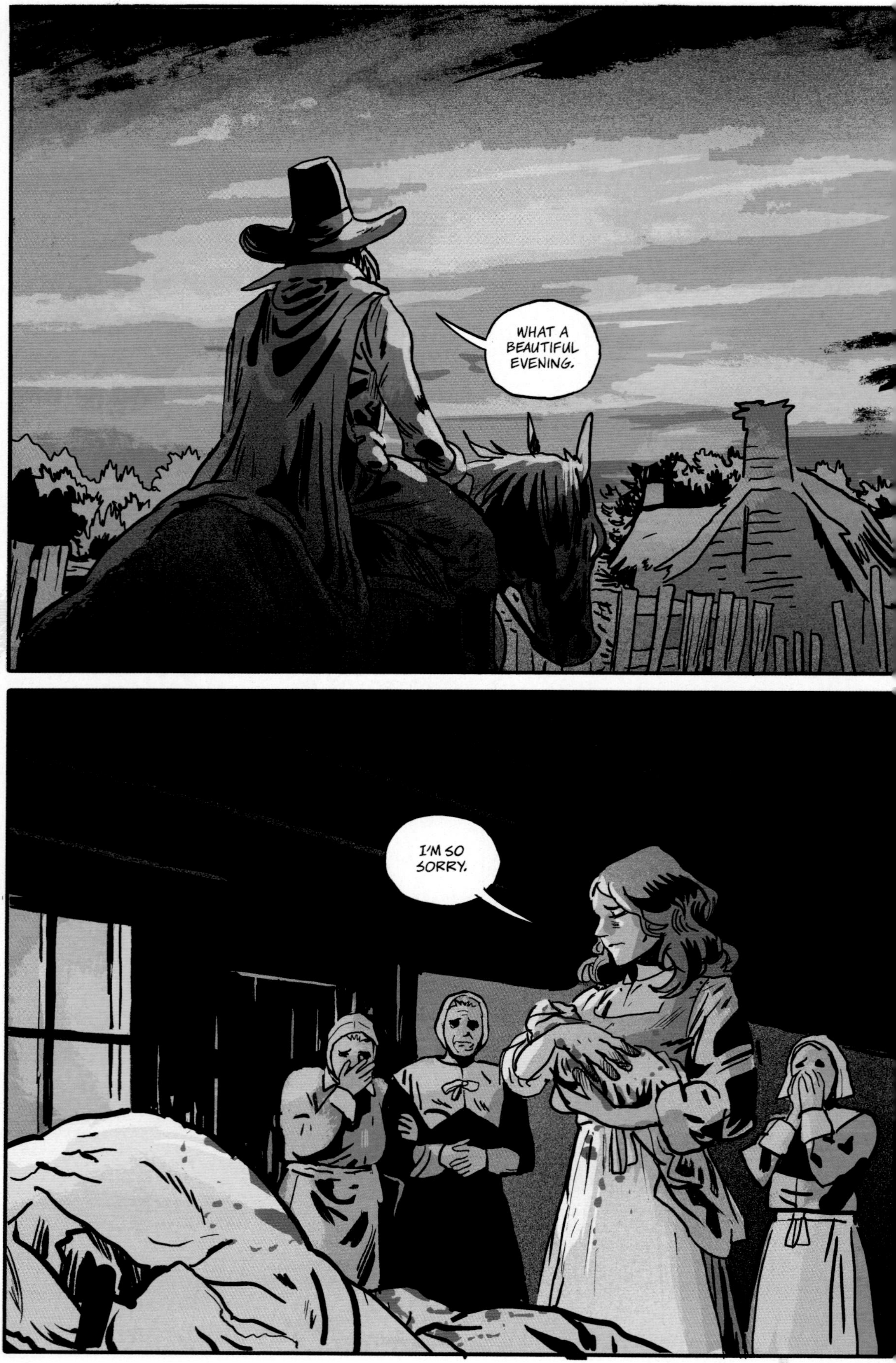
WHAT A BEAUTIFUL EVENING.
I'M SO SORRY.

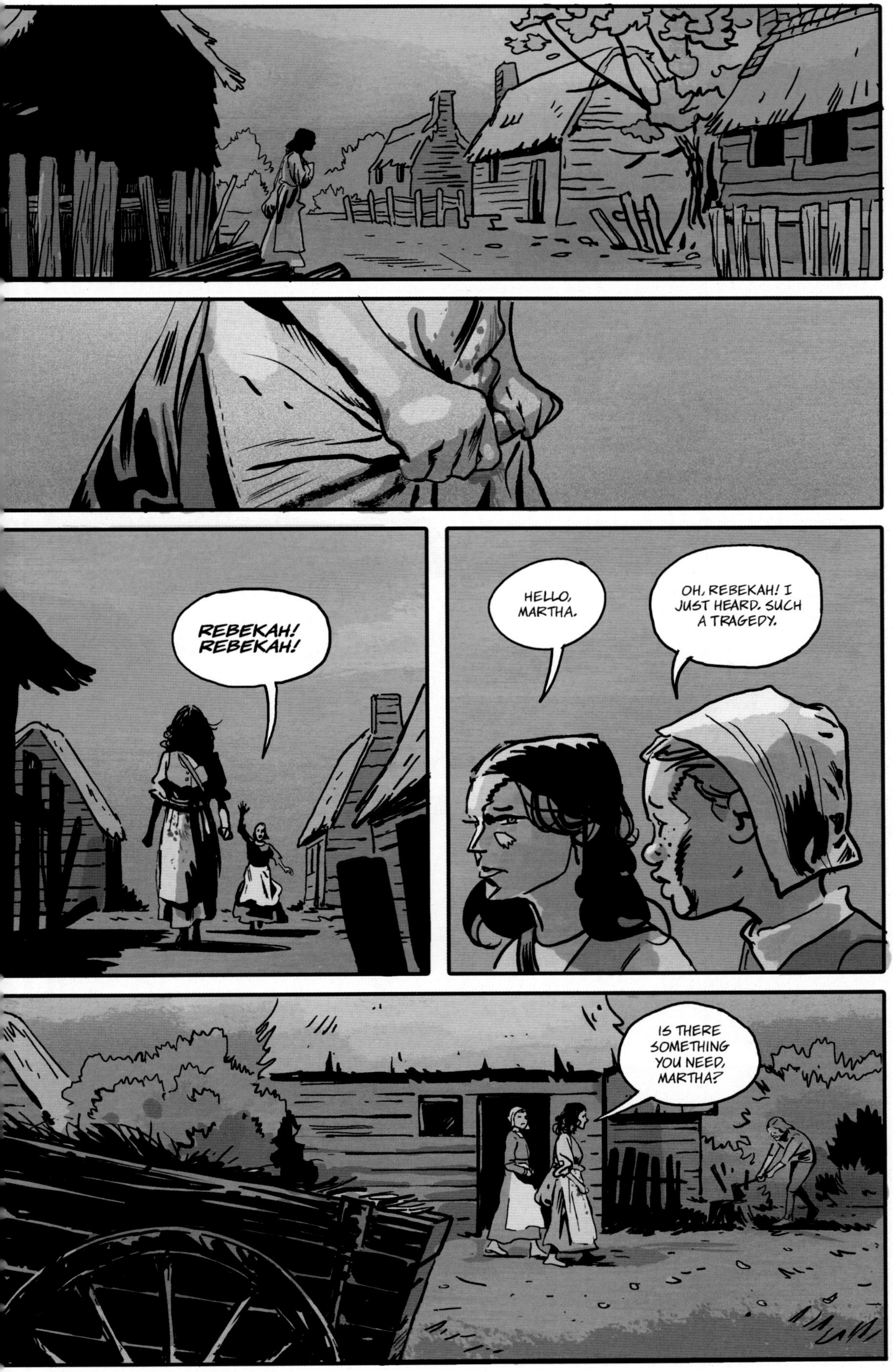
REBEKAH! REBEKAH!
HELLO, MARTHA.
OH, REBEKAH! I JUST HEARD. SUCH A TRAGEDY.
IS THERE SOMETHING YOU NEED, MARTHA?

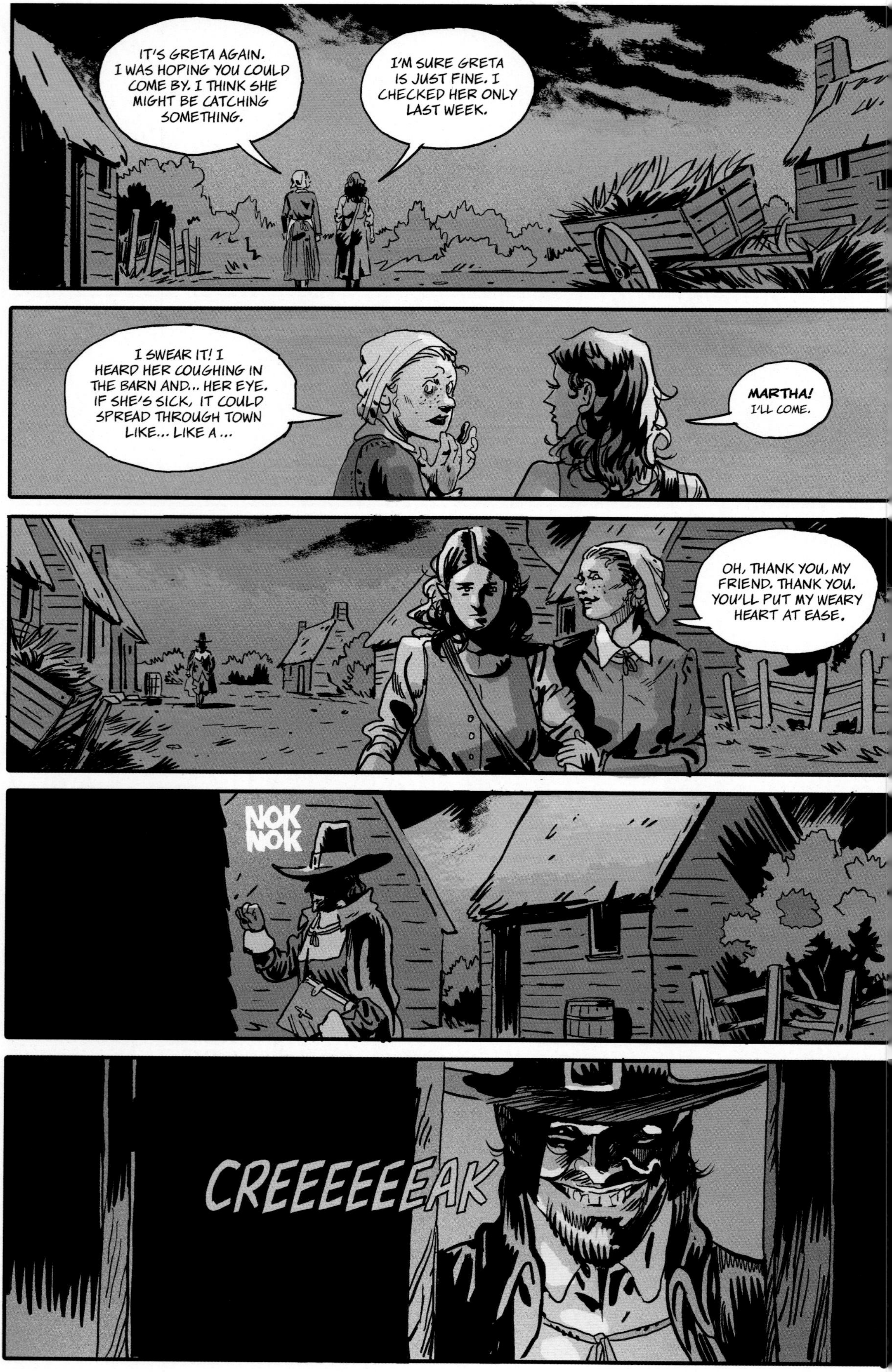
IT'S GRETA AGAIN. I WAS HOPING YOU COULD COME BY. I THINK SHE MIGHT BE CATCHING SOMETHING.
I'M SURE GRETA IS JUST FINE. I CHECKED HER ONLY LAST WEEK.
I SWEAR IT! I HEARD HER COUGHING IN THE BARN AND... HER EYE. IF SHE'S SICK, IT COULD SPREAD THROUGH TOWN LIKE... LIKE A ...
MARTHA! I'LL COME.
OH, THANK YOU, MY FRIEND. THANK YOU. YOU'LL PUT MY WEARY HEART AT EASE.
NOK NOK
CREEEEEEEAK

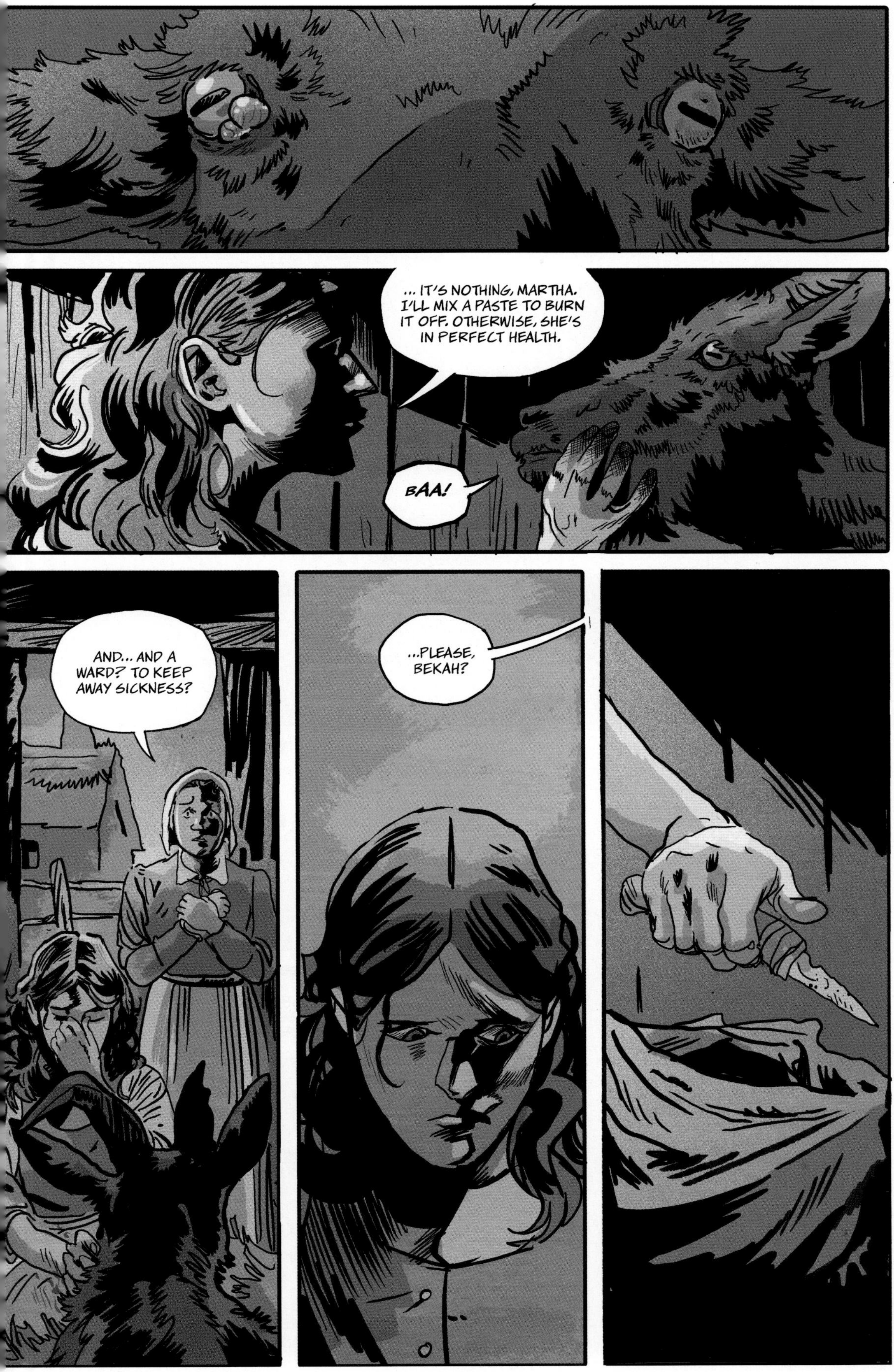
... IT'S NOTHING, MARTHA. I'LL MIX A PASTE TO BURN IT OFF. OTHERWISE, SHE'S IN PERFECT HEALTH.
BAA!
AND... AND A WARD? TO KEEP AWAY SICKNESS?
...PLEASE, BEKAH?

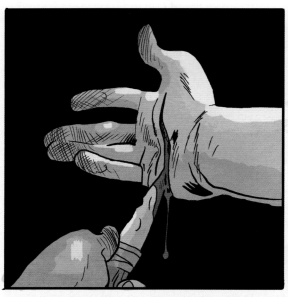

ᕼᕓᐱᒥ, ᒥᛕᏳᒎᕓᒥᒻ, ᐱᕓᑕᒻ.

THIS WILL KEEP HER SAFE.

BAAAA!

I WISH I COULD, SWEET GRETA.

OH, THANK YOU! PLEASE, WILL YOU STAY FOR A TEA? I HAVEN'T SEEN YOU MUCH SINCE THOMAS...SINCE...

NO. I'M EXHAUSTED, MARTHA. I NEED SLEEP.

THURSDAY. I'LL COME BY FOR NOON TEA.

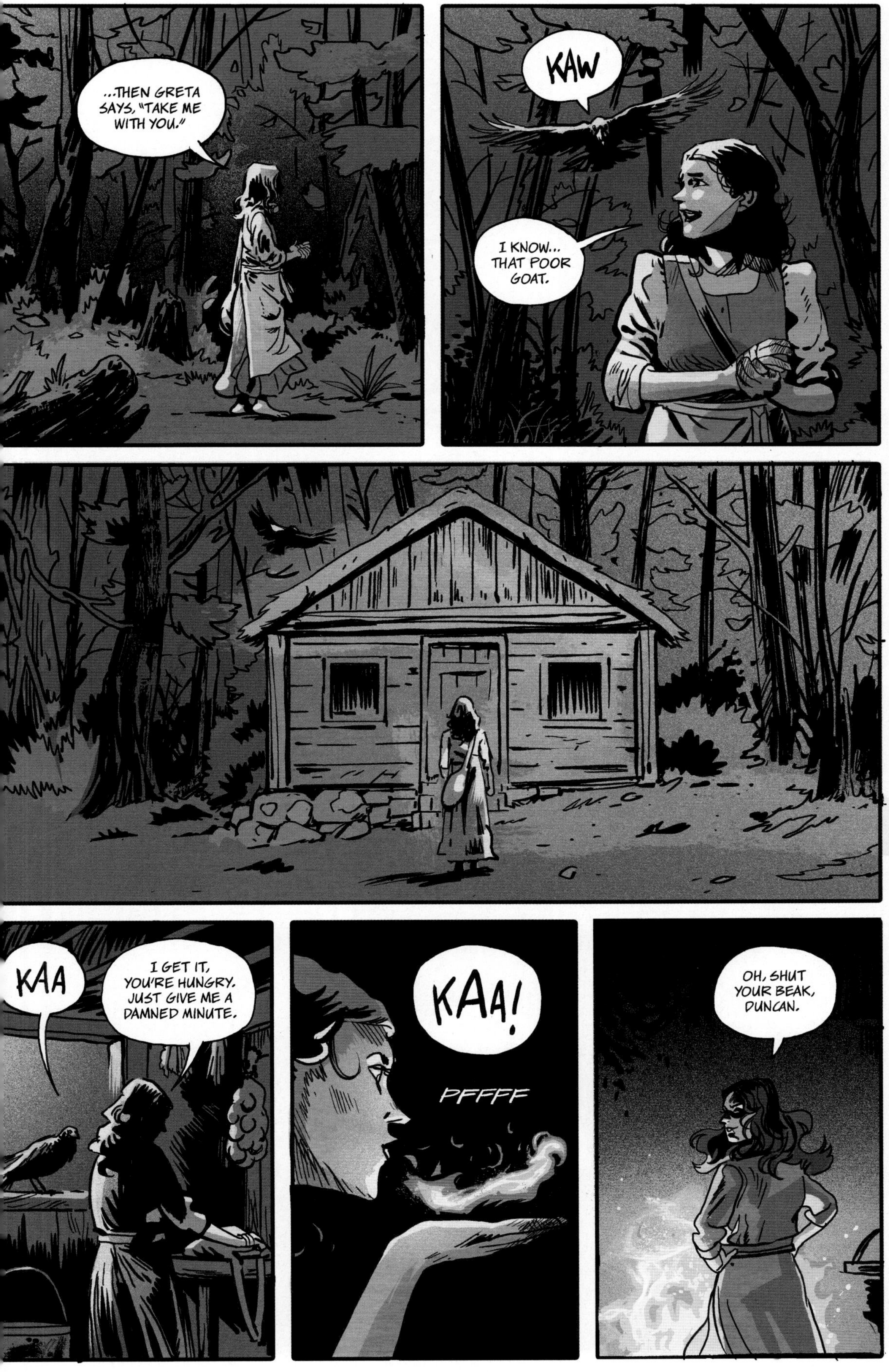
...THEN GRETA SAYS, "TAKE ME WITH YOU."
KAW
I KNOW... THAT POOR GOAT.
KAA
I GET IT, YOU'RE HUNGRY. JUST GIVE ME A DAMNED MINUTE.
KAA!
PFFFF
OH, SHUT YOUR BEAK, DUNCAN.

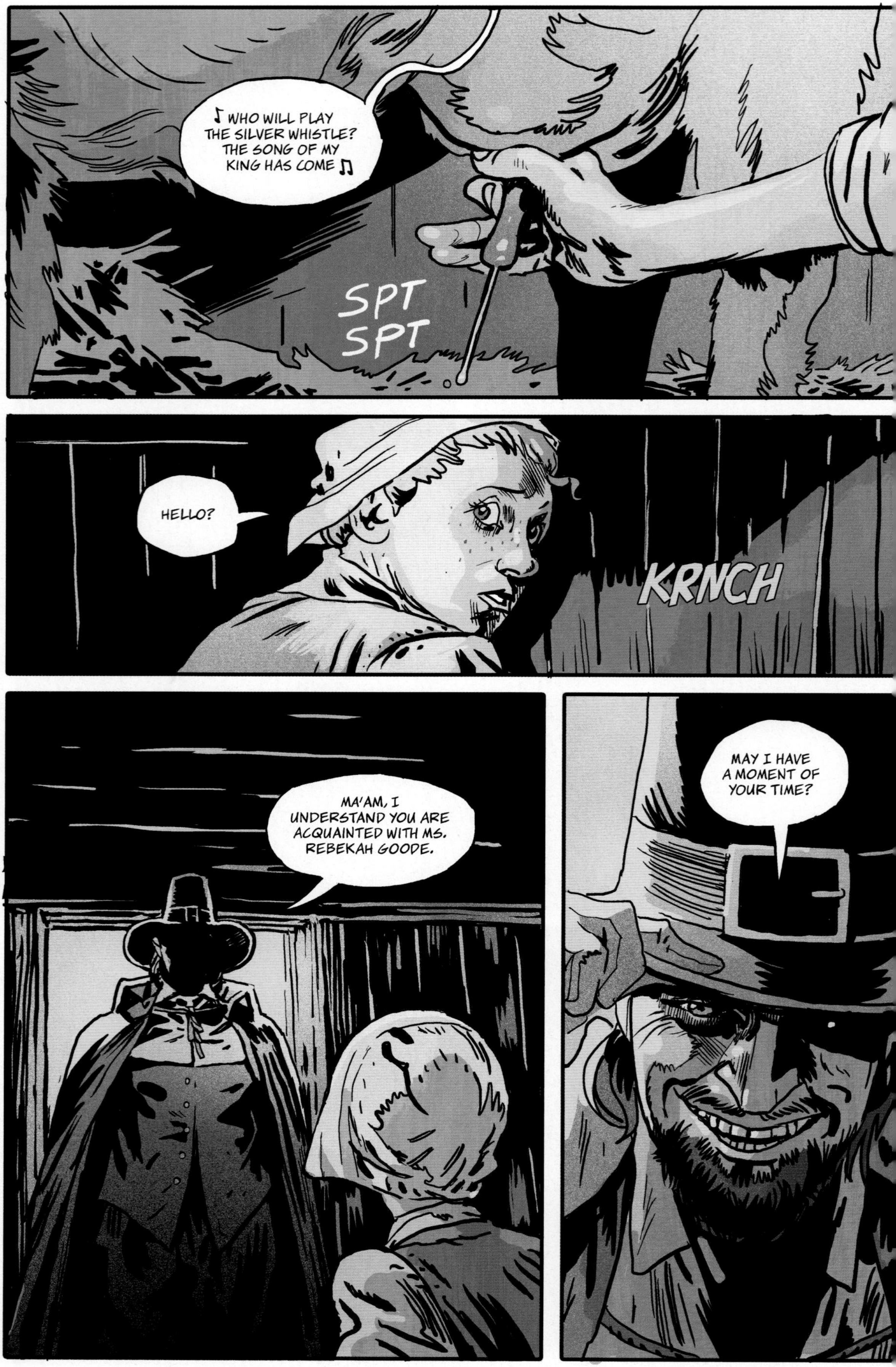
♪ WHO WILL PLAY THE SILVER WHISTLE? THE SONG OF MY KING HAS COME ♫
SPT SPT
HELLO?
KRNCH
MA'AM, I UNDERSTAND YOU ARE ACQUAINTED WITH MS. REBEKAH GOODE.
MAY I HAVE A MOMENT OF YOUR TIME?

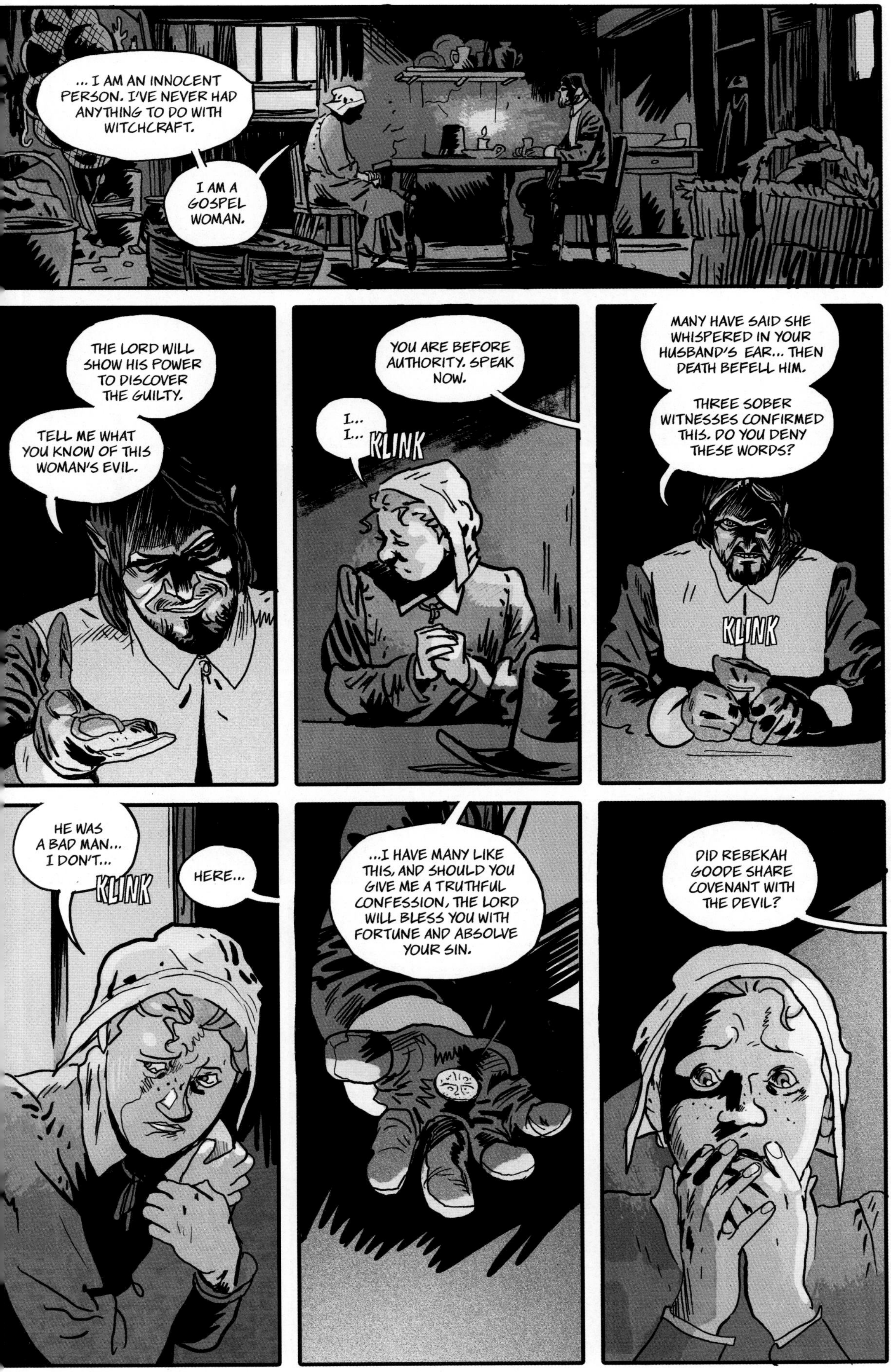
... I AM AN INNOCENT PERSON. I'VE NEVER HAD ANYTHING TO DO WITH WITCHCRAFT.
I AM A GOSPEL WOMAN.
THE LORD WILL SHOW HIS POWER TO DISCOVER THE GUILTY.
TELL ME WHAT YOU KNOW OF THIS WOMAN'S EVIL.
YOU ARE BEFORE AUTHORITY. SPEAK NOW.
I... I...
KLINK
MANY HAVE SAID SHE WHISPERED IN YOUR HUSBAND'S EAR... THEN DEATH BEFELL HIM.
THREE SOBER WITNESSES CONFIRMED THIS. DO YOU DENY THESE WORDS?
KLINK
HE WAS A BAD MAN... I DON'T...
KLINK
HERE...
...I HAVE MANY LIKE THIS, AND SHOULD YOU GIVE ME A TRUTHFUL CONFESSION, THE LORD WILL BLESS YOU WITH FORTUNE AND ABSOLVE YOUR SIN.
DID REBEKAH GOODE SHARE COVENANT WITH THE DEVIL?

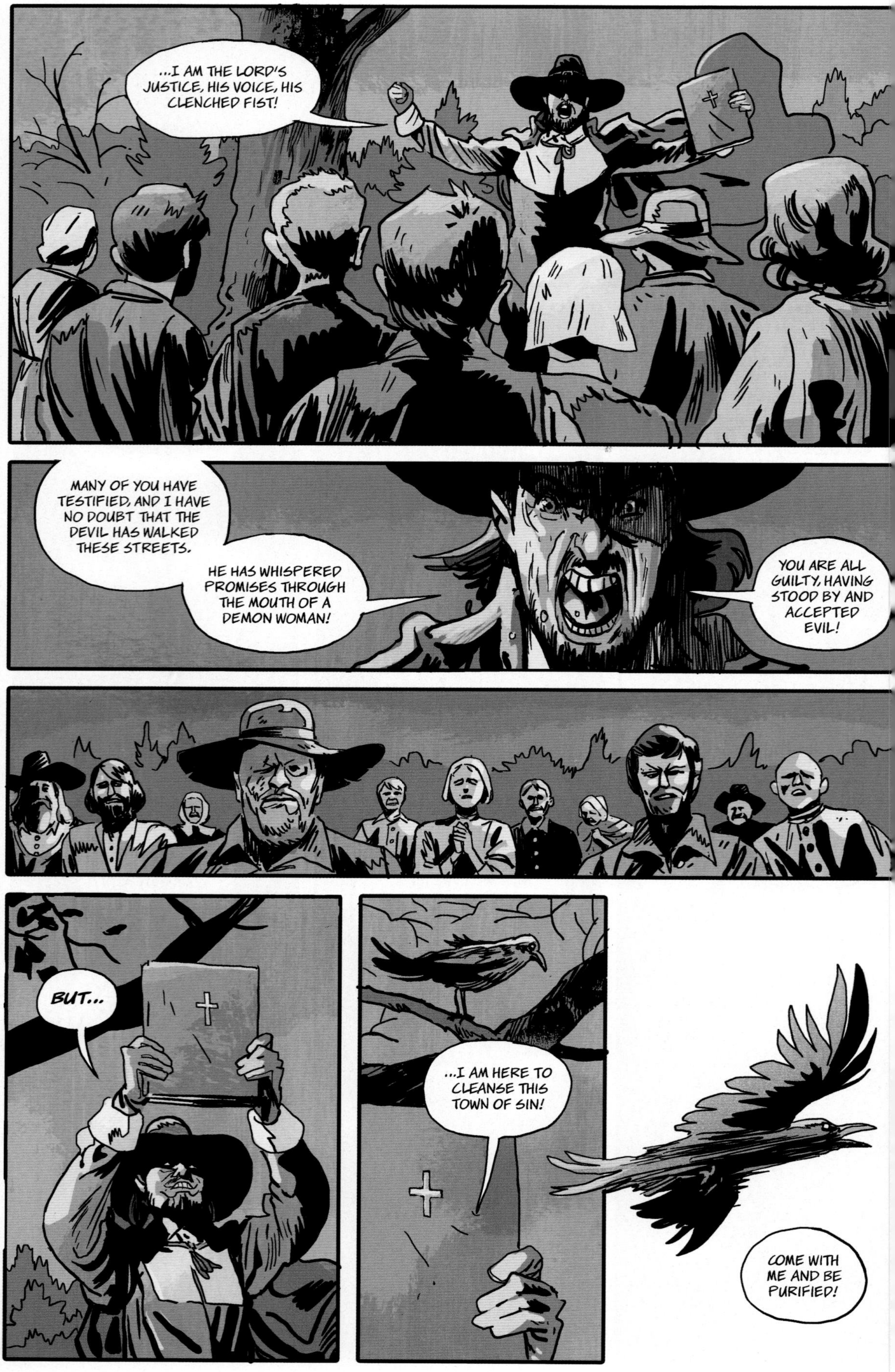
...I AM THE LORD'S JUSTICE, HIS VOICE, HIS CLENCHED FIST!
MANY OF YOU HAVE TESTIFIED, AND I HAVE NO DOUBT THAT THE DEVIL HAS WALKED THESE STREETS.
HE HAS WHISPERED PROMISES THROUGH THE MOUTH OF A DEMON WOMAN!
YOU ARE ALL GUILTY, HAVING STOOD BY AND ACCEPTED EVIL!
BUT...
...I AM HERE TO CLEANSE THIS TOWN OF SIN!
COME WITH ME AND BE PURIFIED!

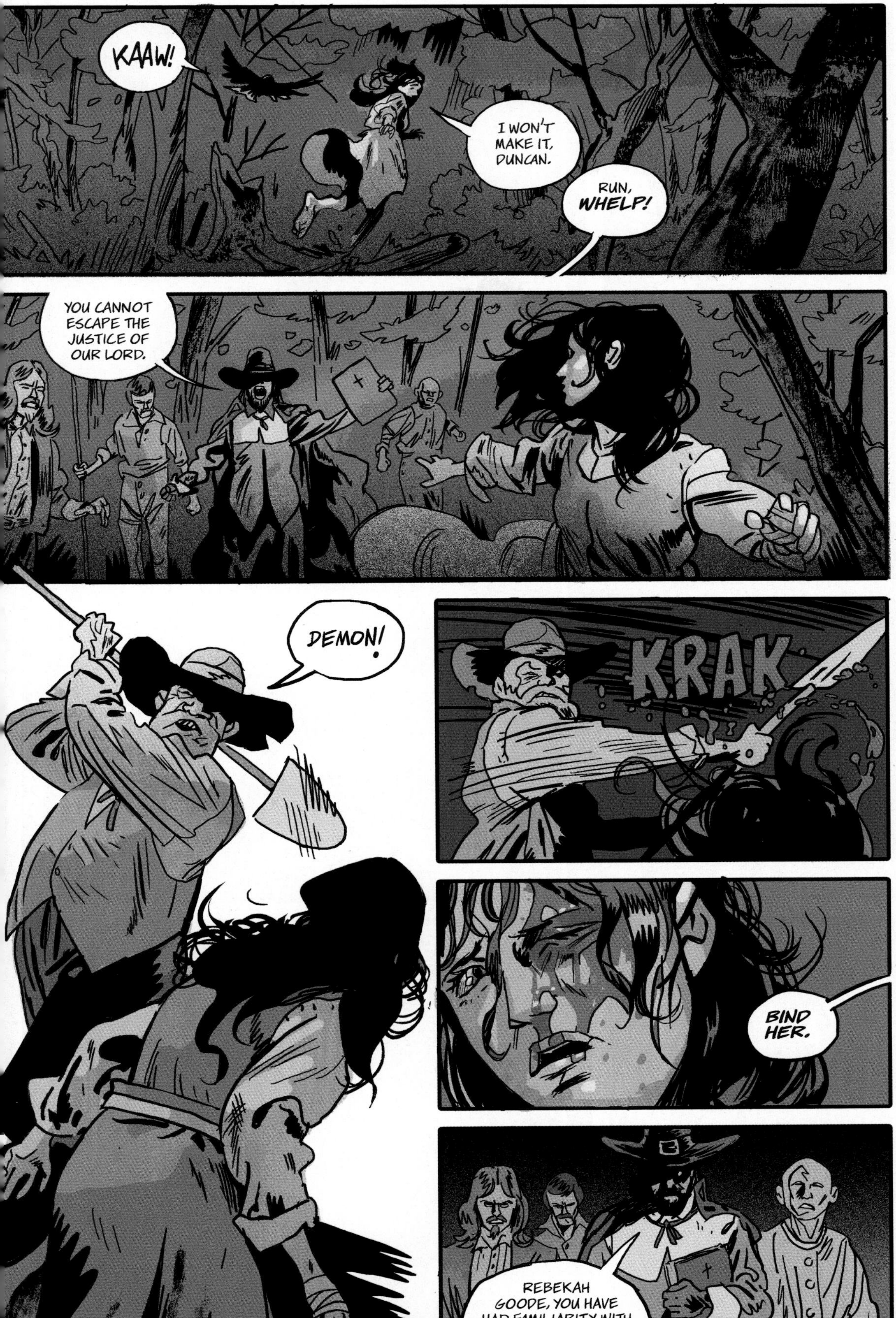
KAAW!
I WON'T MAKE IT, DUNCAN.
RUN, WHELP!
YOU CANNOT ESCAPE THE JUSTICE OF OUR LORD.
DEMON!
KRAK
BIND HER.
REBEKAH GOODE, YOU HAVE HAD FAMILIARITY WITH THE DEVIL. NOW, YOU WILL BE PUNISHED.

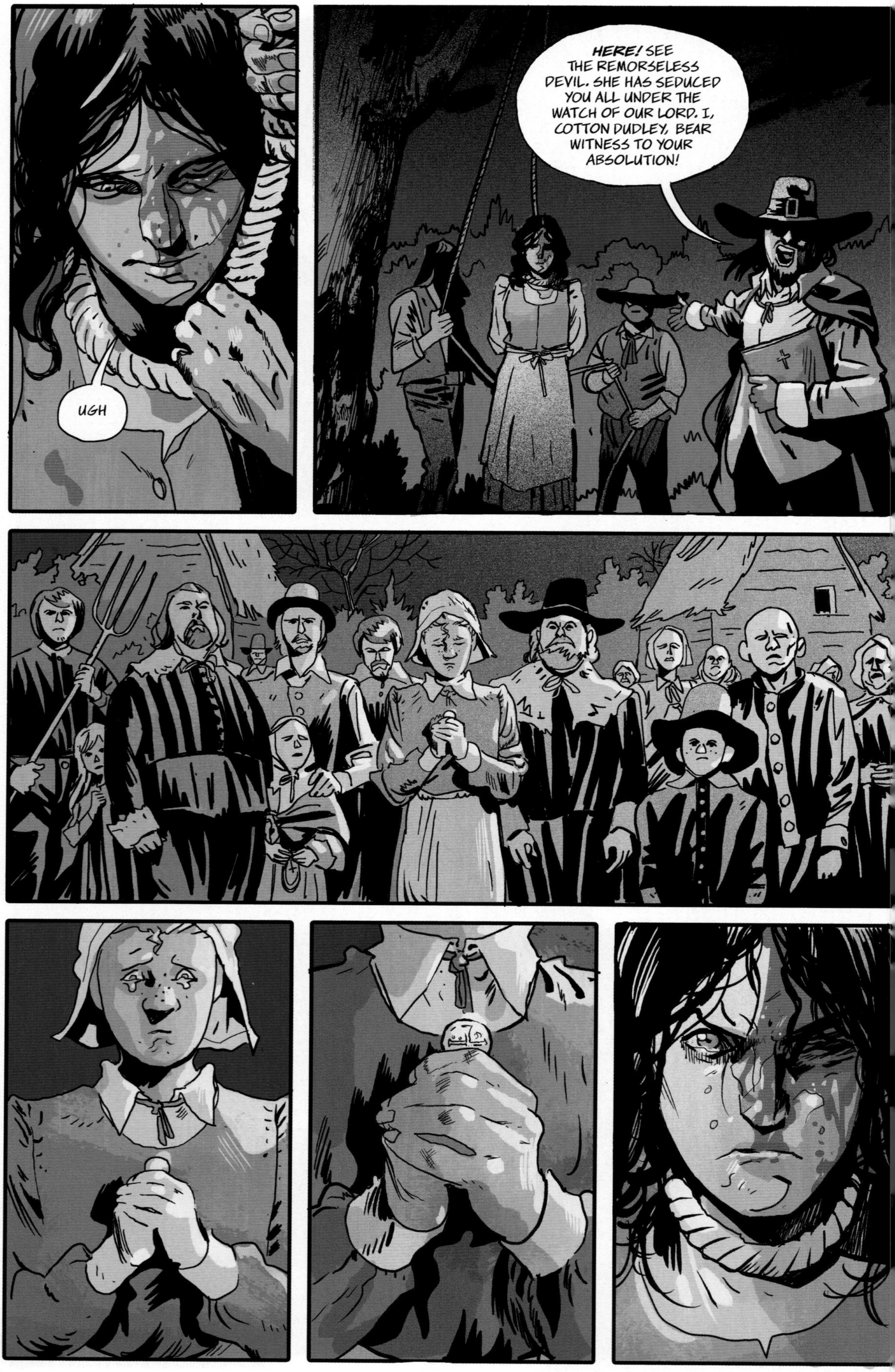
UGH
HERE! SEE THE REMORSELESS DEVIL. SHE HAS SEDUCED YOU ALL UNDER THE WATCH OF OUR LORD. I, COTTON DUDLEY, BEAR WITNESS TO YOUR ABSOLUTION!

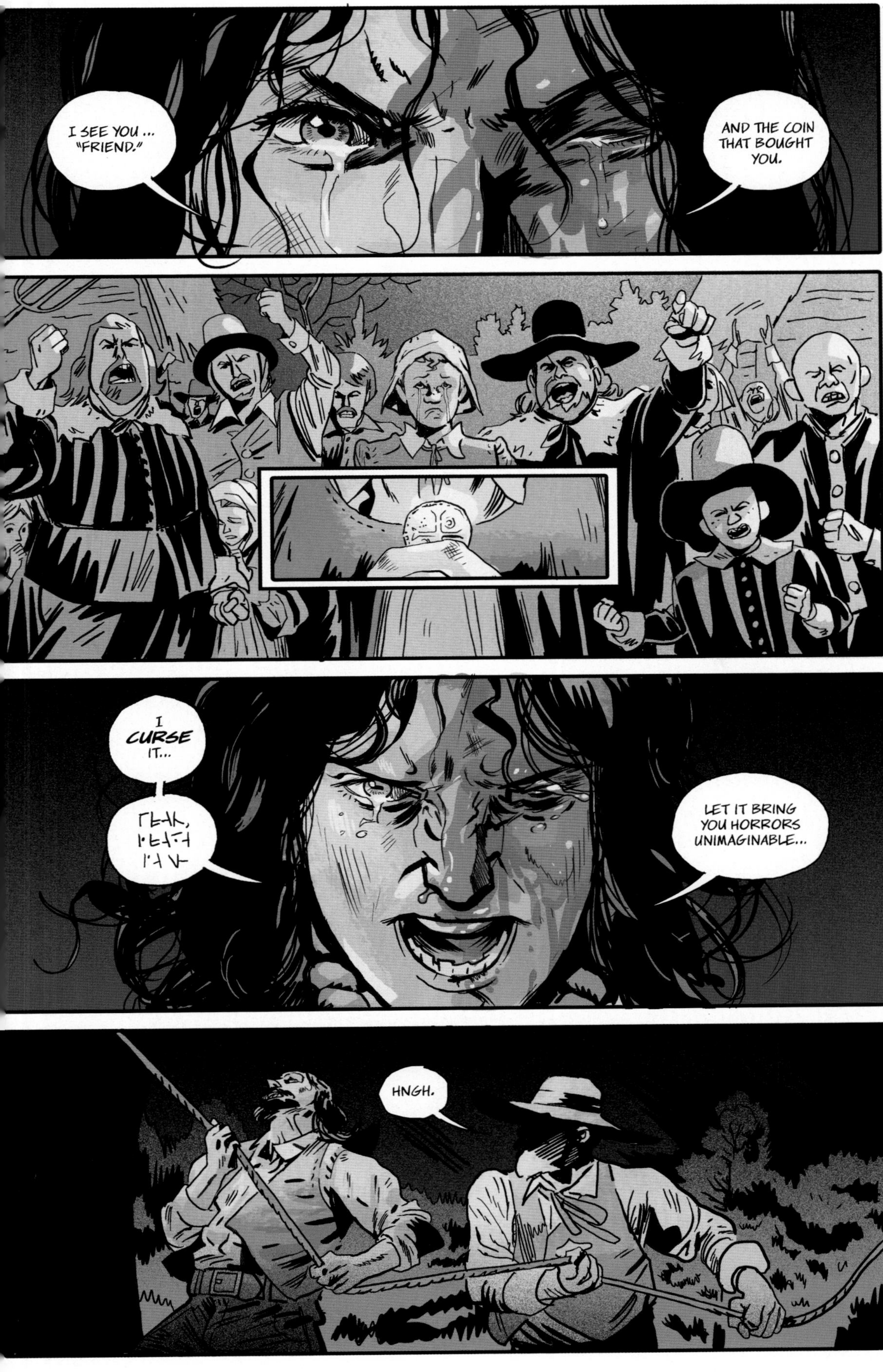
I SEE YOU ... "FRIEND."
AND THE COIN THAT BOUGHT YOU.
I CURSE IT...
LET IT BRING YOU HORRORS UNIMAGINABLE...
HNGH.

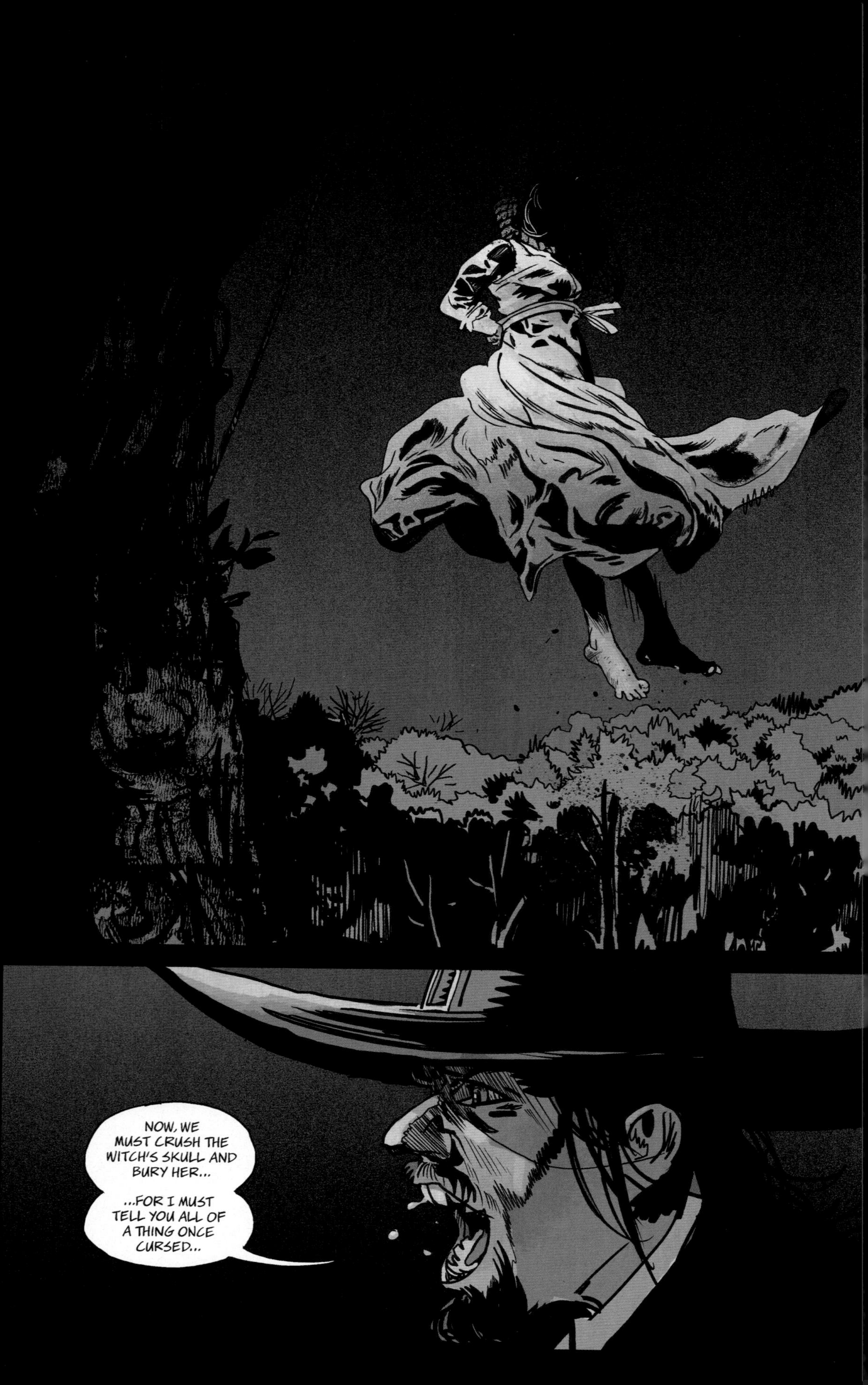
NOW, WE MUST CRUSH THE WITCH'S SKULL AND BURY HER...
...FOR I MUST TELL YOU ALL OF A THING ONCE CURSED...

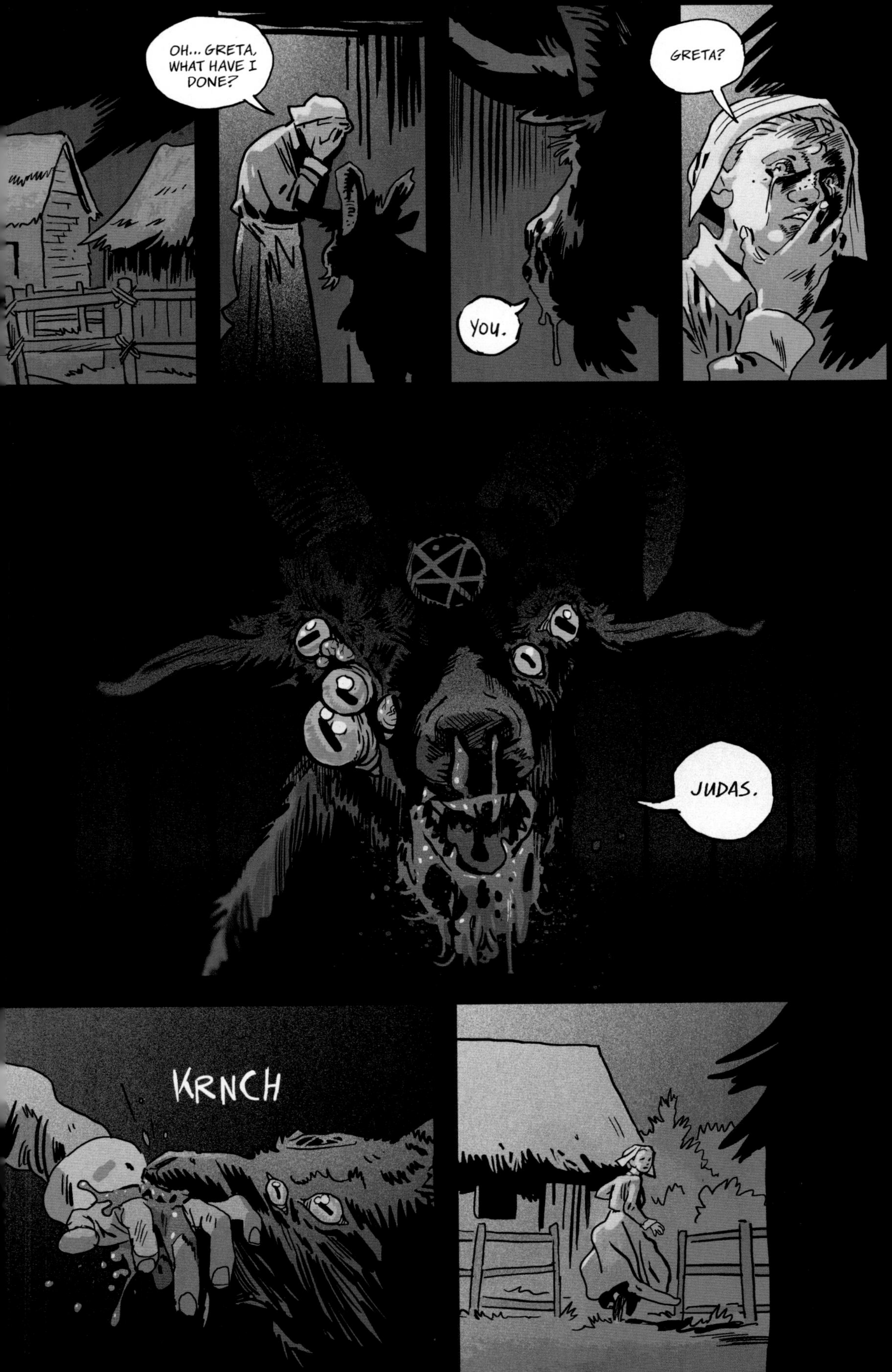
OH... GRETA, WHAT HAVE I DONE?
YOU.
GRETA?
JUDAS.
KRNCH

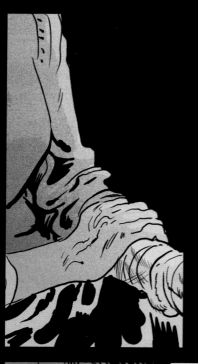

NOK
NOK

OH GOD, IT HURTS.

I HAVE THE REST OF YOUR PAYMENT, MARTHA PORTER. LET ME IN AND YOU SHALL BE COMPENSATED.

DON'T COME IN! I'M SICK, I... I DO NOT NEED YOUR BLOOD MONEY.

IT WAS WRONG, EVERYTHING... WRONG.

I WILL RETURN THIS EVENING. YOU WILL FEEL BETTER IF THE LORD WILLS.

KAA.

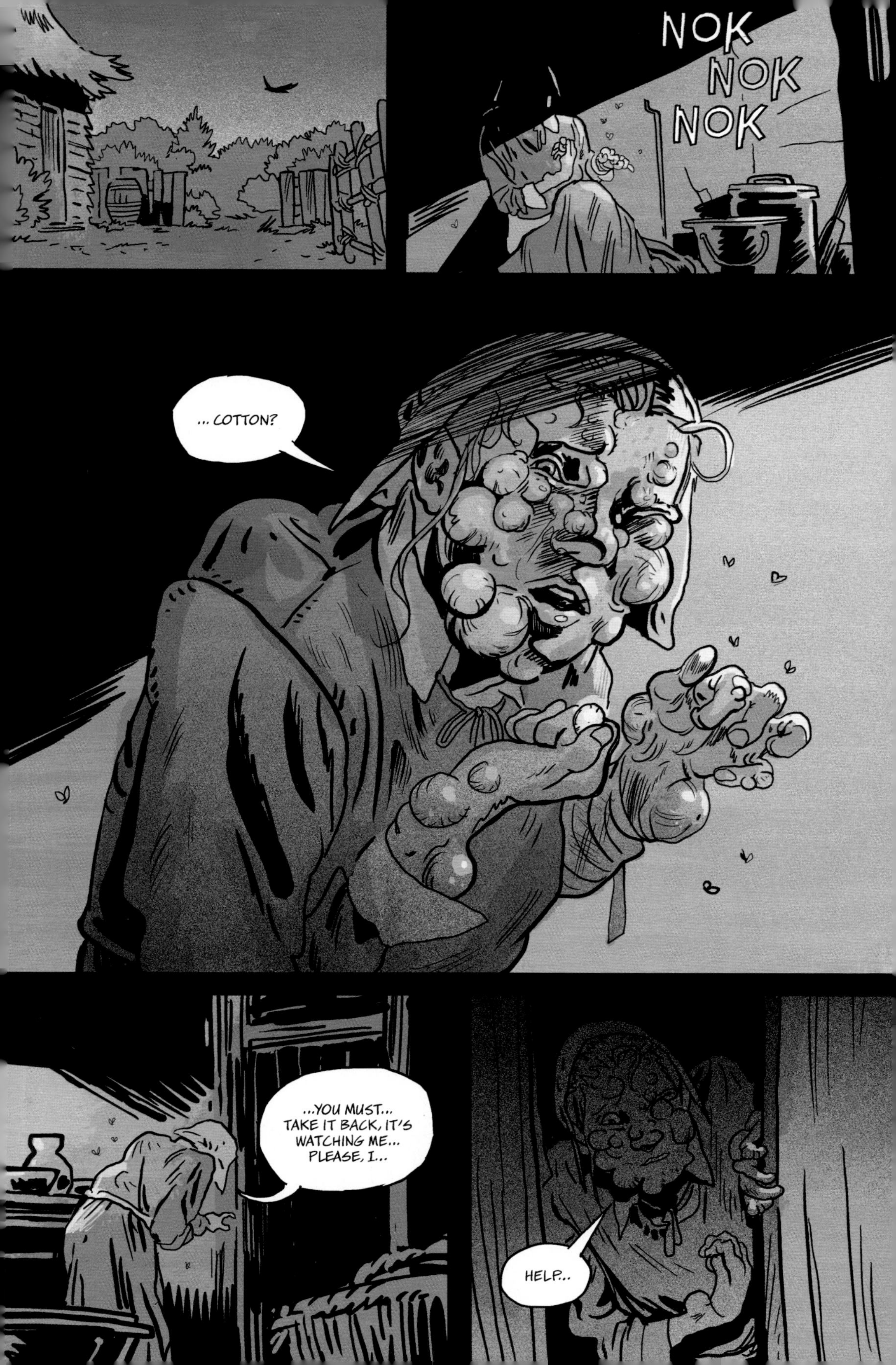
NOK
NOK
NOK
... COTTON?
...YOU MUST... TAKE IT BACK, IT'S WATCHING ME... PLEASE, I...
HELP...

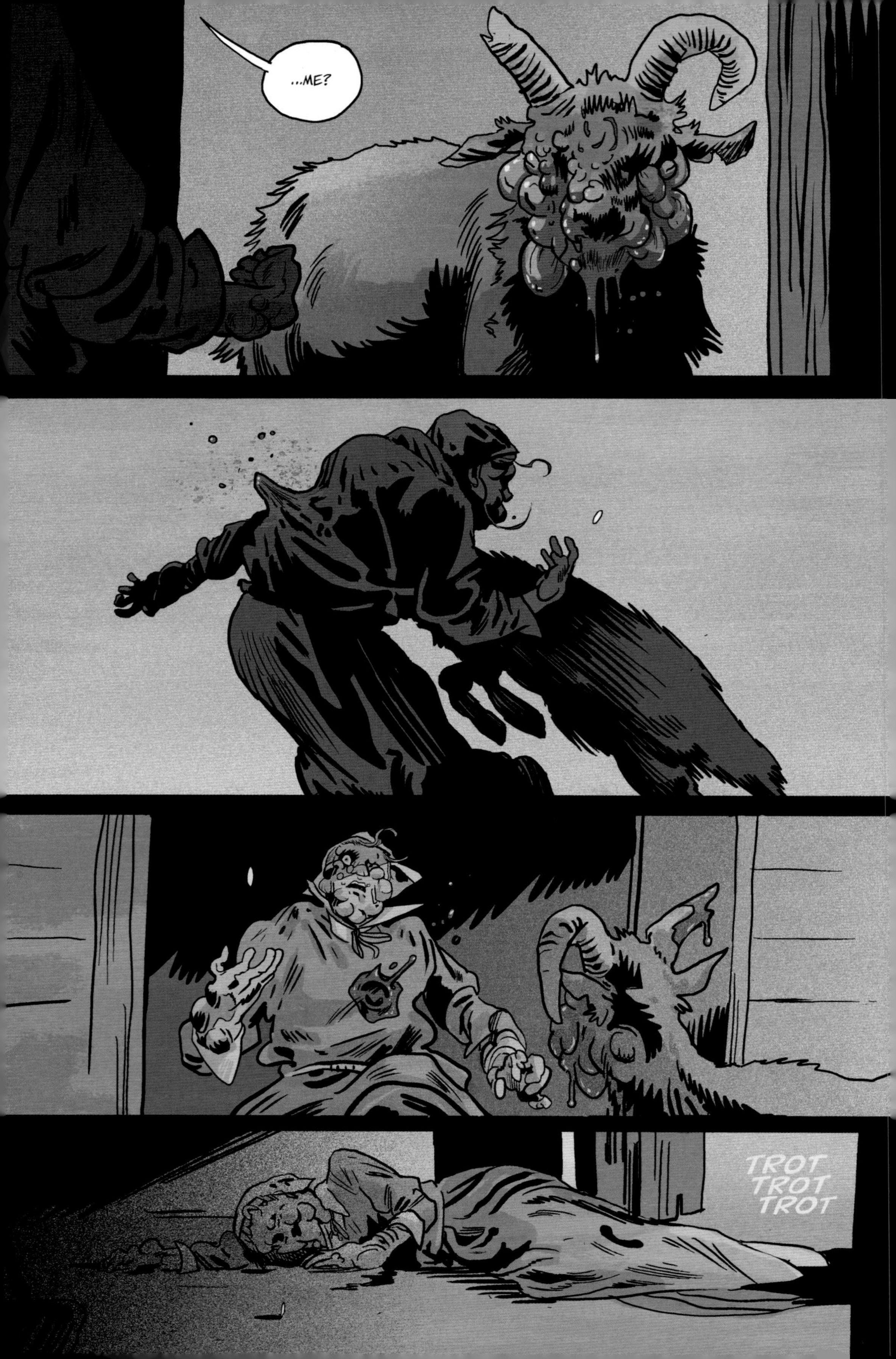
...ME?
TROT
TROT
TROT

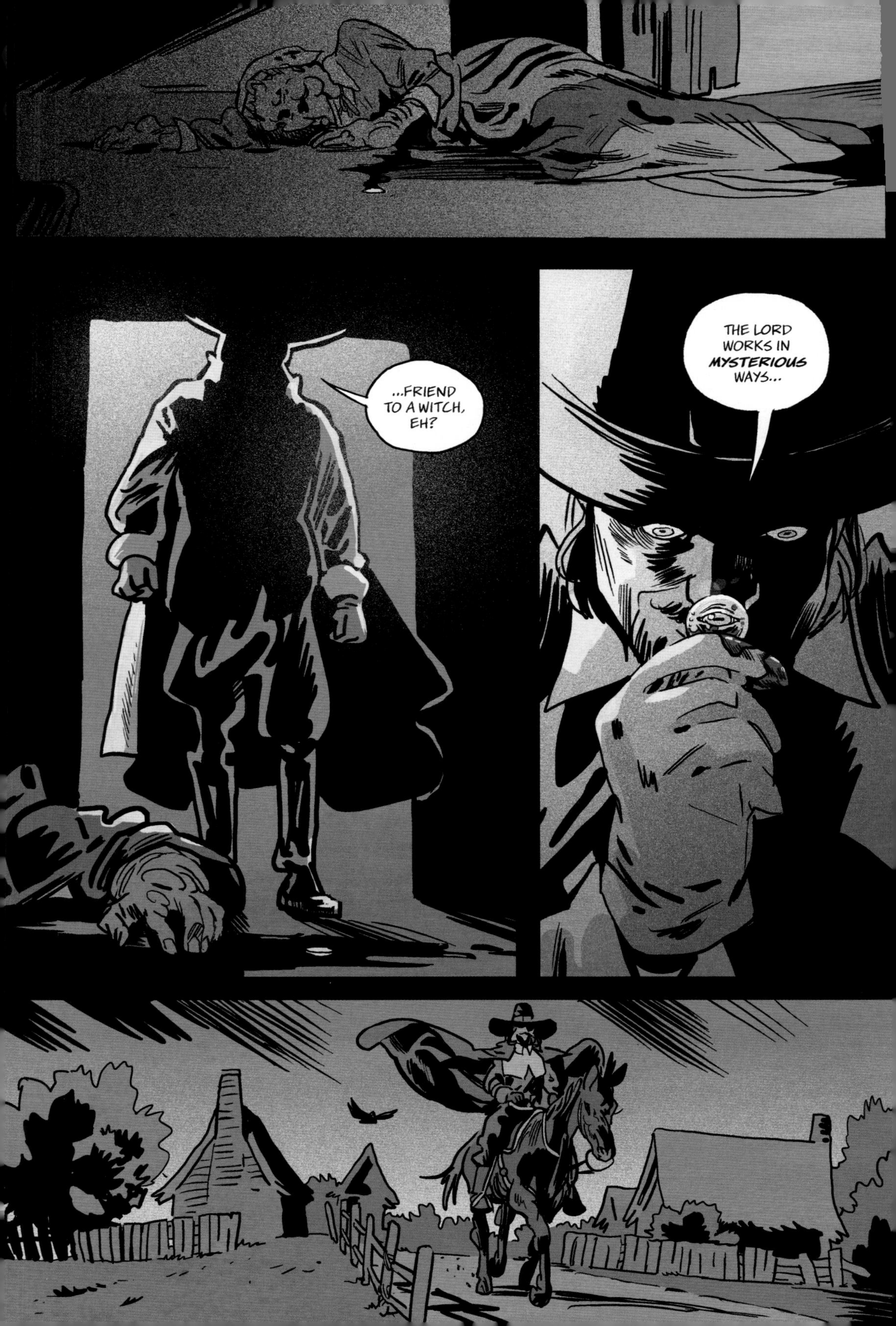
...FRIEND TO A WITCH, EH?
THE LORD WORKS IN MYSTERIOUS WAYS...

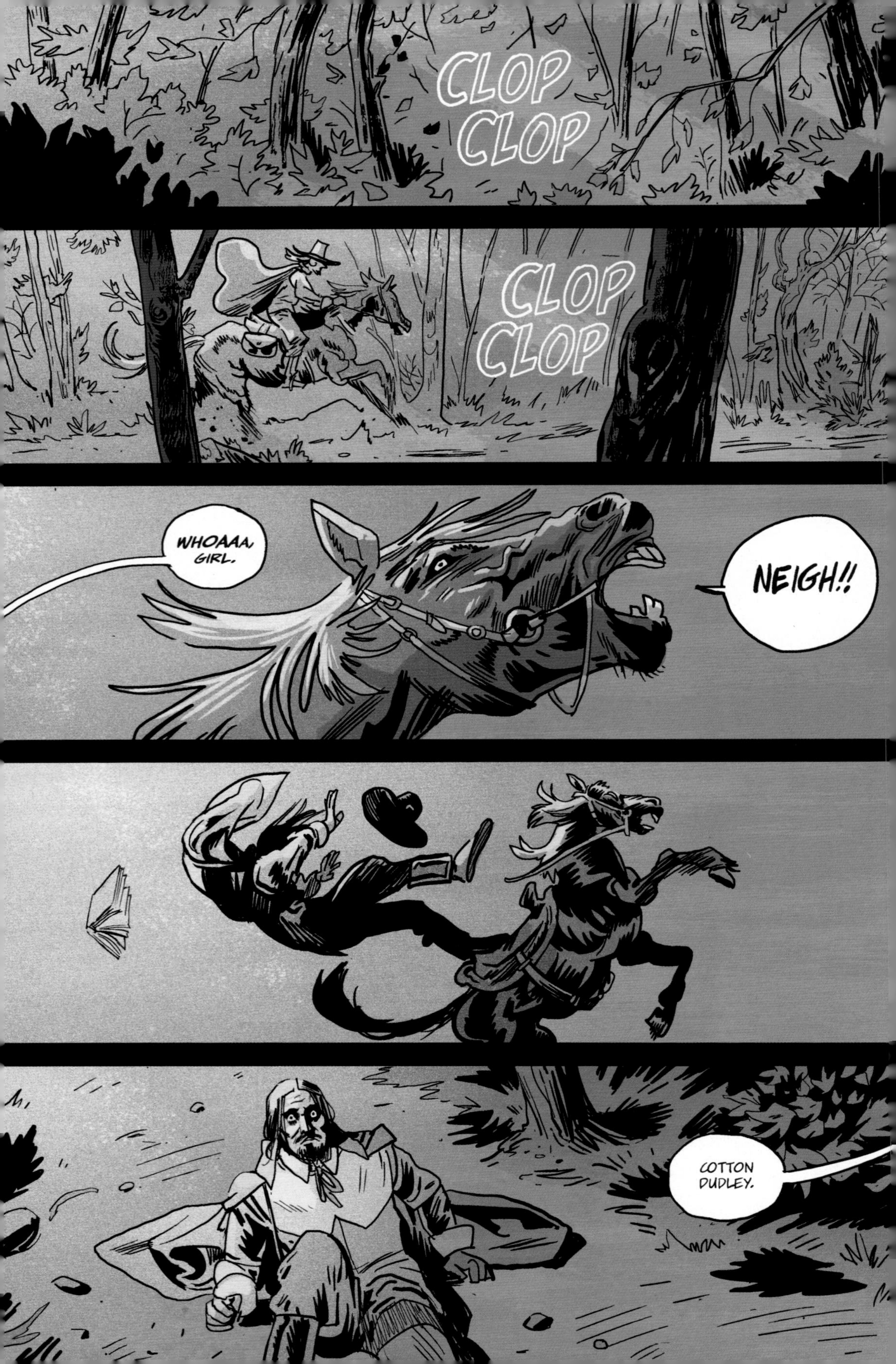
CLOP
CLOP
CLOP
CLOP
WHOAAA, GIRL.
NEIGH!!
COTTON DUDLEY.

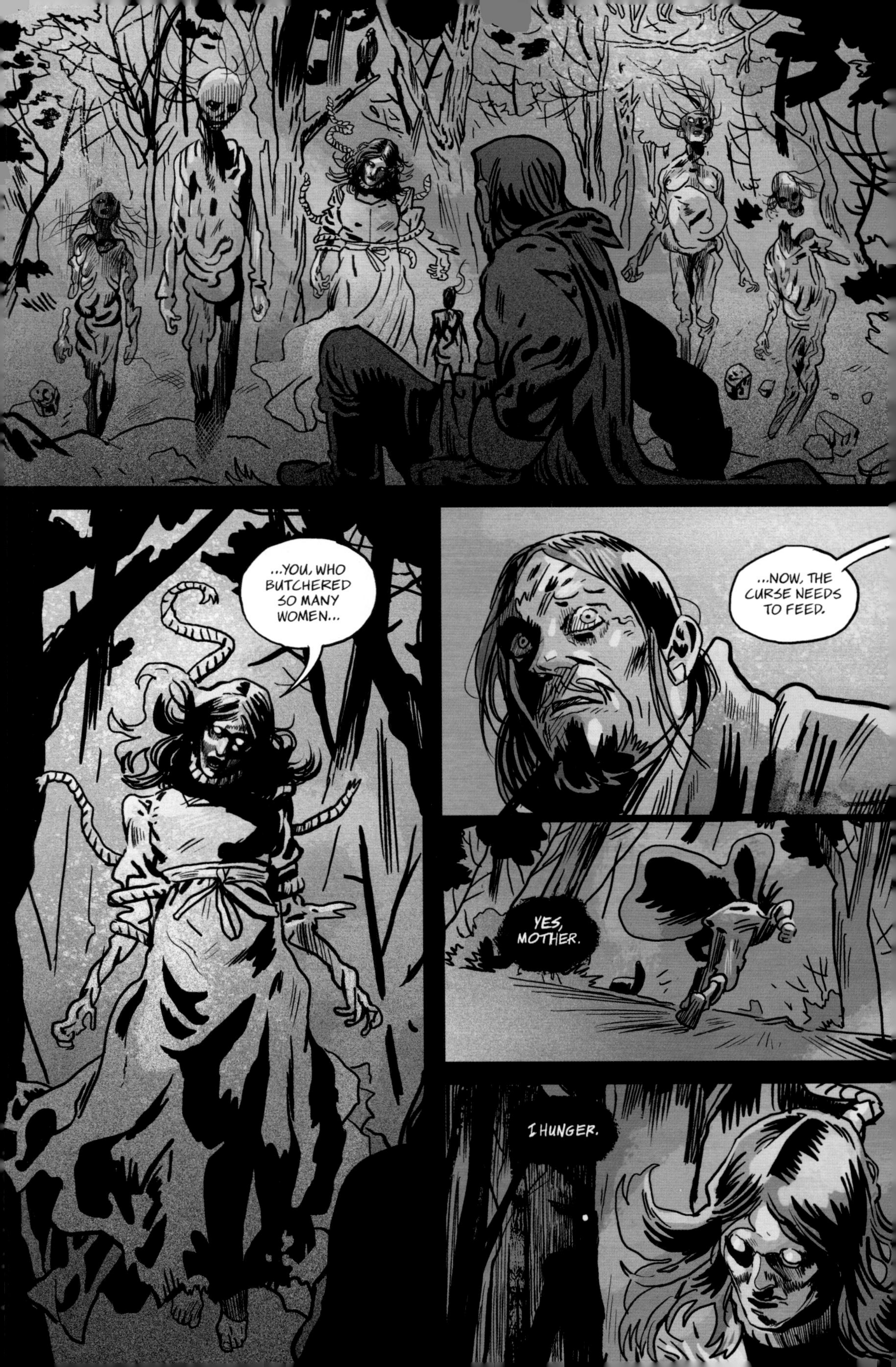
...YOU, WHO BUTCHERED SO MANY WOMEN...
...NOW, THE CURSE NEEDS TO FEED.
YES, MOTHER.
I HUNGER.

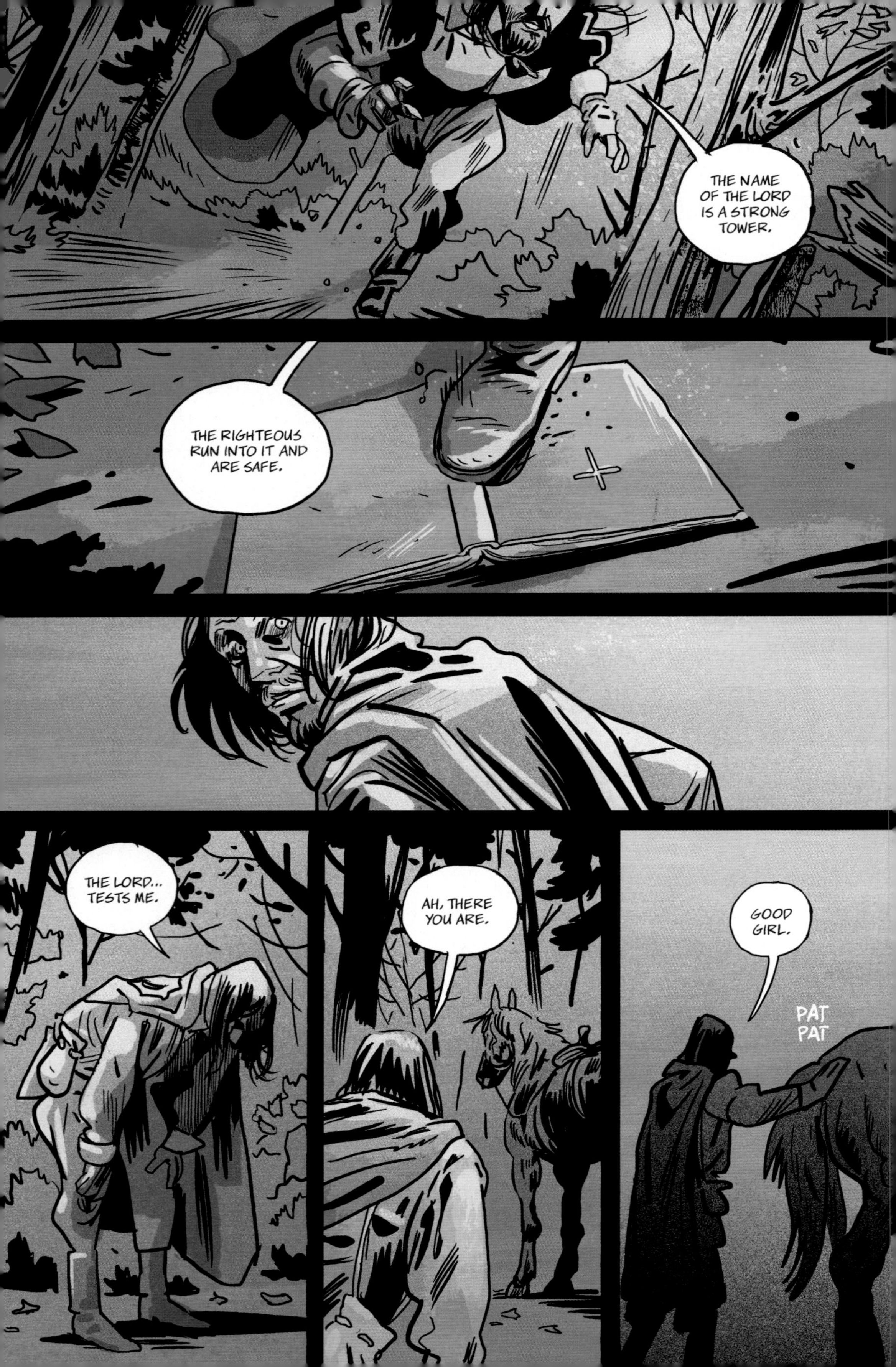
THE NAME OF THE LORD IS A STRONG TOWER.
THE RIGHTEOUS RUN INTO IT AND ARE SAFE.
THE LORD... TESTS ME.
AH, THERE YOU ARE.
GOOD GIRL.
PAT PAT

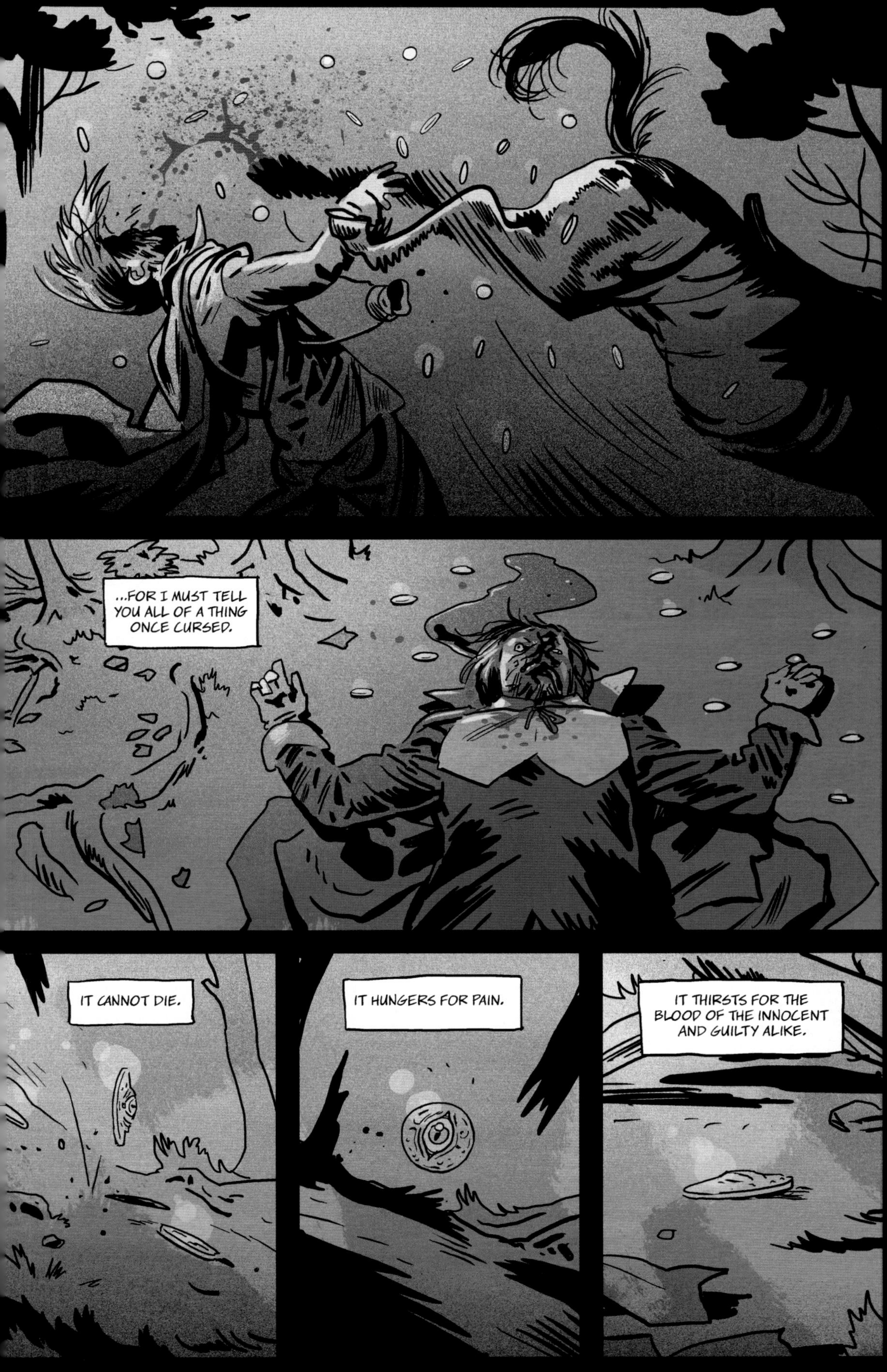
...FOR I MUST TELL YOU ALL OF A THING ONCE CURSED.
IT CANNOT DIE.
IT HUNGERS FOR PAIN.
IT THIRSTS FOR THE BLOOD OF THE INNOCENT AND GUILTY ALIKE.

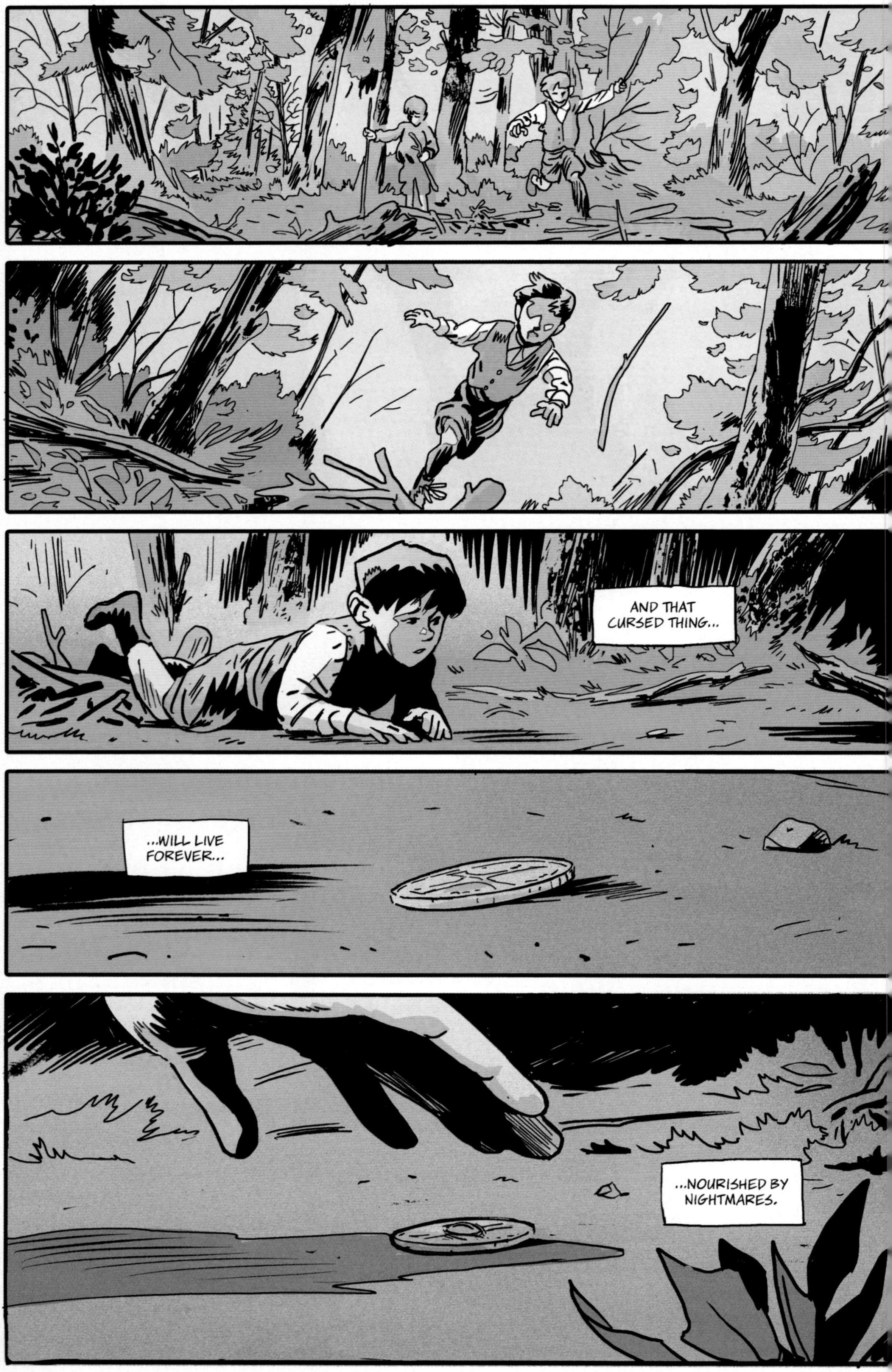
AND THAT CURSED THING...
...WILL LIVE FOREVER...
...NOURISHED BY NIGHTMARES.

"Let it bring you horrors unimaginable."

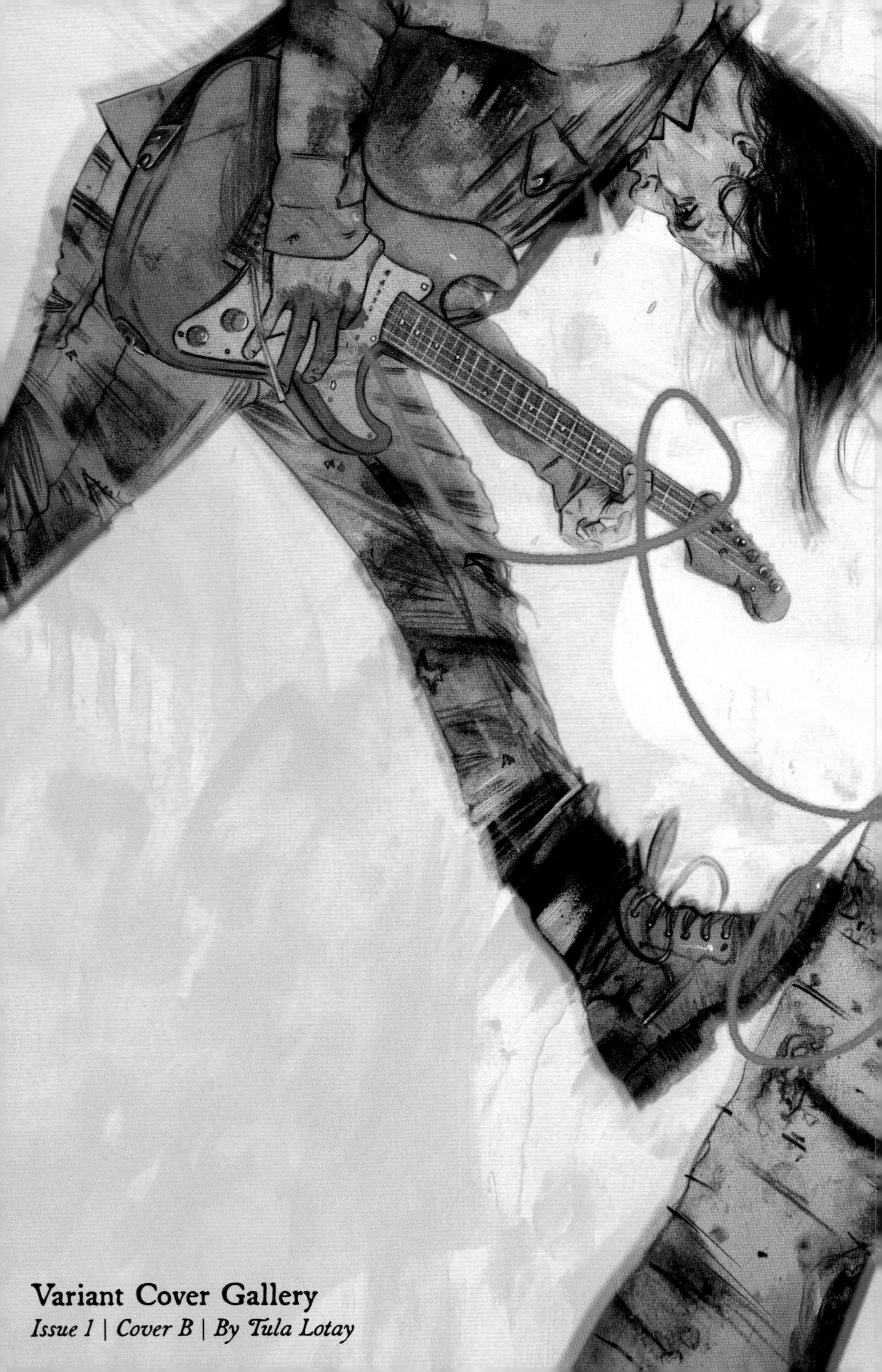

Variant Cover Gallery

Issue 1 | Cover B | By Tula Lotay

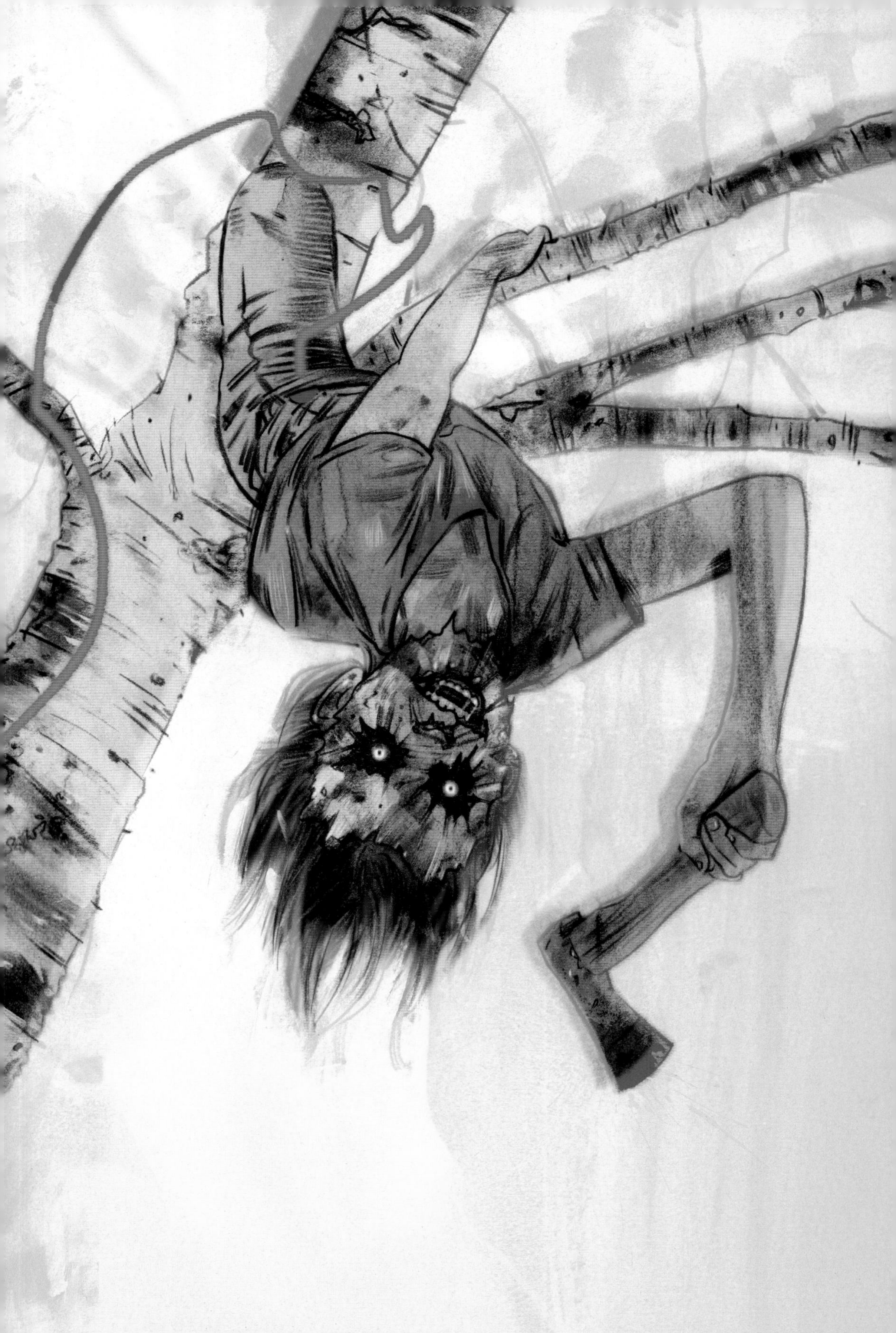

Issue 2 | Cover B | By Tula Lotay

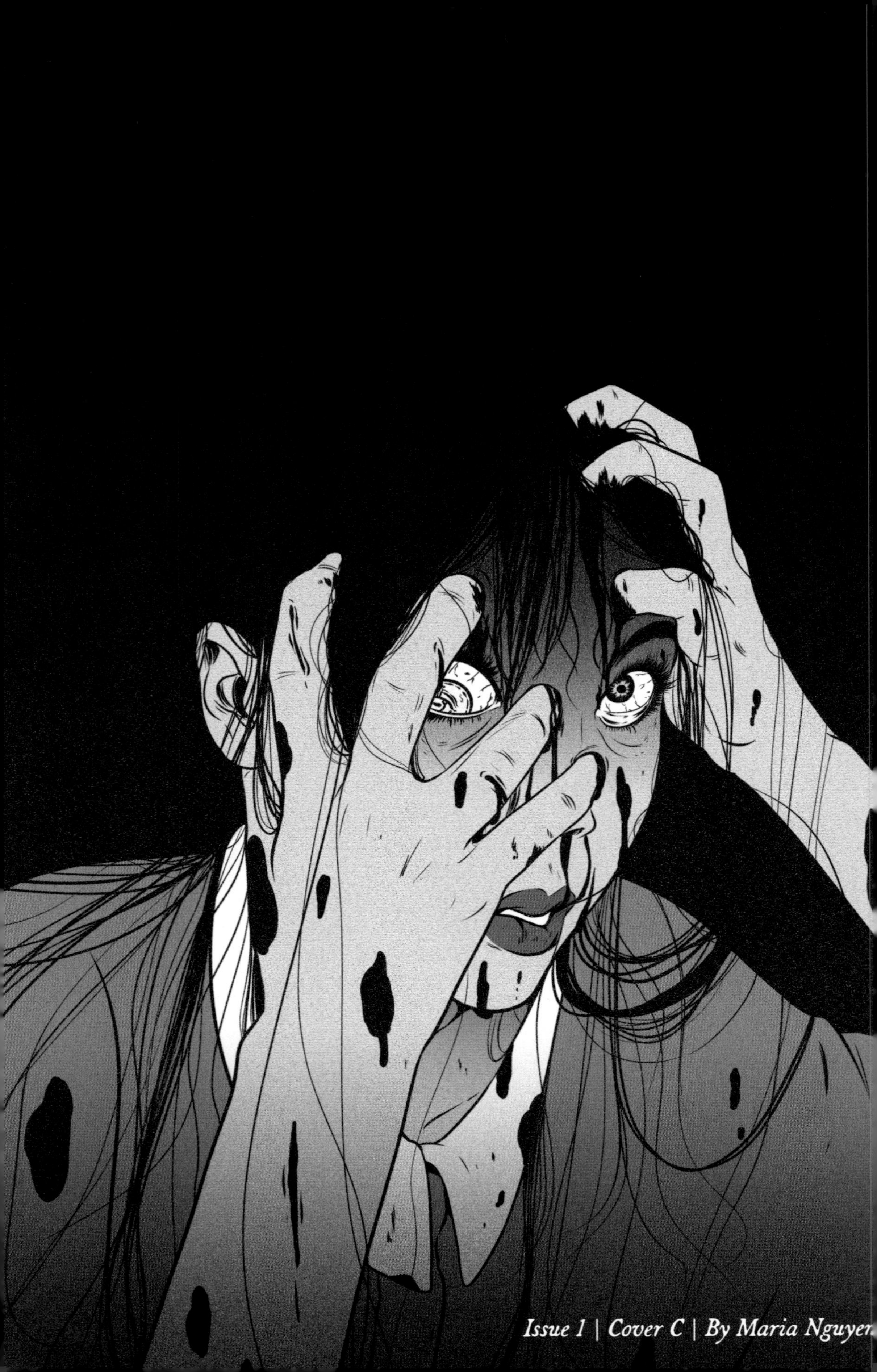

Issue 1 | Cover C | By Maria Nguyen

Issue 3 | Cover B | By Anand Radhakrishnan

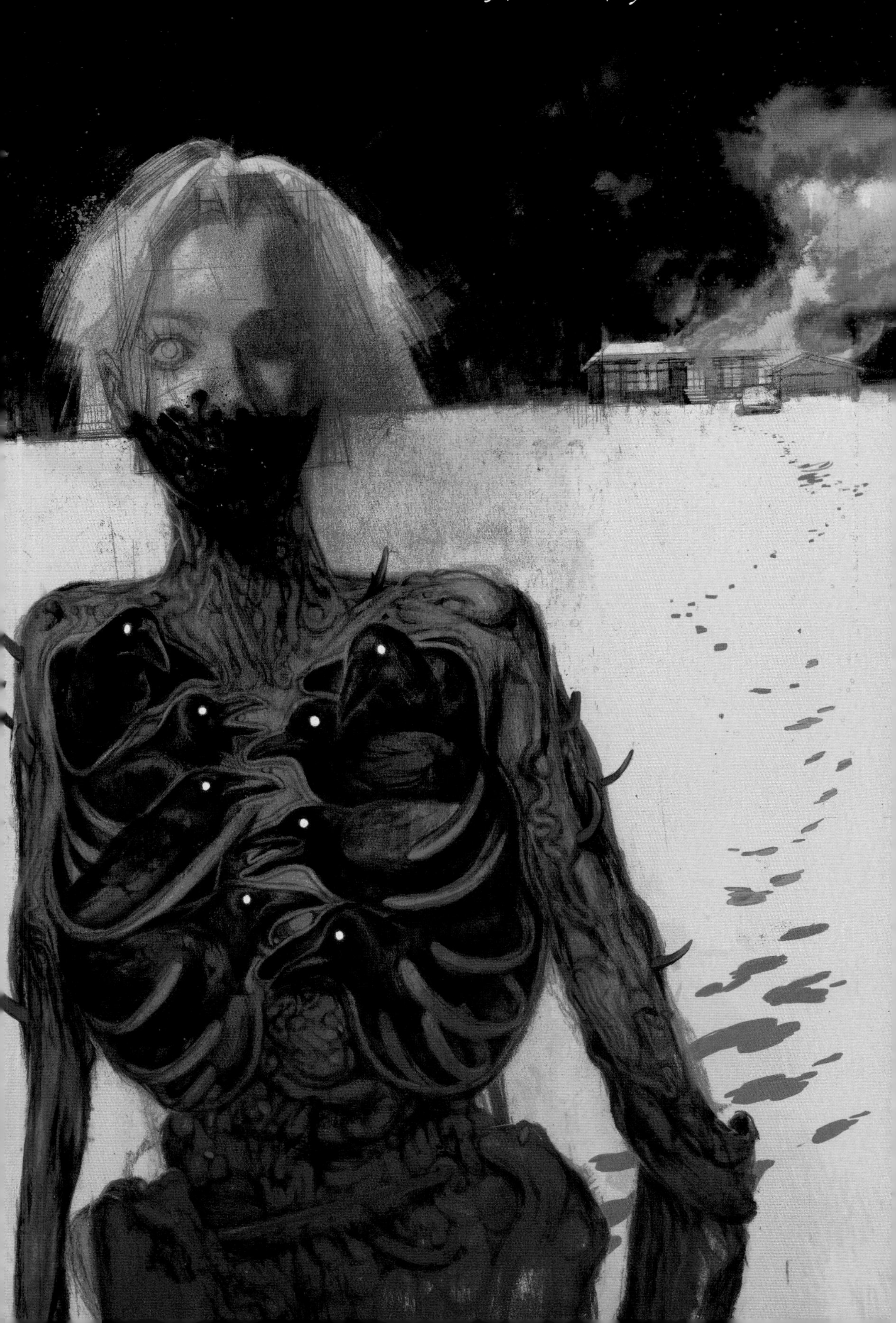

Issue 4 | Cover B | By Christian Ward

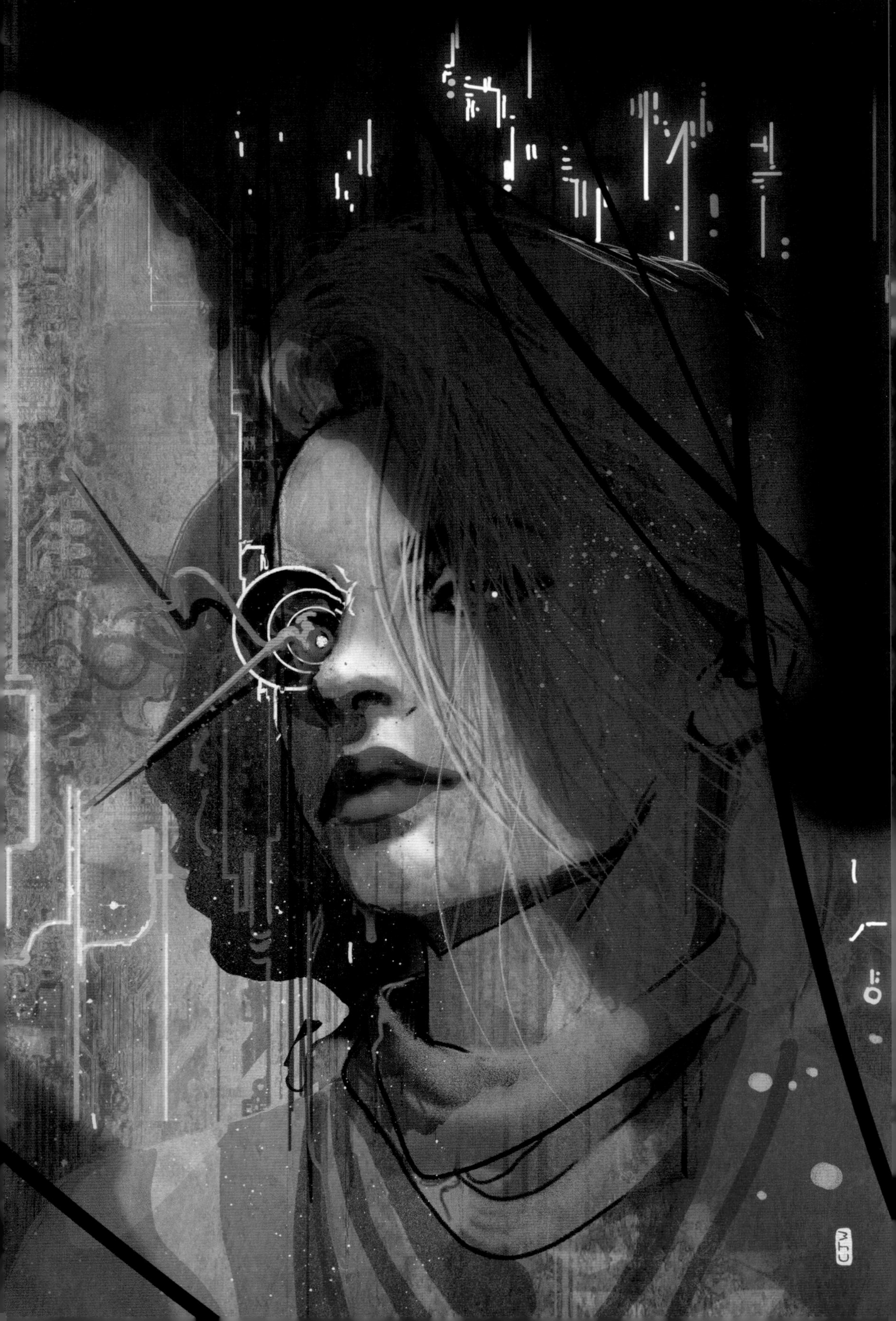

Issue 5 | Cover B | By Maya McKibbin

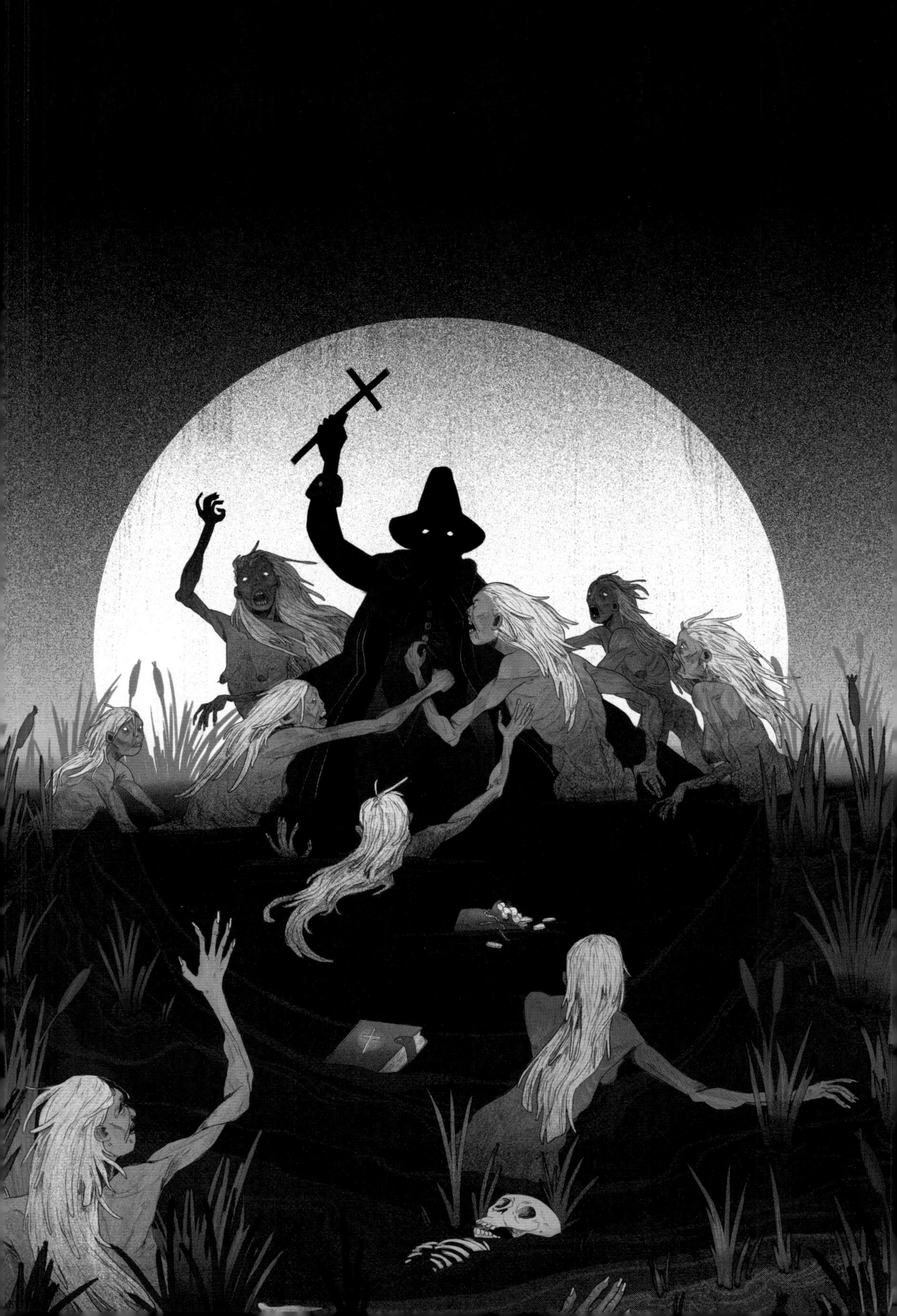

If you liked THE SILVER COIN...
Try these bestsellers...

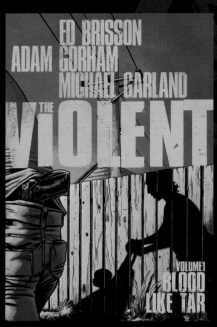

Ed Brisson, Adam Gorham & Michael Garland

The Violent TP Volume One
978-1-63215-714-0

Ed Brisson & Michael Walsh

Comeback TP
978-1-60706-737-5

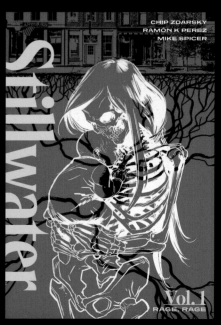

Chip Zdarsky & Ramón K Pérez

Stillwater TP Volume One
978-1-5343-1837-3

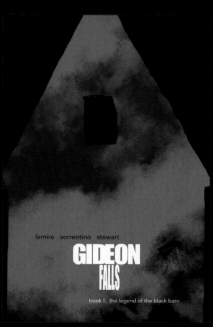

Jeff Lemire & Andrea Sorrentino

Gideon Falls Deluxe HC Volume One
978-1-5343-1918-9